THE 100 BEST
GARDENS IN IRELAND

Overleaf: June Blake's Garden, County Wicklow.

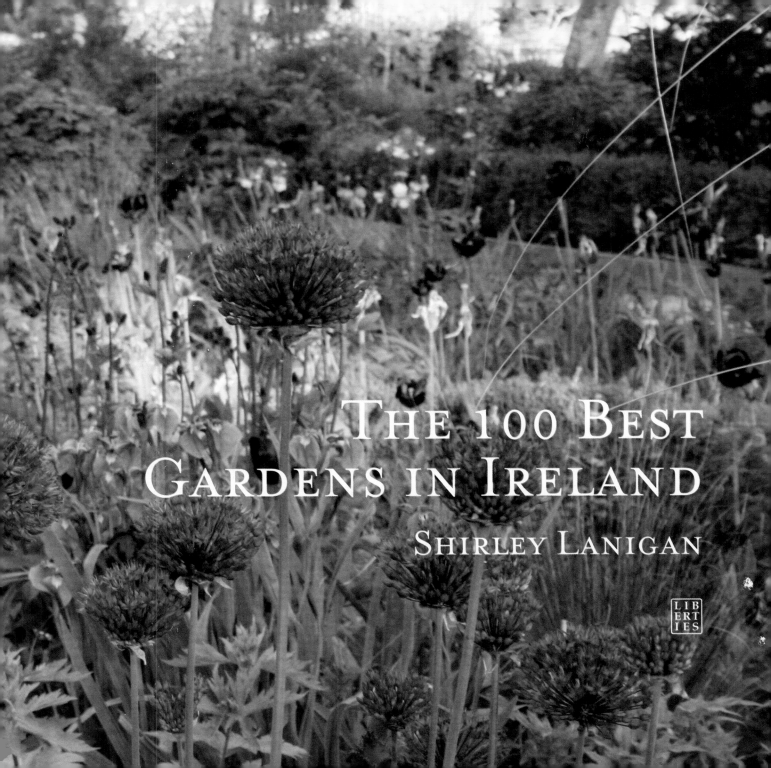

The 100 Best Gardens in Ireland

Shirley Lanigan

LIBERTIES

First published in 2011 by
Liberties Press
Guinness Enterprise Centre | Taylor's Lane | Dublin 8
Tel: +353 (1) 415 1224
www.libertiespress.com | info@libertiespress.com

Trade enquiries to Gill & Macmillan Distribution
Hume Avenue | Park West | Dublin 12
Tel: +353 (1) 500 9534 | Fax: +353 (1) 500 9595
sales@gillmacmillan.ie

Distributed in the United States by
Dufour Editions | PO Box 7 | Chester Springs
| Pennsylvania | 19425

Copyright © Shirley Lanigan, 2011
The author has asserted her moral rights.
ISBN: 978-1-907593-16-1
2 4 6 8 10 9 7 5 3 1

A CIP record for this title is available from the British Library.
Cover and Internal Design by Sin É Design
Printed by W&G Baird

In association with

Previous: Burtown House, County Kildare.

INTRODUCTION

I am constantly told that I have a great job, visiting gardens. But it is not true. Visiting gardens is no job. It is pure pleasure.

Generally speaking, it involves nothing more taxing than trailing around cleverly made, beautiful gardens in the company of interested, engaged owners and gardeners, caretakers and curators, followed by dogs, cats and sometimes fowl. Walking around like this I have picked up more about gardens and gardening than any number of courses or libraries full of books could ever give me. There is always something to learn about how the gardeners achieved their impressive feats, stories about the place and its history and even bits of gossip. Add in cups of tea and cake, the possibility of buying plants at a plant stall and being dispatched with envelopes of seeds and potted-up cuttings which fill the car and turn it into a mobile greenhouse as the trip goes on. Then there is gorgeous scenery, great drives and the fun of trying to puzzle out the best shaped itinerary followed by the not-always-successful keeping of that itinerary. (Driving through a town when its market is on, invariably puts paid to the timetable.)

None of this could possibly be called work or anything like it. I meet people at their best, showing off the thing that they love best. And in nearly twelve years I have only come across one garden owner who chased me away. That in itself says a lot abut gardeners, as I have sometimes turned up unannounced and unknown, having just heard of the garden's existence a few hours before.

So garden visiting is enjoyable. It is also easy and it has become even easier since the introduction of the magic device known as sat nav, when I think of technological wizardry I think of the way a little sat nav with its tiny chip and triangulating abilities, can instantly find a garden that I would have spent ages hunting out only a few years ago. Locking onto the post codes in Northern Ireland, the sat nav is even more impressive. Add in the Internet with Google Maps, Michelin and AA route planners as well as vastly improved roads, and it is now hard to get lost and very easy to land at the right address, on time than it ever was before.

There is work to be done but that only begins back at base, where the rain-splashed spider's scrawl that fills so many notebooks has to be translated into English. Trying to think of a forty-first way to describe shades of green is a bit like work too.

But then it gets easy again with the arrival of an editor who comes in and whisks away the pile and turns it into a book.

As I wade through the notes and photos, handouts and maps, there is usually someone who will ask 'will you do it again?' At that point the answer is usually 'are you mad? Never.' But as the swamp of notes and leaflets subsides and fades into the background replaced by the vision of a nicely bound book, I have to admit that the old road is calling again . . .

Shirley Lanigan
April 2011

Opposite from left to right: Coolaught Gardens, County Wexford, Ilnacullin, County Cork, Glenarm Castle, County Antrim and Ilnacullin, County Cork.

LEINSTER

JUNE BLAKE'S GARDEN

County Carlow

Altamont Gardens | Tullow, County Carlow

Contact: The manager
Tel: (+353) 059 915 9444
e-mail: altamontgardens@opw.ie
www: www.heritageireland.ie
www.carlowgardentrail.com
For walled garden contact: Robert Miller
Tel: (+353) 087 982 2135
e-mail: sales@altamontplants.com
Open: All year. Check web for seasonal hours

Supervised children welcome. Dogs on leads.
Special features: Plant sales in walled garden. Guided tours. Picnic facilities. Partially wheelchair accessible. Toilets. Coach parking. Annual Snowdrop Week. Admission charge to groups only for guided tours. **Directions:** Leave Tullow on the N81 toward Bunclody. Turn left at the sign for Altamont.

The history of Altamont stretches back many centuries. Monastic settlements, a nunnery and several families have lived and left their mark on this riverside site since before the sixteenth century. The house you see today is a dilapidated Georgian ghost that was built over the foundations of an older castle. The garden, however, is the creation of gardeners from the beginning of the twentieth century; first Fielding Lecky Watson and then his daughter, Corona North. The Watsons were Quakers who came to Carlow in the 1640s. Lecky Watson moved into Altamont in 1923, and when Corona North returned home after serving in World War II, she began working the garden. She died in the late 1990s and, as she had planned, Altamont moved into State hands.

Since then, the existing gardens have been well cared for, restored and expanded. The expansion can be seen in the walled garden where you will find the Corona North Commemorative Border. This double mirroring border was made to hold plants that have a special link to the garden, and so there is a lilac which was bought from the nursery at Altamont thirty years ago. The tree grew too big for its intended home in Dublin and was returned to Altamont as a donation for the new border. A special little hellebore came from Helen Dillon (see The Dillon Garden, County Dublin), who had been given it by David Shackleton of the famed Beech Park gardens that once graced Clonsilla in Dublin. Shackleton himself had received the plant from Lady Moore, wife of Sir Frederick Moore, Director of the National Botanic Gardens, in the late nineteenth century. The provenance of this little plant reads like several chapters of Irish horticultural history. Plants with stories are dotted throughout the borders, from a ligularia found by the plant hunter Dr Augustine Henry, to the Tibetan rose collected by Seamus O'Brien (See Kilmacurragh, County Wicklow), representing the current Irish gardening generation. The granite steps dividing the borders were originally part of the quay walls in Dublin, which were removed to accommodate the Millennium bridge in the late 1990s.

The house and garden are reached by a short, wide avenue of beech trees under-planted with mountain ash or sorbus, and daffodils. A huge *Rhododendron augustinii*, named for Dr Augustine Henry, stretches ten metres up the side of the building. To the garden side of the house there is a fish pool set into a slab-stone terrace studded with iris and angel's fishing rod, or dierama. Arched yews straddle the wide path that runs downhill to the lake. In summer, roses teamed with dusty-pink double *Papavar somniferum* fill the beds on either side of the path, walled-in by stretches of 150-year-old clipped box. In spring, sheets of snowdrops, snowflakes, miniature irises and hellebores of all sorts fill these beds. (There are over forty varieties of snowdrop in the garden.) The path ducks under a golden yew arch shaped like Mickey Mouse ears and towards the lake walk where there is a magnificent specimen of white-flowering handkerchief tree (*Davidia involucrata*).

The pump-house walk leads past a range of rhododendrons down to the bund. This is a marl or clay wall that circles the lake, spiked with bright orange Welsh poppies (*Meconopsis cambrica*), and creeping periwinkle, or vinca. The raised wall holds in the lake but, because it seeps in places, the ground around it is damp and an ideal place for candelabra primulas to naturalise.

The lily-covered lake is surrounded by trees. Tree expert Thomas Pakenham (see Tullynally Castle, County Westmeath) declared the *Pinus sylvestris* here to be the 'best specimen of Scots pine in the country'. The weeping silver birch and a Kilmacurragh cypress (*Chamaecyparis lawsoniana*, 'Kilmacurragh') are also remarkably fine trees.

During the Great Famine, one hundred men worked for two years to dig out this lake by hand. One hundred years later, Mrs North and her husband Garry would drain it, digging out a metre and a half of silt and over sixty fallen trees, before filling it again.

A path leads from the lake to the Ice Age glen and arboretum. The glen is home to over one hundred varieties of rhododendron and a number of venerable sessile oaks (*Quercus petraea*). As another reference to horticultural history, many of the rhododendrons came as seed from Frank Kingdom Ward's plant-hunting expeditions to the Himalayas. In spring this area is golden with wild daffodils, which in turn are followed by sheets of bluebells and ferns. At the bottom of the garden the River Slaney cuts through mature woods and the One Hundred Steps lead down to it from the garden.

At the top of the hill, in a sheep-filled field, there is a little temple with views of the Wicklow and Blackstairs mountains.

As in many other historic gardens around Ireland, the *Sequoiadendron giganteum* here was planted to commemorate the Duke of Wellington. In 1852, the seed collector William Lobb brought specimens of this tree to Europe from the forests of northern California. The Duke of Wellington had died the year before, and it was felt that naming one of the tallest trees in the world 'Wellingtonia' in his honour was entirely appropriate.

From here the track leads to a wisteria-covered bridge over the river and on to a rose walk. The visit rounds off with the nuns' walk, an almost over-mature avenue of beech trees under-planted with small wild primroses, cyclamen, arums and ferns.

KILGRANEY HOUSE
HERB GARDEN | BORRIS ROAD, BAGENALSTOWN, COUNTY CARLOW

Contact: Bryan Leech
Tel: (+353) 059 977 5283
e-mail: info@kilgraneyhouse.com
www: www.kilgraneyhouse.com
Open: May to September, Thursday to Sunday and Bank Holidays 2pm-5pm. Unsuitable for children. No dogs. **Special features:** Partially wheelchair accessible. Accommodation. Meals can be arranged. Art gallery. Herb oils from garden for sale. Car park not suitable for coaches.
Directions: Drive from Bagenalstown to Borris on the R705. The garden is signposted.

This is an interesting and singular garden. The house at Kilgraney was built in 1820; it is handsome and one might expect a certain style of Victorian or Edwardian garden around it. But when Bryan Leech and Martin Marley arrived to take over the old house with their elastic vision, they felt that the place could accommodate something more modern. They were right.

The house stands at the top of a tree-lined drive between fields of grazing cattle. The garden, entered by veering off to the side of the house, starts off behind a tall picket fence. This first small area is the vegetable and fruit garden. In here there are neat, raised beds between crushed granite gravel paths. Potatoes, artichokes, beets and other vegetables line out in utilitarian lines, well-tended in neat, labelled rows. The only flowers found in here, between the vegetables, are bright orange marigolds, grown as companion plants for the vegetables to deter aphids. Some medicinal herbs are grouped together in one area and the different parts of this garden are divided by walls of espaliered fruit trees. A huge bay is being trained as a monster cube in the middle of the garden and a big ornamental vine stretches along the sheltering stone boundary wall.

One always comes away from a garden with an idea worth stealing. In this case it's the use of squares of decking as duckboards for stepping across beds without compacting the soil. They are good-looking, inexpensive, very portable and a whole lot more presentable than planks.

The path leads from the busy workspace of the kitchen garden, by way of a set of steps, to an expanse of pale bright gravel surrounded by weathered granite outhouses and a low stone wall sprouting thyme and marjoram. The feature that draws attention here is the striking stone sculpture by Niall Deacon. This work was created by the artist as part of a garden sculpture master class. It looks perfectly at home in this clean, stark area of the garden.

The trail continues around the outhouses, past a ruined bothy with a rogue elder growing through its broken roof. The little bothy doubles as a sun trap and leaning post for a large fig tree. It is here, in a courtyard of sorts surrounded by the back of the house and a range of out-buildings and little cottages, that the main area of the herb garden is sited.

The beds here are full of architectural plants like angelica and fennel. Another bed, hemmed-in by gravel paths, provides a home to two of gardening's rogues – mint and lady's mantle, *Alchemilla mollis*. Dark green mint foliage mingles with frothy lime lady's mantle flowers to make a picture much prettier than the sum of its parts. Square raised beds made of green oak contain medicinal, culinary and traditional herbs and are topped by beautifully made egg-shaped slate pots, planted up with salvia. The dry, free-draining conditions in these structures suit herbs perfectly. Nicholas Culpeper's famous herbal, written back in 1653, was the inspiration and source for many of the species grown in the herb beds.

The 'cloister' garden is memorable. This is the central area, or the 'monastic' garden, so named as it is reminiscent of a cloister at the centre of a monastery. It even includes pews around the perimeter and a little central pond on which to contemplate. The whole structure is also made of green oak. This wood ages beautifully, turning a soft silver-grey as it weathers. The upright, silvering posts are draped in golden hop and vines, both plants that would have been grown in monasteries for brewing and wine making. Sitting in its pews, one overlooks the aromatic herb garden at yet another striking feature: a four-cornered arch of rusting steel spans. The spans are slowly being colonised by a twining jasmine snaking its way up the metal struts. The foliage will eventually meet over the middle of the path and it will be spectacular, but it is already quite a sight. The metal struts were salvaged, as were so many of the materials in this stylish garden.

On warm days the scent of lavender, box, mint and marjoram fill the air. Boxed-in beds of sage and rosemary compete with their own perfumes and on a sunny day the place is heady with herby smells.

At the bottom of this section of garden there is a little pond that is home to a small gaggle of Call ducks and other fancy fowl, quacking about and, presumably, eating slugs. The view from here out over a rolling patchwork of County Carlow fields and the huge horizon beyond them is exceptional.

This garden is a work in progress, and beyond the herb garden they are developing a young fruit garden with a range of apples, pears, plums and quinces. Nearby is an item Bryan is still working on – a Celtic circle garden made from huge boulders arranged in radiating swirls. It will be interesting to see as it is planted up and matures. The historic garden, part of which dates to the 1700s, can still be seen in places, most particularly in the ghost of an ancient beech hedge that was left unclipped for so long that it turned into a Hobbitesque, conjoined set of beech arches.

The planting on the sunny house walls includes big expanses of shell pink roses that stand out brilliantly against the stone. Below these, frothy lavender fringes the building.

The genius of this garden is not in the inclusion of massive numbers of different species of plants, but in the creative use of a restricted palette. A bed full of nasturtium, or hollyhocks dealt with by someone with a good eye is a thing of great charm.

Delta Sensory Gardens | Strawhall Estate, Carlow, County Carlow

Contact: Eileen Brophy
Tel: (+353) 059 914 3527
e-mail: info@deltacentre.org
www: www.deltacentre.org **Open:** Monday to
Friday 9am-5pm, Saturday/Sunday 12pm-5pm.
January to February closed weekends.

Groups welcome by appointment.
Special features: Wheelchair accessible. Garden
centre. Restaurant. **Directions:** In Carlow town
look for Cannery Road, close to the Athy road.
The garden is signposted from here.

There are times when the mere idea of something is enough to get you feeling good about it. The Delta Sensory Garden on the edge of Carlow town is a place that creates that feeling. It is a feast of glorious gardening set in the middle of the most unlikely surroundings of an industrial estate on the outskirts of the town. I think that it is perfect that a plain utilitarian place of work should be graced by something so uplifting and enhancing. Delta seems to have taken on board the desire to share the beauty around. This should happen more often.

The gardens are attached to the Delta Garden Centre, a community enterprise running educational courses and providing interesting employment. The garden is in fact a whole series of gardens, set out around the centre. Some are contemporary, some are more traditional – but all were made as therapeutic gardens devoted to tantalising the five senses.

Each garden was created by a different talent, including designers and plant collectors Jimi Blake, Mary Reynolds, Elma Fenton, Rachel Doyle and Gordon Ledbetter. Anyone who knows their work will know that their styles are wildly different, and these individual personalities are well in evidence in each of the gardens.

A trail leads between the different gardens and there are good design and plant ideas seen everywhere, from elegant living willow walls to well chosen combinations of grasses and perennials. The use of Virginia creeper draping down to the water's edge around the double Koi pond is a clever idea, as is the pebble beach siding around the smaller of the two ponds.

There are examples of indigenous, historic features: such as a Carlow fence and a woven willow wall. A Carlow fence is a unique Quaker innovation, a stone fence made of undressed lengths of local granite. The second feature is an elegant, decorative, living fence.

Mary Reynolds's garden, inspired by Yeats's poem 'The Stolen Child', is a strange, wild garden – a mix of native trees and shrubs, water and bog with a huge, green sculpture at its centre. It is a lightly tended place teeming with wildlife.

For children there is a giant games garden with monster-sized Jenga, chess, lawn darts and croquet. Quiet areas can be found through willow arches in little bowers at the ends of secret hazel walks, behind tall hedges, and in little sculpture gardens enclosed by tall yew walls.

There are classics like the rose garden, made up of standards, swags draped with climbers, ramblers and low growing carpet roses planted in regular patterns, all hemmed-in by box walls.

There are also more modern ideas like the prairie garden, full of tall waving grasses and zinging splashes of flower. An unusual wooden pyramid, with a green roof garden featuring plants like houseleeks and mosses, takes up the centre of the garden. It can be climbed and the bird's eye view from its roof is a good way to spot little garden areas you might like to investigate further.

The scents of flower and aromatic foliage are everywhere, from lavender and sage to roses and honeysuckle. You are encouraged to touch features from spouting, splurting and dripping water features, to rough and polished granite, limestone, wood, glass and metal sculptures. Big balls of stone seem to float on water and beg to be touched.

This is a modern and developing garden being run by the most enthusiastic and friendly staff. It was only started in 2002, the idea of Eileen Brophy of the Delta Centre, and it opened in 2007. It is a garden worth several visits at different times of the year, particulary for anyone new to gardening. Bring a camera and a notebook.

❀ COUNTY DUBLIN

AIRFIELD | UPPER KILMACUD ROAD, DUNDRUM, DUBLIN 14

Contact: The Manager
Tel: (+353) 01 298 4301
e-mail: trust@airfield.ie / info@airfield.ie
www: www.airfield.ie
Open: Monday to Saturday 10am-5pm, Sunday 11am-5pm **Special Features:** Groups by appointment. Tours can be arranged. Supervised children welcome. Guide dogs. Restaurant. Gift shop. Plant sales. Car and farm museums. Occasional market. Courses.
Directions: Travelling from Stillorgan on the Kilmacud Road Upper, Airfield is on the left and signposted.

Airfield started life as a small farm and cottage dwelling in the 1830s. In 1860 and again in 1913 it was extended by the Overend family to make a larger house with a finer garden. The gardens went into decline in the 1950s, as Dublin and its suburbs encroached on the place, until eventually it became an island of neglected green in the city. In 1995 the Airfield Trust was set up with the aim of restoring it. Since then, the gardens have been overhauled, reconstructed and greatly expanded.

Airfield's crowning glory is the walled garden, a flower-and-scent-filled place made of big herbaceous borders, a pond, rose and herb gardens, as well as trained fruit trees.

Hornbeam hedges were planted to divide the larger space into the smaller rooms that now make up the greater garden. It is designed to be enjoyed from the terrace in front of the house when, in late spring and early summer, there are massive displays of tulips, grown in their hundreds through expanses of hardy geranium, alliums and thalictrum. The tulips justify a visit by themselves. Meanwhile, the scent from the huge, flowering wisteria makes a grand accompaniment to lunch on the terrace later in the summer.

My most recent visit coincided with excitement at a flowering of the Millennium plant, or *Agave Americana* 'Variegata'. News of its flowering had been sent out to the press and the woman at the ticket stand even reminded me that I should be sure to see it. It is this sort of interest from staff that makes a visit to a garden like Airfield stand out a little. So the agave in question was duly looked for and the strange plant, with its five-metre flower spike, was worth seeing. It has been growing in the walled garden since the Overends were babies, as can be seen in an old picture showing one of the sisters posed beside it at the turn of the twentieth century. It first flowered in 2010.

Below the large flower beds, the pond is filled with arum lilies and surrounded by ceanothus, lavender and *Verbena bonariensis*. The herb beds, meanwhile, contain all the usual culinary and medicinal herbs like dill, rue, Russian sage or perovskia and smelly curry plant or santolina.

The mixed borders, one of which faces southwest, are held in by box hedge walls. Tipping out over the box there are mounds of white phlox, *Rosa* 'Lady Hillingdon', *Rosa* 'Mme Isaac Pereire', *Rosa* 'Boule de Neige' and *Rosa gallica*. These are all great roses with scents as exotic as their names.

Apart from the agave, there are some plants worth looking out for in here, such as *Acca sellowiana*, a rare shrub that has beautiful red-and-white edible flowers. *Rehmannia elata*, with a pink flower like penstemon, makes its presence known between June and August. The garden also boasts heavily flowering solanum, eupatorium and the Korean shrub *Tetradium daniellii*, which has fine white flowers and interesting fruit.

Tot's Garden was named for Laetitia Overend, one of the sisters who worked the garden. It is a dry shade garden worth studying. In late spring the

ground is smothered in bluebells, species tulips and a mad scramble of perennial sweet pea all choking out any weeds that might fancy their chances. Within it there is a little pet cemetery, with tiny headstones marking the resting places of a whole raft of dogs, cats and newts that belonged to the sisters.

The Victorian greenhouse outside the walls has recently been well restored. Further out, the old orchard has been rejuvenated and medicinal and dye beds have been planted alongside a two-acre wildflower meadow. This was planned in conjunction with Sandro Caffolla of Design by Nature, a man with a passion for and knowledge of wild flowers. There are now thirty-four varieties of wild flower, including field scabious, chamomile, cowslips, and lesser celandine, ox-eye daisies, mallow, hypericum and ragged robin. Because the field runs alongside a wood and has a damp area and a dry, droughty spot, the variety of plants it can accommodate is fairly comprehensive. So there are woodland plants, damp and shade-lovers, as well as sun-worshippers, all growing in one large area like a living guide to native Irish flowers.

The children's garden club outside the walled garden is where junior gardeners learn how to grow flowers and vegetables in a weekly club. They work with the Airfield gardeners and learn from their own experiments. This is a popular, and even over-subscribed idea that could be copied in many gardens near a town or city.

Finally, take a stroll over the farm walk past fields of sheep and Jersey, Aberdeen Angus and Shorthorn cattle. Thousands of native broad leaf trees have been, and continue to be, planted in the woods around these fields.

As a countryside visit set well within the city boundaries, Airfield is unique. The peace and quiet are remarkable and it is with something of a shock that one hits the noisy Kilmacud Road outside the gate.

Ardgillan Demesne | Balbriggan, County Dublin

Contact: Dominica McKevitt
Tel: (+353) 01 849 2212
e-mail: parks@fingalcoco.ie
www: www.fingalcoco.ie
Open: Daily: Winter 10am-5pm, Summer 10am-6pm No entrance fee. Tour charges. Supervised children. Dogs on leads. Partially wheelchair accessible. Tours of the gardens are given from June to August on Thursdays at 3.30pm, or at other times by appointment.
Special features: Garden museum. Castle. Tea room. **Directions:** Travelling north on the M1, take the turn for Balrothery. The demesne is well signposted.

The view from the top of the hill at the entrance to Ardgillan is a breath-catching one. Within the panoramic vista, there is a long sweep of lawn, a gigantic cedar of Lebanon, herbaceous plantings, regiments of clipped yews, terraced rose and flower beds, the house and beyond that the sea and the Mourne Mountains. While adults drink in all that, children will probably be tempted to roll down the hill.

The Reverend Robert Taylor built the house at Ardgillan in 1738 on a site overlooking the Irish Sea in north County Dublin, and his descendants lived there until 1962. In the 1980s the house and nearly two hundred acres of parkland and gardens were taken over by Fingal County Council, which began to restore the formal gardens, using the 1865 Ordnance Survey maps for reference.

Pictures of Ardgillan always include the Victorian greenhouse, the centre-piece of the garden. This too was restored and it now houses a big vine and peach.

But the interesting feature here is the walled garden and its unusual inner free-standing walls. These walls punctuate the two-acres and divide them into several distinct gardens. Some of the walls are whitewashed and niched in an example of pure Victorian ingenuity: whitewash would attract the maximum amount of sun, and the niches improved air circulation behind the fruit trees, which would, as a result, perform better.

The shelter afforded by the walls and surrounding mature woodland renders the climate in the walled garden particularly soft and clement. An indicator of that is the tender specimen of *Dodonaea viscosa* 'Purpurea', which has survived here since 1992. Within the walls there are raised, sunny alpine and scree borders as well as beds dedicated to herbaceous plants, shrubs and climbers, arranged around a cruciform trellis. There is also a well laid-out *potager* and beyond that a herb garden.

Little gates divide and link these, making them feel private and secluded. The old sheds, having been rebuilt, now house a garden museum; gardeners love poring over old, strange and obscure gardening implements.

In addition, there is a maze-like Irish garden with a collection of native plants – gathered or found in Ireland, as well as some bred by Irish gardeners or found abroad by Irish collectors. The collection of Irish fruit trees, being trained along wires, is of particular interest to gardeners today, as growing native fruit varieties is growing in popularity. Knowing that a certain tree was bred in a certain county gives us the chance to pick a variety bred for our particular site and soil. It also goes some small way toward re-stocking small corners of each county with trees that historically belong there.

I love the tiny greenhouses at each corner of the walled garden. They might be dilapidated, but they are picturesque and hopefully they can be restored soon.

There are about 8km of paths through the woods, parkland and gardens. Three features not to be missed are the yew walk, the Lady's stairs and the ice house. The stairs is a quaint pedestrian footbridge which crosses the Balbriggan road and the Dublin-Belfast rail line, supposedly to allow ladies to cross to the sea for bathing. It is, as might be expected, haunted by one of them. The ice house was recently uncovered and lastly, for potentilla enthusiasts, the National Collection is housed in a garden of its own near the house.

THE DILLON GARDEN | 45 SANDFORD ROAD, RANELAGH, DUBLIN 6

Contact: Helen and Val Dillon
Tel: (+353) 01 497 1308
e-mail: info@dillongarden.com
Open: March, July and August,
Every day 2pm-6pm / April, May, June,
September, Sunday 2pm-6pm
Special features: Teas may be arranged for
groups. **Directions:** Signposted off Sandford
Road by the church at the intersection between
Sandford and Marlborough Roads.

It is hard to know where to start with the Dillon Garden. The word 'shrine' might hit the mark. This is a place of pilgrimage for gardeners the country over, not a small number of whom feel that a favourable comparison between a plant in their garden and a specimen here is an achievement to be pointed out at every opportunity. Set in town in a not-too-huge space, it is a garden that fools the amateur into believing that they could imitate and replicate parts of it themselves.

Once you have passed through the front, a cool confection of white barked birch trees over gravel and aeoniums, the huge box of chocolates that is the main garden is reached through a gate in the wall.

The long canal, set into a thirty-metre length of polished limestone, is the first feature to come into view. A perfect circle of unadorned water sits at the top of it like the dot on a letter 'i'. These waterworks replaced what was one of the best-loved lawns in the country – still missed by some people. The canal is perfect however, flanked by two perfect flowerbeds: one of blues, mauves and whites, with goat's rue, tons of campanula, delphiniums, asters, viola, and clematis grown as ground cover. The other contains the vivid reds, oranges, yellows and wines of lobelia, French honeysuckle (*Hedysarum coronarium*), dahlia, cannas, cimicifuga, kniphofia, heuchera, sanguisorba, lychnis, a native called *Valeriana officinalis* and even kale. The water in the middle reflects all this.

These beds can be inspected from every angle and, like the best borders, they are different from every viewpoint and from one end of the season to the other. Annual poppies in all shades spring up between everything at the height of summer, dotting the place with every conceivable shade of dirty-pink, plum and shell. Violas and pansies insinuate themselves into the smallest bit of available space.

Tucked in behind the cool border is the added surprise of a series of raised vegetable beds and big aluminium bins planted up with peas, scallions, Swiss chard and spinach. Helen lines out the vegetables with the same care as the ornamentals, but fans are again divided over the suitability of such a radical approach the Dillon shrine.

On the subject of productive gardening, the latest arrival is a handsome fox-proof hen house set within a grove of bamboo, dierama, pruned-up *Arbutus unedo* and clipped box hedging. This is the elegant *chez nous* of a flock of pretty chickens. I love the pink sweet rose, *Rosa* 'Marie Pavic', that grows outside their fence.

It is almost impossible to see that the outer walls are made of stone, behind the massed climbers, shrubs, old tea roses, azara, tree peonies, potato vine (*Solanum crispum*) and clematis.

Fine statuary, little paths tip-toeing in and around beds, the best garden flowers and 'trained-up' small trees are all features of the Dillon garden – but the aralia garden is something that really stands out. This is a small area planted up with a number of different aralias including *A. Echinocaulis*. On the light-speckled ground underneath the canopy, clumps of ferns such as *Polystichum setiferum* and hellebores are set into expanses of gravel. One of the polystichums here was a present from Cecily Hall (see Primrose Hill, County Dublin). Helen is quick to point out how brilliantly low maintenance this area is – requiring only 'about twenty-four hours a year,' she says frankly.

Trellises and pergolas, arches and walks for clematis, rose and sweet pea, lead in and out of the different garden rooms. Tall foxgloves, teasels and marigolds grow happily in the shade under the arches. There are alpine beds and a cold house that homes frost-tolerant but damp-hating alpine plants. They suffer miserably in rot-inducing, wet Irish weather.

The sunny back of the house is covered with a huge ceanothus that can be seen to best advantage from the end of the garden. At the base of the wall there are troughs full of white petunias, trained box, argyranthemum and helichrysum. Pots of annuals pour into each other like old-fashioned champagne-glass fountains. Dahlias grown here in buckets from spring onwards are then placed elsewhere around the garden in time for their flowering season. The same applies to buckets of agapanthus. A big bed of both black and green aeoniums basking in the sun bears witness to the heat trap the garden wall is.

I likened the Dillon garden to a box of chocolates. If that is so, then it is one without the unloved coconut cream.

The Duignan Garden | 21 Library Road, Shankill, County Dublin

Contact: Carmel Duignan
Tel: (+353) 01 282 4885
e-mail: cbduignan@eircom.net
Open: May to September, by appointment to

groups and for occasional open days through the
Dublin Garden Group.
Directions: On appointment.

How many plants can you fit in a given space? A lot more than you might imagine, and a lot more beautifully than might be expected – if your name is Carmel Duignan. The Duignan garden is a remarkable place, a small-town garden that still manages to contain more beautifully grown unusual and rare plants than many larger gardens worth their salt. It is something of a horticultural Tardis. In the words of an estate agent, it would be described as 'deceptively spacious'. The estate agent would skip quietly past the fact that it is a garden laboured over relentlessly by a hardworking gardener, and that these are the sort of good looks that don't happen by themselves.

From the first instant, a tumble of notable things comes parading past the visitor. In the main back garden, the first sight is a jungle-like combination of schefflera knotted through a tall tree dahlia and *Salvia corrugata*, a plant from Ecuador that is, as its name suggests, corrugated. Carmel says that the dahlia will never flower in this climate, but that it doesn't matter as she grows it for its foliage.

From there the show begins to gather momentum, with gorgeous *Dahlia* 'Admiral Rawlinson', *Fuchsia boliviana*, *Tetrapanax papyrifer* 'Rex' and big trumpet-flowered datura. There is nothing ordinary here.

Carmel has a talent and interest in propagation and experimentation and she takes full advantage of the sheltered aspect the garden enjoys, to raise plants not often seen in Irish gardens. Many of the agapanthus grown here were raised from seed and consequently include some rarities. They are used as spot-plants throughout the garden. But for all its experimentation, this is no haphazard laboratory garden with all the nuts and bolts on show. The arrangements are perfect, and well thought-out combinations of colour and texture, height and shape abound.

The plot is a long rectangle, sloping up gradually with a central lawn dividing deep mixed borders on either side. We stopped to look at a striking black, thorny *Kalopanax pictus*. Not unusual, but also certainly striking, is a pale lilac geranium called 'Rozanne' that Carmel uses in several places at the front of the borders to tie different plant combinations together. Geraniums are useful linking plants for this sort of task.

The colour mixes everywhere are strong and assured, so there will be a vivid yellow tansy with black ophiopogon grass, black dahlias with blood red *Rosa* 'Bengal Crimson' and red cotinus overhead. Carmel has what she calls an 'ecclesiastical love' of red and purple – seen in one corner with a *Clematis* 'Polish Spirit' climbing through red roses. Elsewhere the whites and greens of *Hydrangea* 'Annabel', *H.* 'Limelight' and limy aralias create a cooler look.

Carmel has a great interest in exotics but she is equally in love with plants that have Irish connections, and there are examples of this everywhere throughout the garden. Little paths pick their way, this way and that, past treasures. Among the choicer Irish plants she pointed out are *Clematis* 'Glasnevin Dusk' with dark purple flowers, a fuchsia named after Christine Bamford, who bred fuschias in Wexford, and a *Deutzia* 'Alpine Magician', named by the botanist and horticultural taxonomist for the National Botanic Gardens, Charles Nelson.

It is a garden that one could wander through and enjoy hugely without a shred of horticultural knowledge, simply admiring all the unusual and lovely plants. But for those with a more serious interest, it is a treasure trove of fabulous sights owned by a guide who can satisfy the curious with insight and information.

I left with the intelligence that Carmel also has an allotment, and made a mental note to ask if I might get to see that one day . . .

FARMLEIGH | THE PHOENIX PARK, DUBLIN 7

Contact: Sharon Doyle
Tel: (+353) 01 815 5900
e-mail: farmleighinfo@opw.ie
www: www.farmleigh.ie **Open:** All year.
Thursday to Sunday and bank holidays. There may be closures if required for Government business.

Directions: Drive up the main Chesterfield Avenue in the park in the direction of Castleknock. Near the Castleknock gates the garden is signposted to the left.

The Phoenix Park is a remarkable place. But no less remarkable are the individual gardens within the great city park. Farmleigh, in a hidden corner of the park, was once the property of the Guinness family. It is now owned by the State and came as a stunning surprise to the public when it was first opened to visitors several years ago.

In the short time since it was unveiled, it has become one of the favourite national horticultural treasures, not only as a garden but as a venue for a whole range of garden activities, talks, demonstrations and expositions. But it needs no special activities to make it worth a trip. A simple walk around the grounds and gardens is all it takes to make one fall for the place.

Tended by a small number of seriously talented gardeners, Farmleigh is like a master class in Big House gardening. There is so much about the place that is impressive – particularly the tiny number of people who manage this massive project.

The visit starts properly at the coach yard, a lovely place in itself with a huge wisteria and great oversized, overstuffed window boxes created by Adelaide Monk that are fantastic. But the American red ash *Fraxinus pennsylvanica* just outside the yard is the wow plant here. It is a fine tree at the best of times but breath-taking in autumn when it turns scarlet, and rears above the courtyard like a flaming cloud.

From here, the route leads out to the productive, decorative vegetable and fruit gardens where old and new varieties are grown and tested together in neat rows. The way into the garden proper leads from here up through a fern walk past an unusually pruned-up *Parrotia persicaria*. This is a shrub most often seen with its skirts swishing along the ground but it works very well, taking up a little less space into the bargain, with its trunk unveiled.

The conservatory is next in line. Filled with lemon trees, cannas, and an abutilon, which Adelaide thinks might be the tallest in Ireland. *Dracaena reflexa* is an unusual striped yucca-like plant that certainly calls for attention, and we inspected a banana called *Ensete ventricosum*. Adelaide grew this two-metre tall plant from seed planted in 2009. The exotic good looks of these plants are matched only by the attention to every little detail in their care.

The path to the walled garden runs between a walk of magnolias that feature fine specimens of *Magnolia* 'Elizabeth', *M.* 'Leonard Messel,' *M.* 'Atlas' and *M.* 'Milky Way'.

The walled garden is of course the centrepiece of the garden. It boasts impressive flower and shrub borders, fine statuary set in among well designed walks and all sorts of special plants, from old unidentified tree peonies and daylilies to tall cynaria (artichoke).

Lanning Roper, the American landscape architect, was responsible for the design. He had a great love of sculptural plants and his yew-backed borders here are perfection. I love the cut-flower borders full of lined-up verbena, aquilegia, sweet pea and thalictrum.

Meanwhile, the tulip displays are worth seeing in early summer. Mad orange and shocking pink tulips planted through blue cammasia are just one of the zingier combinations.

There are rose, wisteria and clematis pergolas, gorgeous magnolias, including the great scented *Magnolia kobus*, which is like the best possible version of *M. stellata*.

Adelaide grows so many of the plants in here from seed, a particular love being agapanthus which, she says, 'thrive on abuse'. Their only drawback is that they take a long time to grow and require a great deal of patience.

The greenhouse in here is something of a hub. In summer it is used for growing a number of different chillies and tomatoes; in winter it is hauled into service to mind oleander seedlings, as well as over-wintering semi-tender plants sheltering from the weather. Hauling huge numbers of pots in and out of the greenhouse is only one of the jobs the small team does twice every year.

Outside, vegetables and fruit trees share the space with flowers and the ever-present deep tall yew hedges. There are two miles of yew hedges in this garden, cared for by Noel Ford, who is a perfectionist when it comes to hedging.

On the subject of hedging, the Dutch garden is a marvel. This is one of very few examples of a topiary garden on the island. But this well-clipped feature would hold its own beside any other one might care to compare it with. The contrast between sharp shrubs and sunken beds of fluffy nepeta and tulips makes for quite a sight. And to get to it, the path runs through a cherry walk.

The grounds are extensive and take in lakeside walks and a boat house. Come for special events by all means, but make time to visit it during the year for its own sake, too.

Marlay Demesne and Regency Walled Gardens |
Grange Road, Rathfarnham, Dublin 16

Contact: Michael Church
Tel: (+353) 01 493 7372
e-mail: parks@dlrcoco.ie
Open: February to June, 10am-5pm/July to
August 10am-8pm/September to October,
10am-5pm /November to January, 10am-4pm
No entrance fee. Supervised children welcome.
No dogs.

Special features: Historic house. Craft shops.
Partially wheelchair accessible. Coffee shop.
Tennis courts, golf course, playing fields.
Directions: Leave the M50 at Exit 13. Take the
road signed to Rathfarnham, which leads to
Grange Road. Marlay is accessed from the
car park.

Set in the middle of great expanses of parkland, mature woods and walks, the
Regency walled gardens at Marlay Park are something of a surprise. The rest of
the demesne, while it is a great green oasis in the city, with lots of amenity value,
is essentially a park. But tucked behind a grove of ash, oak and yew, there is a
quaint cottage like something from one of Grimm's tales. Inside is a tearoom,
and through its trellis-surrounded back door, there is a garden to knock the
breath out of the unsuspecting, and even suspecting, visitor. I never walk through
that gate without a heart-skip.

This is a restored garden of real merit. First of all, it is huge. Second, it is
beautifully planted up. And lastly, it is minded with an amount of care and
attention that is quite remarkable. I would almost dare someone to find a point
worth criticising here.

Along the north wall of the first of the three garden sections is a shaded grove
made up of winding golden gravel paths under and between shrubs and trees.
Under the taller storeys there are solid clipped box balls, and architectural foliage
plants like acanthus, sprawling salvia and euphorbia gathered together in groups.
This area is, in essence, the wilderness bordering the formal garden that its paths
lead out to.

Out in the sun, benches painted in soft green *Eau de Nil* line up along precisely edged paths
that slice between perfect lawns, studded with different sized and shaped flower borders.

The order and neatness of the lawns and gravel paths is in sharp contrast to the over-the-top explosions of colour, height and texture in the beds. Mixes of hollyhock scabious, achillea, aconites, stachys and different varieties of hardy geranium seem almost shoe-horned into the beds. The loose flowers are held in by crossed hurdles of rustic sticks about 40cm long. It is so obvious that the gardeners have great fun with flowers here, mixing red and bronze hemerocallis with plum cotinus, cytisus and red achillea.

As if all that weren't enough for the flower-mad gardeners, they have placed huge planters full of colourful flowers, bananas and tree ferns at the points where lawn meets path.

A grotto or 'wet wall' was created on the shaded side of the dividing wall, between beds of arums and ferns. It drips water and is slowly being colonised by hart's tongue fern or *Phyllitis scolopendrium*. Meanwhile, on the sunny south-facing wall, the quaint summer house continues the Grimm's tales look. This house is a mix of thatch and more rustic poles and, like the wet wall and orangerie, it was another popular feature in early nineteenth-century gardening.

The second walled garden is where the vegetable and cut-flower garden is sited. Widely spaced goblet-trained fruit trees stand over perfect circles of earth cut out of the lawn. In the vegetable beds, neat rows of chard contrast with billowing marjoram and parsley. The rustic poles are seen again here, holding in vegetables. I was told that they deter the peacocks, which are lazy birds that are intent on, but easily dissuaded from, attacking the crops. Elsewhere they use box and lavender as edging plants. On the subject of peacocks, it is extraordinary how so many gardeners find these birds — symbols of refinement, beauty and nobility — nothing more than a bit of a pest, willing to eat and damage flowers and foliage as well as bugs and slugs.

The productive beds are just as good-looking as the ornamental areas: the sculptural globe artichoke bed is beautiful and the pear and apple pergola walks are a source of fascination for anyone interested in how to train and shape fruit trees. For those who think gardens take too long to grow, these apple and pear arches were only planted in 2001 and are already impressively mature.

Past chive walls, we hit the raspberry and potato patches, medlar and current bushes, rows of loganberries, plums and pears. With current tastes so taken up with productive gardens, this is a massively popular place with visitors and there were a few people with notebooks out as I walked around, presumably with a view to copying at home some of the ideas seen here.

Leaving this garden you notice the unusual garden sheds with curved walls. These are the old bothies, and today they house tools and pens for the peacocks and other fancy fowl. The way out is under an ancient wisteria that arches over the opening in the wall.

This glorious garden came about as a result of a long and painstaking restoration project. Using old maps and books from the early 1800s, when the first gardens were laid out. The historic layouts of the long-gone garden were unearthed and restored. But the care lavished on the finished product is what impresses most. Medals all round.

PHOENIX PARK WALLED VICTORIAN GARDEN |
THE PHOENIX PARK, DUBLIN 7

Contact: Reception
Tel: (+353) 01 821 3021
e-mail: phoenixparkvisitorcentre@opw.ie
www: www.phoenixpark.ie.
Open: All year
Special features: Admission free.

Wheelchair accessible. Restaurant. Growing demonstrations first Saturday of every month at 10.30am. Veg from the garden can be bought at weekends. **Directions:** Situated in the Phoenix Park, close to the visitors centre near the Castleknock gates. Signposted.

The Phoenix Park is one of the greatest jewels the country possesses. It is at once one of the greatest city parks in the world and home to a huge number of individual entities, including polo grounds and hospitals, the Dublin Zoo, Victorian tea rooms and Ashtown castle, the official homes of both the President of the Republic and the United States Ambassador to Ireland, the headquarters of the Garda Síochána, the official government hospitality venue and the Ordnance Survey Office, herds of deer, playgrounds and Viking burial grounds, historic monuments such as the magazine fort, massive numbers of fine trees, individual parks and gardens, and the workplace of over 2,200 people.

Situated in the middle of the huge park, just beside Ashtown castle, the oldest building in the place, is the walled kitchen garden. This restored Victorian ornamental fruit and vegetable garden is a gem. Enter it from the central main entrance to catch the best first view of the chief feature – the central walk between the double borders. These long beds are stuffed to capacity with changing perennials, from alstroemeria and agapanthus to achillea, aconitum and agastache. And these are only the As. They look good from spring right up to the beginning of winter. I have never seen them looking anything less than lovely. The two beds are corseted at the front by box and backed by wire-trained fruit trees, which will eventually look like giant candelabras.

Behind the trained trees you will find vegetable beds that are so well worked they make perfect demonstration beds, like living textbooks on kitchen gardening. Among these there are herb gardens, rotation beds, soft fruit bushes, lines of strawberries and well arranged lines of lettuce and leeks. Meanwhile a dozen or so rhubarb forcers sit at the edge of a bed waiting for a job of work. From mid-summer on, the little sunflower field becomes more and more dramatic and brash as the neighbouring pumpkin patch fills up with swelling monster veg. Good housekeeping and upkeep are the things that set a vegetable garden apart and this is truly an impeccably maintained garden, one that would send you home with a yen to begin growing food.

The garden is worked by helpful and knowledgeable staff, happy to stop for a few minutes and answer questions. They also give regular demonstrations on growing throughout the summer season.

In the winter of 2011, work was being carried out to restore the long range of greenhouses and vine houses built by Jacob Owen in 1850 on the south-facing wall. This will be visible along the back wall of the garden, down through the double borders, and will be a great addition. Meanwhile, a small orchard of Irish cultivar apple trees is being planted. It is always good to see expansion.

Outside the walls there are some magnificent trees: cedars of Lebanon, giant Scots pines, holm oaks and blue cedars. The miniature maze of box beside the castle is fun for children and from here the choice of things to do and see in the park stretches out in front of you. You can even take a tour on a Segway these days; a novel way to inspect trees.

Don't miss a visit to the People's Garden down at the main entrance at Park Gate Street. This garden came about as part of a forward-thinking civic plan in the 1830s to create a 'Healthy People's Garden', complete with flower beds and drinking fountains of clean water for the citizens to enjoy. The huge rockery here is in the middle of restoration. This has been re-sited three times in its long life, and today it is fronted by unusual ribbon beds where eight rows of bedding are laid out precisely in strings of colour along the ground. Close by, under the shelter of the trees, the unusual modern 1950s shelter designed by Raymond McGrath jars somewhat with the Victorian feel of the Peoples Garden, but it is interesting nevertheless.

Lately, a collection of rare hawthorns has been planted into the laurel lawn bordering the People's Garden, as well as 150 Princeton elms or *Ulmus americana* 'Princeton' planted in an unusual mound system. (The Princeton elm is a cultivar found to be resistant to Dutch elm disease.) On my most recent visit, as we drove on past these, we spotted a huge gorilla sitting on top of a ten-metre pole inside the zoo fence, surveying his world, the fantastic Phoenix Park.

THE NATIONAL BOTANIC GARDENS | GLASNEVIN, DUBLIN 9

Contact: Reception
Tel: (+353) 01 804 0300 / 01 857 0909
e-mail: botanicgardens@opw.ie
www: www.botanicgardens.ie
Open: All year daily (closed Christmas Day): Summer, 9am-6pm/

Winter, 9am-4.30pm. No entrance fee. Car parking fee. **Special features:** Wheelchair accessible. Restaurant. Book shop and visitor centre. Courses and lectures. Guided tours for a fee.
Directions: Situated on the north side of the city on Botanic Road.

To me, the National Botanic Gardens in Dublin is one of the loveliest botanic gardens in the world. It is beautiful at all times of year, functional, well loved by Dubliners and visitors alike, a place of recreation and serious botanical research and conservation, a green lung in the city, a haven for wildlife and a tourist attraction of the first order.

Founded in 1795, the Botanic Gardens constitute Ireland's foremost botanical and horticultural institution. It played, and continues to play, a vital role in the conservation of rare, imported and unusual plants. Throughout its history, all the great gardens around the island have been involved in the division and sharing of plants with the Botanic Gardens, and it has been a great force for good in the world of Irish horticulture.

Education and research have played a part of the work of the Botanic Gardens since soon after its foundation in 1795, when six boys were taken on as apprentices, to be paid *if* their work was considered satisfactory. Today, it is still a classroom and laboratory for the horticulture students that will bring Irish gardening into the future.

The plant collections are a delight, arranged in geographical and scientific groupings in a landscaped setting on the banks of the River Tolka. The layout

incorporates rock gardens, alpine yards, rose gardens, order beds, herb and vegetable gardens, a pond, herbaceous and shrub borders, wall plants and an arboretum.

The four glasshouses include the Victoria house, built specially to house the giant Amazon water lilies beloved of generations of small children. Other houses contain succulents, palms, orchids, ferns and alpines. The curvilinear houses, built by Richard Turner in 1848 and with additional work carried out by himself and his son William twenty years later, are justly world famous. They have been magnificently restored. The wonderful palm house, guarded by the 1870-planted Chusan palm (*Trachycarpus fortunei*) beside it, has also been restored. These elegant houses, with their delicate cream paintwork, lacy iron veins and warm granite bases, are once again the pride of the wonderful Botanic Gardens. A specially developed shade of cream called 'Turner White' was used on the restored houses rather than the previous stark white. The reason for this is that the original paint had oxidised to a similar creamy colour soon after application.

There are so many sights to see at any time of the year throughout the garden. It might be a heavily-laden *Cornus kousa* white with flowers or bracts, or the line of baby Wollemi pines that will one day be an impressive avenue, or the temporary fun of a sun flower maze near the front gate, or the heat of the alpine house full of little gravel-mulched pots of special plants. My own magnet is always the rockery, which is such a beautifully laid-out mature feature. Its mix of gnarled little acers over alpines and small bulbs, low-growing, spreading perennials and sub-shrubs always lures me in.

The most recent addition to the gardens is a walled fruit and vegetable garden. This garden is run on strict organic principles. They grow over two hundred different crops in here, using a range of different organic methods to both feed and protect the plants from pests and disease. It is a fascinating and educational display area. One of the great features here is the willingness of the staff to stop and explain what they are doing to visitors. You will not leave without a tip on how to better grow your own veg at home. Look out for the square-foot beds, devoted to showing how many edible plants can be fitted into a postage-stamp sized border. The green manures are worth inspecting too.

There is always something worth seeing, from a temporary garden-related sculpture exhibition to the gardeners laying out a border of exotics for a summer display, almost using rulers to make sure the spacing between plants is perfect.

The Botanic Gardens have been a favourite haunt of Dubliners for centuries. A whole range of people use them – from painting groups studying and sketching the summer borders, to school classes being hauled along for nature walks, horticultural students studying the well-labelled plants and families out for a Sunday walk. If I lived in Dublin it would have to be next door to 'the Bots'.

Primrose Hill | Lucan, County Dublin

Contact: Robin Hall
Tel: (+353) 01 628 0373
www: www.dublingardens.com
Open: February daily 2pm-6pm, June to end of July, daily 2pm-6pm. Groups welcome by appointment only. Supervised children.

Special features: Plants for sale.
Directions: In Lucan village, turn into Primrose Lane, opposite the AIB Bank. The garden is at the top of the lane. Buses must park in village as they will not fit up the drive.

Primrose Hill is one of the most charming gardens in the country. Attached to a fine Regency house attributed to the famous eighteenth-century architect James Gandon, it is a plantsman's garden, created over the past fifty years by the Hall family. That said, it has the look of a garden from another age; an old-fashioned, quirky, personal and colourful place, chock-full of plants, flowers and scents.

The impressive, hardworking Robin Hall tends this stuffed-to-capacity garden. His mother Cecily began work here in the 1950s when she took on the long-neglected site, turning it into a garden with a particular leaning towards old-fashioned cultivars. The garden now has one of the largest collections of small flowering plants in the country, a famous collection of snowdrops, which can be seen during the spring, many varieties of lobelias and a developing five-acre arboretum.

The beds in the walled garden are beautiful, filled with red lobelia and magenta *Salvia grahamii*, yellow santolina, big Scottish thistles and papavars in a whole range of shades that do battle with each other to great effect in the summer months. Good, gutsy plant combinations stand out everywhere. *Rosa moyesii* sits in the centre of a border beside fine campanula and *Crocosmia* 'Lucifer'. Strong colours are more fun to work with: gold and pink, purple, yellow and plum mix in and out of each other, showing clearly that a gardener can get away with brazen colours if they approach them thoughtfully.

Plants live cheek-by-jowl in these beds and the weeds have only a small chance of moving in, given that their cultivated brethren have accounted for every bit of space.

Tiptoe over the little stone paths between dangling barriers of angel's fishing rods or dierama. This is an assault course made of flowers, with *Anemone hupehensis* and *Digitalis lutea* self-seeding everywhere in the paving cracks, pushing and shoving for those spaces with tall verbena and steely-white eryngium. Masses of early foxglove or digitalis spires are replaced by seas of phlox later in the summer, so it always feels like a crush of flowers.

The ground under Arctic beech (*Nothofagus antarctica*), different birches, tree peonies, mahonia and sweet-smelling philadelphus, is full of gardener's garters, pale yellow sisyrinchium, lilies of all sorts and swathes of hellebores.

The sunny house wall is covered in an aged vine, intertwined with honeysuckle. The two gnarled trunks are like living scaffolding, architectural and lovely. Close by, in a shady spot, the fernery holds a sizable collection of native and exotic ferns, and in front of it the ground is carpeted with golden oregano (*Origanum vulgare* 'Aureum'), which gives off a wonderful smell when walked on.

I left leaving Robin a happy man, as the *Veratrum californicum,* given to him by the people at the Botanic Gardens eighteen years ago, had just flowered for the first time. Patience – the virtue of gardeners.

ROYAL HOSPITAL KILMAINHAM |
MILITARY ROAD, KILMAINHAM, DUBLIN 8

Contact: Mary Condon
Tel: (+353) 01 612 9900
e-mail: info@imma.ie **www:** www.imma.ie
Open: All year (closed 25 and 26 December). No entrance fee. **Special features:** Partially wheelchair accessible. Irish Museum of Modern Art. Bookshop. Restaurant. Guided tours can be arranged. **Directions:** Travelling along St John's Road West by Heuston Station, turn left onto Military Road. The entrance is 200m along, on the right.

Built by James Butler, the second Duke of Ormonde, in the 1680s, the Royal Hospital was modelled on Les Invalides, the retired soldier's hospital in Paris. Similarities between it and the Chelsea Pensioners Home in London are also striking. The Royal Hospital in Kilmainham is considered to be Ireland's finest seventeenth-century building. It is certainly one of Dublin's most striking buildings and a fitting home to the Irish Museum of Modern Art (IMMA).

Lined along the north-facing front of the building, the restored garden stands below the hospital on a shelf of land looking out over the River Liffey and across to the Phoenix Park, which was also laid out by the Duke of Ormonde as a deer park.

It is known as the Master's garden and it is a magnificent place, worthy of a visit over and above any visit to the museum. The garden was an important feature of the hospital's design, when the governors declared that 'a garden should lie all open to the north side of the Hospital for the greater grace of the house' and for the recreation of the retired soldiers.

Its five acres are formal in fashion, in keeping with the French-style building and, as was also the style, it can be seen and studied in full from the main reception rooms. The layout involves four large squares, each sub-divided by horizontal avenues in a *patte d'oie* or goose-foot pattern. Hornbeam hedges along with pleached limes and rows of yew pyramids line the different avenues, which converge on a central pond. Each path leads up to a focal point which will either be a piece of topiary or classical statuary. The planting is sparse and restrained and box hedges, lollipop-trained hollies, statues and soft-coloured golden gravel work together to create a cool, ordered, imposing garden.

The straight lines of trees were quaintly given the name of 'wilderness'. Today the word conjures pictures of wild growth; in the seventeenth century it described a formal wood. The Master of the Hospital, at the time this feature was being laid out, was the Earl of Meath, who was in the process of carrying out similar work to his garden at Killruddery in Bray (see Killruddery, County Wicklow).

At one time there would have been a section given over to vegetables grown by the old soldiers. Today this is represented in a small sectioned-off herbaceous border, running down one side of the garden. Box-enclosed beds full of tulips, irises, nepeta and rudbekia replace the cabbages and onions that the men would have grown.

A wide formal stairway marked by large lead urns leads down to the garden from the viewing terrace. In the planters lined out along the top of the wall, purple and white pelargoniums and aubrietia make small but strong concessions to colour. A group of big chestnuts render this terrace a shady, sheltered place in the summer. The huge walls that drop down to the garden are draped and softened by expansive sheets of *Parthenocissus quinquefolia*.

In a garden such as this, upkeep is everything. A flower border can go untended for a while and still look good; a garden of formal clipped greenery forgives nothing. It must be tended with nail-scissors accuracy. Fortunately for this garden, it is obviously much loved and cared for. It is a splendid place, splendidly minded.

Apart from the classical works in the Master's garden, there are some fine contemporary sculptures arranged about the upper gardens. On the way into the garden you will have passed large works by Tony Cragg and Barry Flanagan. But the most interesting piece is in the garden itself – a work called 'North South East and West' by Linda Benglis. It is temporarily sited in the fountain in front of the restored tea house.

The tea house, an unusual stone and red-brick folly, is the focal point in the garden. It is thought that this was originally built as a banqueting house, and it also housed the gardener and his family in the early twentieth century. The view from it through the garden provides a perfect picture of the hospital and its towering copper spire.

Outside the walls, the large hilly wild flower meadow is cut twice yearly, but otherwise left to nature. This area was the site of the old hospital graveyard. It leads up to the historic Bully's Acre, the oldest graveyard in Ireland.

The gardens at Kilmainham are both historically interesting as well as beautiful. Given that the National War Memorial Gardens are only a short walk away; a trip to both might make an interesting pair of military-related gardens. Add in a trip to all the gardens in the Phoenix Park across the river for a full-scale tour.

The Talbot Botanic Gardens, Malahide Demesne |
Dublin Road, Malahide, County Dublin

Contact: Paul McDonnell
Tel: (+353) 01 890 5609
www: www.fingalcoco.ie **Walled garden open:**
May to September, daily 2pm-5pm
Special features: Historic castle. Museum. Model
railway. Tea room. Craft shops. Tours of garden on
Wednesdays at 2pm, or by appointment at other
times. To see auricula collection visit in April.
Contact for opening details. Partially wheelchair
accessible. **Directions:** Driving from Fairview to
Malahide, turn right at the sign for Malahide
Castle. The entrance is on the left.

The castle at Malahide was lived in continuously by the Talbot family from the 1180s, when the lands were granted to Richard Talbot by the English Crown, until 1973, when the last of the family, Lord Milo de Talbot, died. He left the castle and lands to the Parks Department of Dublin County Council (the demesne is now managed by Fingal County Council).

Despite the lengthy history of the demesne, the gardens are young – they were largely created by Lord Milo between 1947 and 1973. He was a learned and enthusiastic gardener who set out to create a garden full of tender and less common plants, many of them from Tasmania, New Zealand and Australia; all places with which he had connections.

The variety of plants in Malahide is limited by the alkalinity of the soil, which is measured at 6.97 pH. This prevents the growing of acid-loving plants. In Malahide, visitors with alkaline soil in their own gardens for once need not be green-eyed at the numbers of plants on show that they cannot grow themselves. Genera well represented here include euphorbia, crocosmia, hebe, pittosporum, escallonia and the National Collections of olearia and clematis. Great sweeps of lawn, snowdrop carpets in spring, shrubberies and specimen trees are placed handsomely and in abundance around the demesne.

The gardens are divided into the large pleasure garden and the walled garden. The pleasure garden, covering about nineteen acres, is made up of varied rides and paths, in which almost five thousand species of tree can be identified with the help of a guiding leaflet.

The walled garden covers almost four acres and is divided into herbaceous and mixed beds, a spectacularly densely planted pond and the Australian garden, currently being developed using plants from that continent in educational and formal arrangements. The greenhouses and alpine

beds complete the walled garden, which for many visitors is the high point of the visit. The Victorian greenhouse is an interesting reconstruction. This was donated to the garden by nuns in Blackrock in a fine example of recycling. The interestingly designed semi-circular shaped glass panes are made to direct water away from the structure.

The list of superlative plants in this area is a long one, and the visitor falls from one to another. The rare trees include a fine *Cladrastis sinensis* – see it in June to admire its yellow flowers. In autumn and spring, its foliage is golden and dramatic. It was a present to Lord Talbot from Hillier's nursery in England.

The Haggard is a small area within the walled garden and in here one of the loveliest sights is the *Clematis nepalensis*, which carries hellebore-like yellow flowers on bare stems in December. *Rubus lineatus* is another lesser spotted shrub. The greenhouse in this area was built by Lord Talbot in the 1960s and the planting has been held to that historic period. It is full of rare plants, including a nearly extinct *Banksia serrata* which has a remarkable looking bark. The organic regime here involves leaving the windows open from May to October, *Encarsia formosa* wasps and regular misting to stop red spider mite.

'It works,' says Barbara Cunningham, the enthusiastic head of the small but impressive gardening team. One of the most notable things about Malahide is that they work almost completely without chemicals. Getting at the weeds and diseases early and often is the answer, along with an engaged team of workers that manages an impressive work load.

Incredible feats seem to be what this garden is about: Lord Talbot wrote twelve thousand individual cards with the details of each plant he collected and planted in his lifetime. These useful cards were detailed down to the price paid for each plant. They are in the process of being gathered into a computer record which will open them up as an important academic resource.

Out in the pond garden the list of impressives grows, with a *Euonymus lucidus*. This is a tender shrub that lives outside here positioned against a sunny sheltered wall.

In the quaintly named chicken yard the rarities include a collection of Chilean plants like a *Berberidopsis cordifolia*, embothriums and an ancient looking gnarled leptospermum that overhangs the gravel path like an arch. The tower here was thought to be a fourteenth-century building. Recently, they discovered that it was a seventeenth-century pigeon house built to stock birds for the castle's kitchen. Outside the wall of the chicken yard are the olearia collection and an *Escallonia revoluta* that experts from Kew say is the biggest in Europe.

Development and discovery are constant and ongoing here. Most recently, the uncovering of eight fireplaces along the wall in the Alpine garden gave rise to some interest. These were used to light fires that would create smoke, and thus deter frost from the tender plants in the little garden. Wonderful.

County Kildare

Burtown House |
Ballytore, Athy, County Kildare

Contact: Lesley Fennell
Tel: (+353) 059 862 3148 /
086 263 1485
www: www.burtownhouse.ie
Open: April to September. See
website for annual details.
Special Features: Gallery and
Artist's studios. Shop. Lunches or
refreshment can be arranged.

Partially wheelchair accessible.
Coach parking. Supervised
children. **Directions:** Travelling
south on the M9, leave at junction
2, then turn right onto the N78
signposted for Athy. Take the
second turn to the left, signposted
'Irishtown'. Burtown House is the
first gate on the left.

One of the notable features about the garden at Burtown House in Kildare is the fact that it is tended by three generations of one family: artist Lesley Fennell, her son and daughter-in-law, James and Joanna, and her mother, Wendy Walsh, Ireland's finest botanical artist.

But this is no case of too many cooks: Burtown consists of several separate garden areas around the Georgian house, each worked by different family members. Lesley, however, is the chief gardener in charge of most of the gardens, including the big sunny borders around the walls of the house, the rock and woodland gardens running out from the buildings, the formal hedging and topiary areas, the orchards, water gardens and rose walks.

The show around the buildings, and up against the house, is one of bustling drifts of irises, peonies, thalictrum and alliums. The wall planting here includes a huge, ancient wisteria and an unusual scarlet-

flowered *Schisandra rubriflora*. Growing on the north-facing wall, this plant reaches out about three metres. It thrives in the dry shade and even managed to survive the awful winter of 2009-10, enduring temperatures of minus sixteen.

The lawns that spread out from these borders are in turn bounded by shrub borders that hold some very special plants, including a tree peony named for Lesley's mother, *Paeonia* 'Wendy Walsh'.

We took a wide gravelled walk between trimmed and trained young yews away from the house, to a cross path under a long pergola. The formality of the yew walk balances the busy pergola, which is laden down under mature *Rosa* 'Albertine' and clematis. These are under-planted with honesty or *Hesperis matronalis*, tulips, pink mop-head hydrangeas, miniature irises and double primroses. On the far side of the pergola is an old-fashioned orchard, with a collection of venerable-looking apple trees growing over a meadow studded with daffodils.

The next garden, which belongs to Wendy Walsh, is attached to a converted stone outhouse. It features a sunken stone slab patio, full of self-seeding wild strawberries, hardy geraniums and *Alchemilla mollis*. The *Magnolia wilsonii* and some other light shrubs form a grove to one side of this, adding some height without enclosing the area too much. The family are related to the Shackletons, and a number of phloxes from Beech Park, the famous Shackleton garden in Dublin, seem appropriate here against the sunny wall. This feels like a garden just made for sitting in on a baking-hot day.

Beyond the stone house is the oldest area in the garden – the big wood. This is set on an island surrounded by streams. It is a magical sort of place whose damp banks are full of trilliums, ferns, hostas and impressive *Cardiocrinum giganteum*. Lesley added some pretty *Anemone nemorosa* 'Lucy's Wood' and an unnamed white double anemone to the wild or 'wooden enemies'. Erythroniums and epimediums also do well under the tall beech trees, the homes of numerous bat, bird and owl boxes.

The next garden is in the old stable yard. This is a sheltered, high-walled square where James has been experimenting with a formal planting of pruned up and staked two-metre-high ligustrum or privet under-planted with lavender around a square of lawn. Its marked formality is an interesting contrast to the looser feel of the garden outside the walls.

The walled kitchen garden is close by, dominated by a viewing tower in the middle that must be the best possible place for games of 'king of the castle'. Meanwhile, down at ground level, the business of producing purple sprouting broccoli, leeks, peas, beans, asparagus, currants and rhubarb goes on.

Moving from the kitchen garden back toward the house, the path takes in more flower gardens and an almost secret, semi-wooded area of acers, bamboos, shade-loving plants and a great spreading white-flowering cherry. With a flat head about ten metres across, it casts a gentle shade over large spreads of aconites, bluebells and lily-of-the-valley.

Before I left, Wendy showed me a tree that has a special place here: an Oregon maple or *Acer macrophyllum*. This is a baby of the famous maple in Front Square in Trinity College. Along with some other seedlings, Lesley's father found it on a rubbish tip in the college and transplanted it to an altogether finer life in a field below the house at Burtown, beside a beech and bluebell wood.

Coolcarrigan House |
Coolcarrigan, Coill Dubh, Naas, County Kildare

Contact: Robert Wilson-Wright
Tel: (+353) 045 863 527 0r 086 3351021
e-mail: rww@coolcarrigan.ie
www: www.coolcarrigan.ie
Open: By appointment only. Supervised children welcome. Dogs on leads.
Special features: Lunches and tours by arrangement. **Directions:** Drive from Clane to Prosperous and continue to the crossroads by the Dag Weld pub, from where Coolcarrigan is signed. Go through Coill Dubh. Pass the church. The garden is a short distance along on the left, marked by black gates.

The Wilson Wright family has been gardening at Coolcarrigan for six generations. Today, the results of that work are seen in the classic Victorian garden, rockeries, lily pond, herbaceous borders, lawns, greenhouses and an impressive collection of shrubs and trees, which today stands at many thousands.

The present owner, Robert Wilson-Wright, is the most recent member of the family to continue the tradition. Minding an inheritance is important, but Robert also displays an infectious enthusiasm for the garden that stretches well beyond simple guardianship. In the last decade, he has added a further six acres and two hundred and fifty species of trees to the growing venture. Pooled knowledge and work over such a long period lends this garden a special place in Irish horticulture as well as its own unique personality.

A visit begins with the more intimate area around the house. The chief attraction here is a classic border, an assembly of blue delphinium spires, bell-like campanulas, geums, dahlias, blue *Clematis integrifolia*, California tree poppies (*Romneya coulteri*) and a host of other border flowers that are on the go from early summer to late autumn. It is flanked by a striking strawberry tree (*Arbutus unedo*) with tiny white flowers, edible strawberry fruit and a trunk like a huge cinnamon stick.

Nearby, the long, well maintained greenhouse is divided into separate smaller houses. A memory of its being perfect on previous visits must have been mistaken, because recently Robert took it apart, restored and raised the roof height, so that today it is even more impressive. Along with the original grape vine, planted when the greenhouse was built in 1900, there are rich scented ginger lilies, peaches and a collection of passion flowers, which includes the banana passion flower (*Passiflora antioquiensis*). This plant has slender, deep pink flowers that frill out like tutus. Another specimen is the bizarre-looking *Passiflora quadrangularis*, the flowers of which feature filaments like purple-and-cream-striped jellyfish tentacles. In here there are also succulents and a pineapple guava with edible and fairly tasty flowers.

The view from the greenhouse takes in a naturalistic pond cut straight into the turf. The planting around the rim is sparse and for the most part restricted to grass. A few lilies decorate the water, but generally restraint has been shown and the main body of water remains clear to reflect the sky and trees. In the surrounding damp lawns there are wild orchids in almost weed-like numbers.

There are several varieties of wild orchid scattered throughout the grounds. We spotted pyramidal orchids (*Anacamptis pyramidalis*), common spotted orchids (*Dactylorrhiza fuchsia*) and common twayblade or *Listera ovata*. Naturalists will be delighted to see red squirrels, spotted fly-catchers and stoats. Robert has implemented a light touch policy in the care of the extensive lawns and meadows, and the effect on the wild flower population has been remarkable. He carries out just one cut in the summer. This is both time- and labour-saving as well as being beneficial to the habitat.

In the thicket beyond the pond we climbed in between shrubs to see a rare *Berberis valdiviana*, with unusual long yellow flowers and another rarity close by, *Syringa pinnatifolia*. This was a plant that the expert Roy Lancaster fell in love with when he visited the garden many years ago. Long after the visit, when re-introduced to the Wilson-Wrights, he remembered them as the owners of the shrub. It is that special.

While the main garden at Coolcarrigan is based on limestone, there is one area where the soil is acidic. This is due to a pocket of

bog. The peaty bed here has been planted with rhododendron, azalea and spring bulbs for an early-year show of colour. Many of these are planted around two newly created lakes Robert made since he took over the garden.

The arboretum, for which the garden is justly well known, has benefited from a long-time relationship between the family and the British plantsman Sir Harold Hillier, whose knowledge contributed hugely to the significance of the Coolcarrigan tree collection. Since Robert took over the collection, he has started to collect a number of rarer oaks from South America.

He is also working on thinning the larger old park trees to allow light spill down onto newly freed-up space in the lower levels where choice, berrying cotoneaster, magnolia, rare *Heptacodium miconioides*, *Nyssa sylvatica*, and varieties of sorbus need to be accommodated. We walked through the best barley sugar-smelling *Cercidiphyllum japonicum* I have ever encountered to discover that the tree was almost fifty metres away.

In the walled garden he has developed a Nuttery, with cobnuts and hazelnuts, Irish apple varieties, damsons and medlars.

Before leaving we went to inspect the new area, another arboretum, where Robert has been creating paths through a large meadow and planting new trees to create vistas, focal points and dramatic punctuations. How it will look in twenty years he has no idea, but hasn't this always been the way with planting long-term features like arboreta? Heart, soul and finance continue to be poured into both the upkeep and advancement of the garden.

THE JAPANESE GARDENS AND ST FIACHRA'S GARDEN |
KILDARE, COUNTY KILDARE

Contact: Frieda O'Connell
Tel: (+353) 045 521 617 / 522 963
e-mail: japanesegardens@eircom.net
www: www.irish-national-stud.ie
Open: February to 23 December, daily 9am-5pm. Guide dogs only.

Special features: Wheelchair accessible. Guided tours. Self-guided tours in ten languages. Café and shop. **Directions:** Situated on the edge of Kildare town, signposted clearly off the N7.

In 1906 Colonel William Hall Walker of Tully, County Kildare, a man with a keen interest in Japanese gardens, brought a Japanese gardener, Tassa Eida, along with his family, to Ireland to create a Japanese garden on the Kildare plains. Tassa worked with forty men for four years to develop the garden. The stories about his stay in Ireland are legion. He arrived as a man who neither drank nor backed horses and left, years later, a poor man with a taste for both. But he also left a wonderful Japanese garden. In 2010 it celebrated its hundredth birthday and some members of his family travelled back from Japan to see the garden their ancestor built.

The miniature landscape is heavily laden with symbolism and meaning, based on man's journey through life from birth to death. Reading the symbolism is optional, however, and the

place can be enjoyed simply as a garden full of mature shrubs, trees, topiary, gnarled little piceas and splayed cherries, waterside planting, paths and statuary. The garden is seen from a winding path that trails up, down, over and around rocky outcrops and past trees with carefully exposed root runs. By making choices about which path to take, one can visit different areas of the garden, each of which is related to a time in the life of man. A delicate old teahouse, the site of occasional tea-making ceremonies, sits high on one outcrop and overlooks the different gardens. The little building is surrounded by bonsai, some of which have been in the garden since its creation in 1906.

The paths are rocky, moss-covered and fern-studded, sometimes picking their way up little hills, sometimes partially submerged as stepping-stones through the hosta-lined stream. There is even a little raked gravel garden.

Although not a huge garden, it is one of the busiest in the country, attracting over 130,000 visitors a year. If you want to avoid the crowds, time your visit – go on an off-season Monday or Tuesday. The garden does not depend on flowers or plants that should be seen in the summer, so a trip off-season will be just as rewarding, and perhaps even more enjoyable, particularly in early autumn when the acers begin to colour. The structure of the garden, combined with the many and various textures and shades of foliage, is its main attraction.

Attached to the Japanese Garden is the larger St Fiachra's Garden. This is a woodland garden designed by Martin Hallinan of University College Dublin and dedicated to St Fiachra, the Irish saint, known in France as the patron saint of gardening. This large, wild place has an artless and natural feel. The design is made up of simple walks through plantations of native oak, ash and willow. A large lake, fed by natural springs, dominates the centre of the garden. The water in the lake has been trained over small waterfalls and there are rock pools sited about the edges.

Simplicity is again the keyword for the planting by the lake. The woods are under-planted with spring bulbs, wild garlic and wood anemone. These are all plants which will spread and naturalise under the light-speckled canopy. Fossilised trees stand like sculptures, giving an air of history and something ancient to the place. Three beehive huts have been sited at one end of the lake, reminiscent of the monastic cells in which St Fiachra and his monks might have lived. Inside one of the huts is the curious Waterford Crystal Glass Garden, with plants made from crystal.

While you are at the Japanese Gardens you can also visit the Irish National Stud. Remarkably, people need to be told to be sensible: there is a sign at one of the fences reading 'DANGER! Horses bite and kick'.

Lodge Park Walled Garden and Steam Museum |
Straffan, County Kildare

Contact: Mr and Mrs Robert Guinness
Tel: (+353) 01 627 3155 / 628 8412
e-mail: garden@steam-museum.ie
www: www.steam-museum.ie
Open: May to September by appointment / June to August, Wednesday to Sunday and bank holidays 2pm-6pm. Supervised children welcome.

Horticultural and agricultural students free entry.
Special features: Wheelchair accessible. Steam museum. Shop and tearoom, no entry fee.
Directions: Straffan is signposted from the Kill flyover on the M7, and from the Maynooth flyover on the N4. It is approximately 8km from both places. Follow 'Steam Museum' signs

Before even entering the garden you have to be intrigued at the sight of a weather vane swivelling above a clock tower in the courtyard: it is a lovely fat pig, painted with the quartered family crest, cheerfully pointing out the direction of the wind. The garden entrance is then reached past a tall stone wall with a small hole in its base through which the resident hens can trot in and out to get to their house, safe from the local hen-hating spaniel. You cannot but enter in expectation of a good visit. Open the heavy iron gate that leads inside, duck under tendrils of hanging *Vitis coignetiae* and quite suddenly, in contrast to the cool, unadorned exterior, you are in a perfect old-fashioned walled garden, full of surprises, flowers and flourishes.

The walled garden at Lodge Park dates to the 1770s but it was restored in the 1940s and again in the 1980s. It is a charming, relaxed flower garden run by Sarah Guinness and talented gardener Patrick Ardill.

A visit begins at the top of the long rectangular garden, along a path that runs its length, with various gardens leading away from the path to the centre of the garden. The first picture is of a white garden full of frothy cream-coloured potentilla, agapanthus, sedum, lamb's ears, phlox, stock, anemone, white borage, rock roses and white variegated agave. This secluded little garden room is built around an ornamental stone well-head. The greenhouse next to it is unusual. The outer wall is marked by a water-spouting lizard, spurting into a small rectangular lily pond. The path around the little pond is edged with billowing argyranthemums and an exquisite red passion flower (*Passiflora antioquiensis*). On a warm day the sound of water and the passion flowers make this corner feel quite exotic.

Meanwhile, the path continues on, under an iron 'spider web' arch covered by *Rosa* 'Francois Juranville' and on past a lean-to greenhouse on the south wall. From early spring this small house is an Aladdin's cave full of cuttings and baby plants. In the early months of the year, there is not an inch of space to be found between pots of plectranthus, little argyranthemum cuttings, alpine pelargoniums and salvias. They spend their first months in this warm nursery alongside a huge bird of paradise or *Strelitzia reginae* before being planted into the large containers that stand outside the steam museum through the summer. Patrick has an obvious talent for creating the sort of eye-catching planters that even people who do not like planters will love.

Outside this propagation house, on the red-brick south-facing wall, gold- and green-gages have been trained, soaking up the heat.

The double north-to-south borders are quite new. Backed by *Sambucus niger* 'Black Lace', they have been planted up with purple and blue irises, salvias, eupatorium, forget-me-nots and cornflowers. Alliums, particularly *A.* 'Purple Sensation', add an extra zing to the more solid colour blocks. *Verbena bonariensis* is allowed to seed about and it has an effect like purple gauze over the borders. This is a gorgeous feature and, at only three years old, it looks much more mature. The black elders are pruned once a year in spring and this encourages them to produce the best dark foliage. The font, from St Jude's Church nearby, stands in the middle of the wide grass path.

Beyond, one can see a sharply clipped beech hedge with an opening that invites investigation. But the path, bordered by huge, perfectly clipped yews and its own beckoning gate in the distance, keep one on the main trail, down past a line of good-looking shrubs, including magnolia, garrya and abutilon, a tall trachycarpus and knotty corokia. In front of and under these there are runs of alstroemeria and more alliums.

Then there is the *roseraie*. Designed by Sarah's husband, Robert Guinness, this great big crown of metal struts supports a whole range of roses from *Rosa.* 'Rambling Rector' to *R.* 'Belvedere' and *R.* 'Alister Stella Grey'. Up close, it is like a floral maze and it is completely gorgeous from mid-June.

Eventually, the path reaches the gateway and beyond it the herbaceous border and tennis court. In contrast to the darker double borders, this is all pinks and pale blues. There are campanulas and crambe, nepeta and early daffodils and they all stand in front of an impeccably trained, gigantic *Rosa* 'Felicite et Perpetue'.

Making our way back in to the main garden, around and through the *roseraie*, we arrive at the north bed, where the damp- and shade-loving plants do best. There are lines of different hydrangeas, like *Hydrangea aspera* 'Villosa' and *H. paniculata* sharing with the *Schizophragma hydrangeoides* and Irish yews. Beneath these, hostas and hellebores smother the ground and keep all weeds at bay with their exquisite flowers and large, leathery leaves. The perfect beech hedge, seen earlier, is here again, visible from the other side. The opening in it draws the eye back out to the sunny borders, past a line of espaliered apples and the old apples and quinces in the orchard.

I left with the picture of a fine specimen of *Rosa* 'Francis E. Lester' beside the vegetable beds, trained over pillars to keep them manageable and producing great flowers. One could be happy forever in this lovely place.

COUNTY KILKENNY

KILFANE GLEN AND WATERFALL | THOMASTOWN, COUNTY KILKENNY

Contact: Susan Mosse
Tel: (+353) 056 772 4558 / 772 7105
e-mail: susan@irishgardens.com
www: www.kilfane.com **Open:** See website for
annual details. Groups of ten welcome all year.
Supervised children welcome. No dogs.

Special features: Sculpture trail. Teas
Wednesday, Friday and Sunday during open
season. Picnic area. **Directions:** 3km off the
Dublin–Waterford road (N9), signposted to the
right 3.5km from Thomastown.

*© Royal Society
of Antiquaries.*

Green gardens and woodland gardens done well are probably easier to love than any other type
of garden. But they are probably harder to make a success of than great flouncing flower gardens.
The very restraint required to make them work is exactly where their charm lies. Kilfane Glen
is my favourite woodland garden on the island. Walking through it is like visiting the illustrations
in a book of fairy tales.

The main body of the garden is a beautifully restored romantic garden, originally laid out by
the Power family in the 1790s. Many of the features of the classic romantic garden can be found
within the thirty-acre plot: there is of course the woodland, deep in the middle of which is a
glen with its own perfectly placed artificial waterfall, a *cottage orné* and hermit's grotto. The
waterfall leads into a meandering stream which runs through the wood, crossed at several points
by rustic bridges.

The original garden had become lost, swallowed up by choking *Rhododendron ponticum* and
laurel. But in the early 1990s, looking at an 1805 print that showed a glen and waterfall with a
little ornamental cottage seemingly on their land, owners Susan and Nicholas Mosse began to
investigate. Their explorations in the rhodo-choked woods eventually proved that the print was
no work of imagination, but an historic document. Down in the glen, at the centre of the garden,
they found the footprint of the *cottage orné*, which had been razed to the ground in the middle
of the nineteenth century. They painstakingly rebuilt it, bringing in the late, famed designer

Sybil Connolly to design the interiors of the little thatched cottage. The porch and outer walls of the cottage were planted with honeysuckle, jasmine and climbing roses in peat pots, in a manner faithful to the original planting.

Outside the cottage, and visible through the leaded windows, the artificial waterfall once again pours out over a cliff. The ancient pumps were found to be in working order and were clanked back into commission to send water tumbling into the glen for the first time in nearly two hundred years.

Apart from the old wood garden, several new gardens were created, including a blue orchard. At its centre, crab apples have been grown in a circle and underplanted with grape hyacinths or muscari and bluebells. The facing wall backs a blue bed of agapanthus, monkshood, delphinium and aubrieta. The gateway in the centre of this wall leads into the pool garden and a clematis wall made up of *Clematis* 'Mrs Cholmondeley', *C.* 'Star of India' and *C. tangutica*. The formal pond looks down on the all-white moon garden. Tender angel's trumpets (*Datura arborea*), tall, waving bugbane or cimicifuga and white under-bellied New Zealand flax *Phormium tenax* add a little 'oomph' to the other white and silver border plants. Susan says her preferred time in this little garden is in the late evening, when the whites glow and it all looks ghostly.

Behind this garden there is a bamboo walk, a sort of hall of mirrors hidden in a laurel walk, and the vista, a view of Slievenamon through a clearing in the trees.

A contemporary sculpture trail is also in the process of being created. Two of the finest British sculptors, Bill Woodrow and David Nash, have made pieces for the garden. So too has William Pye, whose copper water vessel is the centrepiece in the vista. It brims with water, reflecting the surrounding trees. Set beside it is Lynn Kirkham's living willow bench.

In the end, the most appealing features in Kilfane are the many paths that weave through the woods, going up- and downhill, running past rushing, gushing streams, under dark tunnels of trees and past little stepping stone features in openings in the woods.

This is probably not a place for those expecting miles of herbaceous borders, but it would certainly not be improved by the addition of fifteen different varieties of delphinium.

WOODSTOCK | INISTIOGE, COUNTY KILKENNY

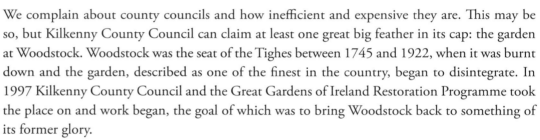

Contact: Claire Murphy
Tel: (+353) 056 779 4033 / 775 8797
or John Delaney 087 854 9785
e-mail: woodstock@kilkennycoco.ie
www: www.woodstock.ie
Open: All year. October to March,
9am-4.30pm / April to September,
9am-8pm. Groups welcome. Car parking charge.

Supervised children welcome. Dogs on leads.
Special Features: Partially wheelchair accessible.
Guided tours can be organised. Tearoom June to
September. Playground. Buggy service to the
walled garden during the summer. Contact
for details.
Directions: Situated 2km west of the village, up a
steep hill to the left of the two village churches.

We complain about county councils and how inefficient and expensive they are. This may be so, but Kilkenny County Council can claim at least one great big feather in its cap: the garden at Woodstock. Woodstock was the seat of the Tighes between 1745 and 1922, when it was burnt down and the garden, described as one of the finest in the country, began to disintegrate. In 1997 Kilkenny County Council and the Great Gardens of Ireland Restoration Programme took the place on and work began, the goal of which was to bring Woodstock back to something of its former glory.

A spectacular monkey puzzle avenue, made up of thirty-one pairs, thought to be the longest in Europe, was restored. New, young monkey puzzles (*Araucaria araucana*), were planted where older specimens had fallen. A decade on, they still look like tiny babies, sitting on tuffets of earth beside their huge relatives. Planting them proud of the ground is thought to help them establish better.

A second avenue of noble fir or *Abies nobilis,* almost half a kilometre long, running at an angle from the monkey puzzles, was disentangled from a great thicket of rhododendron, laurel and bramble. The first avenue had always been apparent. The noble fir avenue, on the other hand, had been completely obscured by the rhododendron. Returned to their glory, together they impart a sense of grandeur to an already grand place.

All over the pleasure grounds, clearances have revealed gardens not seen properly for nearly a century: the yew walk and kitchen gardens, only barely discernible until recently, were saved and restored. A box parterre was also replanted outside the walled garden. This leads up to the rebuilt Turner-designed greenhouse. The dovecote is still in a good state of repair, while nearby the skeletons of rows of cold frames, melon-houses, greenhouses and sheds can be seen. The ornamental dairy, a strange-looking item that was submerged under centuries of soil build-up, is now clearly seen, and the big Victorian rockery has also been restored. This rockery was created when 200,000 cubic metres of soil were removed from in front of the house to make way for the sunken winter gardens. These have been re-grassed, but once they were elaborate confections of fashionable plants.

The walled garden is a real pleasure after so many years of neglect. Today, its expansive beds of vegetables, mixed shrub and herbaceous beds, trained fruit and well maintained paths are a delight.

The work has been and is still being carried out largely by John Delaney and his small band of gardeners, and Woodstock is flourishing under this impressive team. They garden through the growing season and, when the garden jobs are in short supply in winter, they take on projects like the building of new children's playgrounds and the reconstruction of lost features such as the bamboo rustic bower – with the help of conservation experts. The bower is an unusual feature, clad in sasa bamboo, which was grown and harvested in the garden by the team. The patterns in which the canes are arranged are gorgeous.

They also restored a lacy iron rose pergola nearby over a recent quiet winter. This is now planted up with *Rosa* 'Madame Alfred Carriere' and *R.* 'Blush Noisette'.

A red squirrel whipped up a tree as we walked past and John told me that there is a healthy population the garden. The pine martens prey on those greys misfortunate enough to venture into the garden, but they cannot catch the more nimble reds that meanwhile thrive on monkey puzzle seeds.

Although the once-famed collection of trees has sadly become depleted over the years due to storm damage and neglect, there are still massive wonders ranged about the grounds, including examples of *Sequoiadendron giganteum* (Wellingtonias), *Thuja plicata* 'Zebrina' and *Cryptomeria japonica*. Planting is ongoing, in part to make up for the lost trees.

Long woodland walks wind their way through the huge estate, leading in one case to a Gothic teahouse perched in the trees, with a panoramic view over the valley, woods and river below. It is easy to go back in time and imagine enjoying tea up here, with servants of course to ferry the tea tray and picnic things up the tiresome hill.

As I left, John showed me a re-instated Turner-designed gate that was donated back to the garden by a kind lady, Mrs Carr, from Inistoige.

❁ County Laois

Gash Gardens | Castletown, Portlaoise, County Laois

Contact: Mary Keenan and Ross Doyle
Tel: (+353) 057 873 2247 / 087 272 8337
e-mail: gashgardens@eircom.net
Open: May to September, Monday to Saturday, 10am-5pm (Closed Sunday, except by appointment.) Groups by appointment. Not suitable for small children. **Special features:** Teas can be arranged. Nursery.
Directions: 1km off the Dublin-Limerick N7 road at Castletown, signed.

For years Gash was well known as the domain of Noel Keenan, the man who single-handedly developed this interesting garden. Today the garden continues to be worked by his daughter, Mary, herself a plant expert of note. Mary is developing and carrying the four-acre garden into the future, adding to its existing features and creating new ones, working with the natural assets and even the drawbacks of the site as she makes new garden features.

For anyone who has visited Gash before, the most memorable feature of the garden must be the moon house. This is a little cave set in the base of a large rockery at the entrance to the garden. It peeps out through a circular stone opening into a cascade of water coming from above. The roaring noise created from the crashing water is invigorating but the moon house is only one, albeit the most spectacular, of a number of water features at Gash. There are ponds, streams and rivulets criss-crossing the garden, travelling in all directions, dividing and linking different garden rooms, feeding the roots of damp-loving plants and dictating the sort of plants that do best here.

There is a fine collection of good-looking trees, from *Metasequoia glyptostroboides* and liquidambar to spectacular flowering *Cornus mas* and *Cornus kousa*, planted through the garden. They each look individually good and together they create fine combinations. This is a garden full of strong statement plantings, as seen in the group of three white-barked Himalayan birch, *Betula utilis* var. *jacquemontii*, underplanted with red heathers.

The style is flowing and informal, taking in an easy mix of natural-looking rockeries, alpine beds, borders made up of herbaceous perennials, ponds and streams, mixed shrubs and flowers, laburnum walks, damp and shaded ferneries. One of the stand-out planting schemes here is the unusual circle of *Hydrangea* 'Annabelle' around an inner circle of *Hydrangea sargentiana*. Mary explained that she grows *H. sargentiana* for its strong foliage, and to get it to put on its best leaf show she cuts it back hard every year.

Her enthusiasms are scattered through the place, as in the little collection of Solomon's seal and related plants by one of the streams. These include an evergreen cousin, *Disporopsis pernyi*, and *Polygonatum verticillatum*, a plant that looks like a fern but has flowers and red berries. Overhead, a *Salix magnifica* with big leaves and dark stems certainly cuts a dash. Not for nothing is it called the 'magnificent willow'. She also loves big grasses, and uses them in substantial drifts throughout the place. *Stipa gigantea*, *Miscanthus sacchariflorus* and bull rushes planted in numbers are eye-catching plants. They create a strong, visual statement as well as a background rustle at the slightest breeze.

The garden was extended out into the countryside with the planting of a mixed maple walk along the bank of the River Nore. This stretches for a quarter of a mile along the water's edge.

The simple desire to go for strolls by the river gave rise to this feature, one that will be there for centuries. It was difficult to get to the water through the fields, so making a maple walk seemed like an attractive solution. Once the trees were planted, the plan expanded and they created a linked water garden with several small waterfalls.

Mary continues to plant and expand: the latest features are two natural-style ponds. She made one in an outlying paddock that constantly flooded and another in the centre of the garden where the ground is always wet. When it comes to water, the wisest route is to go with it, rather than argue with nature.

HEYWOOD GARDEN | BALLINAKILL, COUNTY LAOIS

Contact: The Manager
Tel: (+353) 057 873 3563
e-mail: heywoodgardens@opw.ie
www: www.heritageireland.ie   **Open:** All year
daily, during daylight hours. No entrance fee.

Supervised children welcome. **Special features:**
Partially wheelchair accessible. Guided tours by
appointment (fee charged). **Directions:** 7km
southeast of Abbeyleix, off the R432 to Ballinakill
(in the grounds of Ballinakill Community School).

Edwin Lutyens was an architect whose work with the great plantswoman Gertrude Jekyll is well known to garden lovers. He created a small number of gardens in Ireland with and without the help of Jekyll. Along with the National War Memorial Garden in Islandbridge in Dublin, the formal garden at Heywood ranks as the best known of his Irish projects. Lutyens's garden at Heywood is a small but spectacular place, set in the middle of a greater demesne in the rolling Laois countryside and it is known and admired by garden visitors everywhere. Visiting today, it seems incongruously attached to a modern secondary school. The reason for this is that Heywood House, the property to which it was attached, was destroyed by fire in the 1950s. The formal garden, which today appears slightly adrift of the world, was once overlooked by the large house. Lutyens's garden is a little gem, created at the beginning of the twentieth century on several levels of an embankment standing out from the now demolished Heywood House.

The main attraction of this formal garden is the sunken, circular, terraced garden with a central lily pond surrounded by spitting lead turtles and a wonderfully over-sized fountain shaped like a huge champagne glass, out of proportion to the pond. Gertrude Jekyll designed the planting and, while her plans have been lost, a study of her famous garden at Hestercombe in

England gave the gardeners at Heywood the direction they needed. Herbaceous perennials such as calendula and nepeta, pink phlox and Japanese anemone, *Viola cornuta* 'Huntercombe Purple' and silver stachys, peonies and bergenia, low shrubs and *Rosa* 'Nathalie Nypels' are signature plants of Jekyll. They fill the beds around the circular pond in two terraces, each backed by low walls and ledges.

There is a handsome summerhouse in grey, lichen-covered split limestone covered in jasmine in which to sit and enjoy the garden room. Set into the sheltering outer walls, circular windows, each frame a perfect vista, like landscape paintings on a drawing-room wall. The views include rolling parkland, distant church spires, the village nearby and cattle that seem to have come straight from central casting. The compositions are worthy of Constable, and when the church bells in the distance ring it is pure heaven.

Leaving the formal circular garden, the path leads through an ornate wrought-iron gate to a short avenue of pleached limes and a pergola on a high ledge above and overlooking the lake, woods and wider pleasure grounds. The wall is cut with niches for pieces of sculpture. To the side of the path, lawns surrounded by more low stone walls and herbaceous borders also float above the fields below. Visitors with children should note that the low walls mask steep drops on the other side. The whole garden sits on a raised ledge overlooking the parkland. Small children should not be left alone here.

Linked to these two main areas there is a maze of small garden rooms. Walking between the little enclosures you will come across hot borders full of geums, gold helianthemums and rudbeckias, kniphofia and papavars. There are also sundial rooms, little iris and hellebore gardens wrapped in yew hedging with stone bird baths and hide-and-seek hedges that create a sense of mystery and secrecy.

But the Lutyens garden is only part of a larger garden at Heywood, and within its formal surroundings there are several small features that point to an older, different style of garden: the ionic pillars in the pergola came from the old parliament building in Dublin (today the Bank of Ireland at College Green). There is also a carved Coade stone shell-fountain in one of the little garden rooms and the plaque in the summerhouse with lines from an Alexander Pope poem. All these fragments of stone date to the 1770s and are thought to have come from a folly once situated in the older garden out in the pleasure grounds:

In the 1990s the land came into the hands of the State. There followed an amount of detective work by the then Park Superintendant, Patricia Friel. Using historic records, she began to research that older garden, a substantial romantic demesne that dated from the late eighteenth century, which had been almost forgotten. The years since have seen it unearthed and restored; the discovery has added hugely to an already fine garden.

Heywood's most recent discovery down in the woods is an excellent example of late eighteenth-century romantic garden design. It was created by Frederick Trench, a tenant of the original house and the man responsible for the first gardens at Heywood. He was a fashionable, well travelled and educated man and his garden reflected the fashionable tastes of his time. It was made up of trails or rides past a series of features: a sham castle, gothic follies peeping out from beyond woods and hills, orangeries, rustic and quaint stone bridges, artificial lakes, serpentine pools and streams. (The sham ruin came as salvage from Aghaboe Abbey, a ruin about 20km away.) It is wonderful that this charming wild and romantic garden has been saved from oblivion. The two gardens together make up one of the most satisfying garden visits I know.

County Louth

Beaulieu House and Garden |
Beaulieu, Drogheda County Louth

Contact: Gabriel De Freitas or Malcolm Clark
Tel: (+353) 041 983 8557
e-mail: info@beaulieuhouse.ie
Open: May to September, Monday to Friday 11am-5pm / July to August, Saturday and Sunday 1pm-5pm. Not suitable for children.

Special features: Partially wheelchair accessible. Historic house. **Directions:** The garden is on the right turn towards Baltray (R167) off the Drogheda to Termonfeckin road (R166), 2km from Termonfeckin.

Beaulieu House was built in 1628 on the banks of the Boyne, refurbished between 1710 and 1720, and bears the distinction of being the first non-fortified house of its kind on the island. The style of the redbrick house is unusual for Ireland and looks as though it might have been borrowed from northern France or Holland. In fact, the bricks used to build it came from the Netherlands. The drive up to the house is short, wide and straight, in keeping with the Franco-Dutch style, fairly singular in County Louth or indeed in the Republic as a whole.

The walled garden is set close by the house and is bordered by a mature wood. The Dutch artist Willem Van der Hagan, who painted several canvasses that can be seen in the house as well as an allegorical work on the ceiling of the drawing room, was also reputed to be a designer of walled gardens. If he designed it, that would date the garden to before 1732.

To get to the garden you take a path, bordered by golden yew and fuchsia, which passes a small temple-like building and a faded and fragile old greenhouse with a small grotto and fernery. The garden is likewise a faded gem that has been managed by one person for many years. The late Mrs Sidney Waddington, a tiny, delicate-looking but determined woman, worked the garden for decades, up to her mid-eighties. Today the manpower available to take care of this grand, old, ghostly garden is just as scarce, although a gang of interested Jack Russell terriers, and maybe even some geese, will accompany visitors around.

On stepping into the walled garden the visitor is greeted by a huge border on a wide ledge which looks down over the rest of the garden. Many of the plants in the border are old cottage varieties that have been grown here for generations. This is part of what makes the border so atmospheric and attractive. The flowers include white galtonia, variegated mallow, asters, phlox and rust-coloured phormium. Plants like exotic *Cautleya spicata*, which marries red stalks, red-veined leaves and vivid yellow flowers, and the Maltese cross (*Lychnis chalcedonica*) in a shade of red that scares off more timid gardeners, are just two among the bolder plants in the south-facing border.

At eight metres deep, this bed holds an enormous number of plants in creative and sometimes surprising combinations of leaf and flower: white agapanthus beside cream and green variegated sage, waves of anemone and the honey bush (*Melianthus major*) are thoughtfully mixed. Big pink crinum lilies and common kale, or *Crambe cordifolia*, like sprays of gypsophila, make another memorable combination. A sundial that seems hours out of synch as it trundles along at its own pace, stands head-high among the flowers. Losing time in Beaulieu seems a perfectly natural thing to do.

The path running the length of this dreamy old border leads down towards a rustic summerhouse that looks like something the Crooked Man from the nursery rhyme might have lived in. But before getting to it you walk past a knot garden made of intricate walls of box surrounding splashy roses, purple heliotrope and antirrhinum. Two huge Irish yews, nearly three hundred years old, hide a shady foxglove and hellebore garden to the side of this formal bed. Mrs Waddington planted a eucryphia here in the 1950s, which she declared 'almost too full of flowers'. She was right – it is. Its branches sag under the weight of blossoms.

Both border and knot garden sit on the raised ledge at the top of the garden. The level drops down to where the productive vegetable and fruit garden is sited. The bank down to this area is covered in meadow grass, hardy cranesbill and other wildflowers. Down below, paths run under rose-covered arches and trellis with trained apple trees into the vegetable and working kitchen garden. It is obvious that there is no large staff available to mind the Beaulieu gardens, but despite manpower shortages and the resulting slightly scruffy look, this is a garden with a truly magical atmosphere.

KILLINEER HOUSE AND GARDEN |
KILLINEER, DROGHEDA, COUNTY LOUTH

Contact: Charles Carroll
Tel: (+353) 041 983 8563
e-mail: charlescarroll@hotmail.com
www: www.killineerhouse.ie **Open:** Contact for annual dates and times. Groups at any time.
Special features: Historic house. Partially wheelchair accessible. **Directions:** Travelling north from Dublin on the M1, cross the suspension bridge over the Boyne. Take the first left signposted for Drogheda and Monasterboice. At the roundabout, take the exit for Drogheda. Go straight through the next roundabout, in the direction of Monasterboice. At the third roundabout turn left for Monasterboice. Continue for approximately 1km. The garden is on the right, marked by olive green gates and a gate lodge. Ring the bell on the gate pillar.

On a hill looking south over the town of Drogheda is the beautiful garden of Killineer. The house was built by a merchant from the town in the mid-1840s, when seventeen acres of grounds were laid out as a garden. I would bet that today Killineer enjoys the distinction of having the most extensive laurel lawn on the island. This is a remarkable-looking expanse of laurel grown as a hip-high 'lawn' through which tall oak, beech and ash trees as well as more rarefied magnolia and *Cornus kousa* emerge and rise to produce a canopy overhead. Driving uphill toward the house, this is the first feature that greets the visitor. The second is on the other side of the drive: a wide expanse of glass-smooth water, a man-made lake.

The house, standing at the top of the hill, looks sideways toward the laurel lawn and straight down over sloped and stepped lawns to the bottom of the hill. It takes in views of the lake, a little temple-like summerhouse and stands of specimen trees including a big *Thujopsis dolabrata* and *Chamaecyparis lawsoniana* 'Triumph of Boskoop'. These have been pruned so that when one walks through the garden, their lifted skirts allow one see beyond them to views of the water and the greater gardens beyond. A greater proportion of the garden at the bottom of the hill is light woodland and, in the woods, the damp ground is festooned with candelabra primulas. Charles Carroll has been busily encouraging their spread. He says this is an easy task because there are two underground streams that feed the two lakes and keep the ground sufficiently moist.

In other areas, carpets of white lamium or dead-nettle spread out under the trees. Charles is not so pleased with that, but it still looks good and its pale foliage is spiked with ferns like dramatic *Dryopteris affinis* 'Cristata'.

Down here, one of the plants that must be seen is the fourth biggest holly in the country. The strange knobbles on its trunk are indicators of its great age. Nearby, the spongy, bark path runs under tunnels of rhododendron, among which there are red-leafed *R. arborea* and *R. sinogrande*. Everywhere, newly planted baby acers, magnolias and rare rhododendrons have been placed. Charles continues to develop the garden, ensuring its good looks well into the next century.

He loves his trees and witness to this is the Caucasian wingnut or *Pterocarya fraxinifolia*, which fell in a storm. Using a tractor, some friends, and plenty of rope, he managed to right the casualty and today it is heading skywards again.

The walled garden, dating back to Regency times, is behind the house. This area is the domain of Mrs Carroll, while Charles works the greater grounds. Deep, varied, mixed borders run around the walls and a mix of flower and vegetable borders criss-cross through the one-and-a-quarter-acre space. *Hoheria glabrata* and *Hydrangea aspera* 'Villosa' and roses provide a permanent structure for the more fleeting herbaceous flowers. It is a charming, bustling kitchen and flower garden.

The word 'substantial' best describes these gardens, with their sweeps of lawn, well trimmed hedges, and stands of trees and shrubs. The woods, shot through with little streams, surround the more tended, cultivated areas and there is a great sense of a wild yet subtly reined-in garden.

COUNTY OFFALY

BELLEFIELD HOUSE | BIRR ROAD, SHINRONE, COUNTY OFFALY

Contact: Angela Jupe
Tel: (+353) 0505 47 766
e-mail: angelajupe@iol.ie
Open: By appointment.

Special features: Garden design service.
Occasional plant sales.
Directions: 1km north of Shinrone on the N492.

Angela Jupe is something of a force of nature. It was sad to hear that she had moved, a few years ago, from Fancroft Millhouse, the beautiful garden she had created outside Roscrea. However, within a short time, news of a new and developing garden on the outskirts of Shinrone leaked out along with word that it was *Angela Jupe's* new garden. The garden expert seemed to be turning into something of a serial garden restorer. That new garden is Bellefield and it is now open. As with the garden outside Roscrea, this is a brand new creation made on the neglected site attached to a fine old house.

The house sits at the top of a drive between fields of grazing horses, culminating on a little meadow studded with scarlet tulips – a stylish start if ever there was one. A new orchard garden is being created to the side of the house, but the garden proper begins through the courtyard behind the house in the old walled garden.

When Angela arrived, to have called the walled garden a 'neglected mess' would have been kind. A 'mature walled wood' might have been more appropriate. Scores of mature, wild, self-seeded trees and brambles meant that the only way the garden could be accessed was on all fours. But Angela had moved here specifically because it had a walled garden and so a clearance was enthusiastically embarked upon. She held on to a small number of the trees to ensure that the new garden would start life with a certain level of maturity. These trees also give the place a quirkier look than if it was all uniform, symmetrical and perfect.

The walled space is divided into two areas, on two different levels. The first section, set out on the lower ledge is home to the long greenhouse/sun room. This is where Angela grows some exotics, a vine and, in the summer, tomatoes. The area in front of it is formal, with a wide central gravel path and rill dividing two neat sections of lawn backed by shrub borders.

Stepping from here up to the main area, there are long mixed borders running in all directions. These are largely colour co-ordinated. Down one wall there is a seventy-metre-long mixed border full of purple lupins and campanulas, plum-coloured poppies, rich pink campanula and blue nepeta. The stone wall behind the bed supports a range of roses and clematis in the same range of shades. The original renegade trees are allowed to elbow in on the action at a few points. They contribute to the informal, individual style of the garden. The bed turns corner and continues on down the length of the next wall. Fruit bushes, grown decoratively, feature strongly here. The space between the black, white and red currants has been used to grow strawberries. As the border turns corner again, the accent shifts to some of Angela's collection of peonies. These old garden favourites are one of her passions and she grows some wonderful species and hybrid peonies, many of them collected on her travels in France.

Down the middle of the garden is a pair of brilliant early summer iris beds. These are overlooked by the *pièce de résistance* – a rather wonderful, Indian-inspired summerhouse. This is a towering confection made from salvaged items Angela has acquired over the years. Within it there are old leaded windows that were salvaged from a convent, as well as the most wonderful copper cupola bought in a salvage yard in England. Angela thinks it came from India. The interior has been decorated using mosaic tiles. It sings of fun and whimsy and suits the flower-filled atmosphere in this seemingly effortlessly stylish garden.

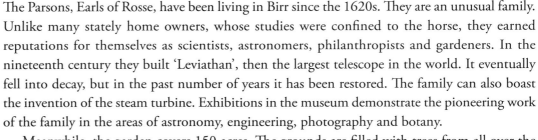

Birr Castle Demesne | Rosse Row, Birr, County Offaly

Tel: (+353) 057 912 0336
e-mail: mail@birrcastle.com
www: www.birrcastle.com
Open: All year daily. See website for seasonal hours. Groups welcome. Supervised children welcome. Dogs on leads.
Special features: Telescope demonstrations during the summer. Gift shop. Museum. Gallery. Tearoom. Tours can be booked.
Directions: In the town of Birr, signposted.

The Parsons, Earls of Rosse, have been living in Birr since the 1620s. They are an unusual family. Unlike many stately home owners, whose studies were confined to the horse, they earned reputations for themselves as scientists, astronomers, philanthropists and gardeners. In the nineteenth century they built 'Leviathan', then the largest telescope in the world. It eventually fell into decay, but in the past number of years it has been restored. The family can also boast the invention of the steam turbine. Exhibitions in the museum demonstrate the pioneering work of the family in the areas of astronomy, engineering, photography and botany.

Meanwhile, the garden covers 150 acres. The grounds are filled with trees from all over the world, including arguably the most impressive *Cornus kousa* in the country and a huge *Sequoiadendron giganteum* up which I spotted a red squirrel running. This collection of special trees is largely planted between great spreads of wild flower meadow, which adds immeasurably to the charm and unity of the grounds.

The Rosses subscribed to many of the great plant-hunting ventures of the nineteenth and early twentieth centuries, including the Kingdom Ward, Wilson, Augustine Henry and George Forrest expeditions. Michael, the sixth Earl, travelled to Tibet himself to collect plants, and after his marriage in 1937, he and his wife Anne went collecting in China. Many of the special trees that came about as a result of these expeditions grow in Birr today, labelled and easily identified. Among them is what could be the first *Metasequoia glyptostroboides* brought to this island.

Inviting filigreed iron gates lure visitors from the park into the formal walled garden. The smallest hint of what may be seen inside is gleaned when one spots the restored greenhouse in the distance at the end of a long path. This walled garden was largely redesigned in the 1930s by Anne to commemorate her marriage to Michael. She was an enthusiastic gardener, her family being the owners of the famous English gardens, Nymans. In here, the most famous plant is

Paeonia 'Anne Rosse', a yellow tree peony that came about as the result of a cross made to create a flower specifically for his wife.

Hornbeam *allées*, older than the 1936 garden, form a 'cloister' around the inside of the walls. Michael planted snowdrops under the hornbeams as a young man while home on leave during World War I. The cloisters have 'windows' cut into them, providing glimpses of the parterres of box, planted in complicated patterns. These incorporate the big 'R' for Rosse.

There is a rose garden to one side of the box parterre. It is a romantic little garden, full of old French roses, mainly cultivars from the 1820s to the 1890s. The list of names reads like creatures from a bodice-ripping novel. So we have *Rosa* 'Duchesse de Montebello', *R.* 'Belle Poitevine' and *R.* 'Petite de Hollande' in flounces of pinks, dusty mauves and plums.

A romantic air continues with the delphinium border. This is a long wall bed, filled obviously with all sorts of delphiniums in blues, jewelled purples and pale lilacs. They are supplemented

with catmint, tree peonies, thalictrum, inula and aconitum or monkshood, a relative of delphinium that, unlike its finer relation, does not need staking. Beyond this sea of flowers, a Greek goddess standing in a little bower is afforded some privacy in the shape of clematis and sweet pea drapes.

Other features that stand out are the gnarled wisteria arches, iris and paeony beds and the famed two-hundred-year-old Tallest Box Hedges in the World according to the *Guinness Book of Records*, with their strange smell. This is a remarkable scent. When you know that what you're smelling is box, it smells good. But, like basil and Parmesan cheese, it is curiously unpleasant, and reminiscent of cats, when the source of the smell is unknown.

The way back out to the greater garden is by a path under a yew avenue. One route leads through the trees to a Victorian fernery. Overhead, a dense tree canopy creates the perfect dark, spooky atmosphere for a collection of ferns and tree ferns. They look perfect in the damp green light, growing between wet, moss-covered stones, beside ravines and bridged streams. The narrow goat-track path picks though these, rising and falling as it travels past the exposed roots of beech trees which crawl down the bank. This is the height of Gothic romanticism. After heavy rain, when the stream is high, the roar of water over the little falls has to be experienced to be believed.

Out in the open, in front of the castle there is a new garden feature called the whirlpool spiral, made of lime trees. First planted in 1995, this spiral travels in ever-decreasing swirls, its shape reminiscent of a galaxy of stars. When it is mature it will look wonderful from the air.

Birr has many of the usual features expected in a great pleasure garden including, not a shell house, but a shell well, set deep in the woods. The mixed borders leading up to the castle and tucked in under the outer walls of mock fortifications are flowing and easy, herbaceous and informal. These are full of buddleia, echinops, white iris, tradescantia, snow-in-summer or *Cerastium tomentosum* and Japanese anemone. Do not miss the big, gnarled, pinned-up *Magnolia delavayi* behind the flowers.

Inside the castle walls, the high and low walks are equally lovely to wander beside, above and along the river. Waterfall point looks down the spring-flowering bank to the gushing River Camcor below, and on towards a small suspension bridge that leads across to groves of cornus, acer, willow, cherry and pine on the other side of the river. This elegant bridge, a legacy of the family's engineering endeavours, was built in 1810.

Leaving the garden, one passes the castle gates, also built by Mary Rosse in 1850, with three ugly monsters to guard it, and a huge rose beside the portcullis.

County Westmeath

Belvedere House and Garden |
Tullamore Road, Mullingar, County Westmeath

Tel: (+353) 044 934 9060
e-mail: info@belvedere-house.ie
www: www.belvedere-house.ie
Open: All year from 10am. See seasonal closing times on web. Children welcome. Dogs on leads.
Special features: Café. Garden centre. Gift shop. Events.
Directions: 5km from Mullingar on the N52.

On hearing the history of Belvedere, one could be forgiven for thinking that they were listening to the plot of a particularly gruesome Gothic novel. This is the deeply unpleasant story of the three Rochford brothers, their three homes, Belvedere, Tudenham and Gaulstown, and their terrifying sibling rivalry. The brothers' lives seem to have been one long run of despicable carry-on, with stories of misfortunate wives locked up for decades, debauchery, duels, fights, vicious, quarrelsome feuds and casual cruelties. One can imagine an intriguing sort of oppression still hangs around Belvedere as a result of such a history of conflict. On my first visit, in the late eighties, it certainly had the feel of a woebegone sort of place.

The family history can still be seen today in the garden of Belvedere, in the bricks and mortar of the Jealous Wall. This well-named building is the largest Gothic folly on the island and a visible reminder of the Rochford feuds. It was erected as a mock ruin by Lord Belvedere to obliterate the sight of his brother's home, Tudenham, built next door to, and bigger than, Belvedere.

Several centuries on, the dilapidated gardens and deserted Georgian house were taken over by Westmeath County Council in the nineties. They then underwent a serious programme of restoration and were opened to the public in 1999. Today, Belvedere is a centrepiece attraction and source of great pride in the county. It is a big, busy tourist attraction that hosts all sorts of country events, concerts and fairs. The restored gardens, along with the Jealous Wall, are well worth visiting.

More than a decade on from the restoration project, the work has settled in and bedded down, making the gardens appear as mature as if they had never faded. At the front of the Georgian house there is a formal terrace. This imposing feature steps down from the building in a series of sloped spans of lawn, gravel ledges, heavy balustrades and statuary. It is all very self important-looking. Savage lions glower down from the steps, with shields decorated with coats of arms. Trained yews add to the formality. This feature was added in Victorian times, the faithful copy of a more famous stone terrace at Haddon Hall in Derbyshire, England. Lough Ennell is clearly visible from here, spread out in front of the house and lawns. At the side of the house, a wild-looking rock and wood garden tumbles downhill. It is all a suitably sombre backdrop for the Jealous Wall.

The seven-acre walled garden was also built, not by the Rochfords, but by a later owner, Charles Marley, in the nineteenth century. He and subsequent owners stocked it with a great variety of rare shrubs and trees. The larger space is divided into five rooms, each with a different mood or feel. The Bell Gate leads into the garden and its chief feature, a double border. This is backed by walls of yew and fronted by box hedging. The borders were designed to look good for much of the year. Spring bulbs give way to iris, catmint and grey, sharp-leaved globe artichokes, like monster thistles. *Cornus kousa* and different species of daphne provide a permanent skeleton between the drifts of more transient herbaceous plants.

The Himalayan garden came about when one of the earlier owners participated in plant hunting expeditions. It boasts blood-red flowered *Rhododendron thomsonii* and Himalayan blue poppies (*Meconopsis grandis*). It is in the rose garden where one will find the famous pink climbing rose named for the garden, *Rosa* 'Belvedere'. The greenhouses, meanwhile, are filled with the exotic perfumes and frilly blooms of an orchid collection.

The garden rounds off with the fruit, vegetable and herb garden. Some of the wall-trained fruit trees are particularly impressive specimens. The small pond and fountain pond full of Koi, collared by masses of flowers, probably shares joint place for prettiest sight in the garden, along with the view over the garden, with its maze of walks and paths, small hidden summerhouses and fairy gardens complete with ugly troll bridges.

In order to encourage more bees and butterflies, the walk down to the lake was planted up with fuchsia, shrub roses, buddleia and eucryphia. Mature maple and ash mark the edge of the deeper woods. Down here is where they uncovered, reinstated and restored a number of old cobbled paths.

Lough Ennell is itself as grand a body of water as such a house would require, with a wildflower meadow running up to the water's edge. On the way back to the house the path passes a fine weeping beech tree and blue cedar. A network of paths runs around the 160 acres of park leading past fine trees to more follies and viewing places.

TULLYNALLY CASTLE | TULLYNALLY, CASTLEPOLLARD, COUNTY WESTMEATH

Contact: Valerie and Thomas Pakenham
Tel: (+353) 044 61 159
e-mail: tullynallycastle@eircom.net
www: www.tullynallycastle.com
Open: May and June, weekends and bank holidays. August daily, 2pm-6pm. Groups at other times by appointment. Supervised children welcome. Dogs on leads.
Special features: Guided tours of castle. Tearooms open weekends, bank holidays or by appointment. Plants for sale.
Directions: Situated 1.5km from Castlepollard on the Granard Road (N52).

For anyone with an interest in trees, Tullynally will hold a special significance. It is the home of Thomas Pakenham, author and world-renowned tree expert. Travelling towards the castle, up the oak avenue, past elegant skeletons of fallen trees re-sprouting with new shoots, this feels exactly as the home of a tree enthusiast should, and serves to whet the appetite for this magnificent place. Tullynally was built in the 1600s by the Pakenham family and they still live here.

Today the castle is largely nineteenth-century Gothic in style and it overlooks a park and garden that have been in almost constant development since the arrival of the family so many centuries ago. There are records of plants being brought to Tullynally from plant hunting expeditions in the 1700s and you walk between garden features that date to almost every era since then. It is exciting to see that the pioneering planting continues into the early twenty-first century. This bodes well for the future of this horticultural treasure chest.

Tullynally Castle is the biggest castellated house in Ireland. The building is sided by a yew hedge, cut like battlements, overlooking the terraces and parkland. Austere stone rails form a barrier between a stone terrace close to the house, where the only softening effect comes in the shape of a big wisteria climbing the house wall and an apron of agapanthus and orange and yellow Welsh poppies self-seeding in cracks between the flagstones.

The romantic landscape and garden beyond this date to the eighteenth century. Among its most beautiful features is the grotto. This curiosity is a little stone bower perched up on a bank and tucked under a canopy of trees. It is ghostly and atmospheric, crowded with native ferns growing between outcrops of rock.

The walled garden, where the flower and kitchen gardens are sited, is home to a sunken lily pond with a fountain that is completely mossed over and surrounded by lady's mantle (*Alchemilla mollis*), geranium, fern and the strongest-scented marjoram. This is a Victorian device called a 'weeping pillar'. Two Coade-stone sphinxes guard the entrance to the flower garden. These were bought by Lord Longford in 1780, and known as the Merry Maids.

The kitchen garden covers a huge eight acres. It was built in the eighteenth century, when manpower was in no short supply. However, by 1840, when labour was still cheap, it was already being described as 'impossibly large for these times'. There were originally twelve greenhouses ranged along the long brick wall. Today there are only two left and one hot-bed house for melons and pineapples. The summerhouse, built in the 1920s, is flanked by two substantial borders. A curve in the borders forces the visitor to move along the whole length to see the contents of the beds properly. This is a design that makes the walker earn their reward.

Apples trained along the walls provide productive decoration. The avenue of blended, humped yew and box walls, knotted through with ivy and mahonia are known as the 'tapestry hedges'. They feature so many contrasting textures and shades of green and must be one of the loveliest examples of hedging to be found anywhere.

A hot border of orange, red and gold daylilies, nasturtium and crocosmia is like a blazing fire against the strong green yew foliage.

Some of the huge area in the walled garden is today given over to a family of llamas that Valerie Pakenham told me are good grazers – or lawn mowers – and easily minded as well as being interesting to look at.

Past Queen Victoria's small summerhouse, the track leads to the 'bridge over the River Sham', well named because it is not a river at all but a serpentine lake masquerading as a river. Even the Sham's crocodile, standing on an island in the 'river', is bogus, and the ducks and black swans showed no interest in or fear of the wooden croc. The summerhouse, too, falls into the same category: Queen Victoria never visited the garden, and this is a copy of one made for her elsewhere.

The path leads into the Tibetan garden. This is on the site of an old American garden planted by the second Countess of Longford in 1830 with acid-loving plants like camellia and azalea. Following a visit in 1834, the novelist and diarist Maria Edgeworth wrote of this feature:

'I never saw in England or Ireland such gardens . . . she has made the most beautiful American garden.' The acid-loving plants eventually succumbed to the lime soil in the area however, and the American garden was no more.

Fortunately, the more recently planted Tibetan garden has been more appropriately placed. This is an exciting project, the product of a seed-collecting trip made by Thomas Pakenham to Yunan in China. Two years later, the fruits of the trip were planted out. There are new and interesting species of blue Himalayan poppies, yellow *Primula florindae*, Tibetan birch and species tree hydrangeas among them. As we made our way through the jungle on a golf cart, we could spy four-metre-tall *Cardiocrinum giganteum* grown in among dogwoods with *Lilium auratum* and some recently discovered species rhododendrons.

The trail goes on past a pagoda surrounded by lime-tolerant Chinese plants like sorbus, white pine, betula and philadelphus. It also takes in what looks like a gingerbread house as it makes its way down to a viewing point.

The development continues and the most recent additions include a new magnolia garden with thirty-six different species, set deep in the woods.

In the meantime, a recently discovered rock wall full of ferns and moss has proved to be an exciting feature. Valerie explained that it came about as a result of the spoil left over when the River Sham was dug out in the 1860s. A rockery was draped over the stone to disguise it, turning leftovers into a feature. Until recently, it was lost under ivy. Today they are replanting it.

The adventure goes on, with Valerie in charge of maintenance and weeding as Thomas forges ahead, constantly planting new and unusual plants in the magical wood garden.

There are many remarkable trees here, but two are famous: a Champion Tree in the shape of a common beech that measures thirteen metres tall with a girth of seven metres, and the 'Squire's Walking Stick', an unusually tall, stick-straight oak. It was planted in the mid-1740s by a previous Thomas Pakenham.

County Wexford

Ballymore Garden |
Ballymore Schoolhouse, Camolin, County Wexford

Contact: John and Sylvia Mulcahy
Tel: (+353) 053 938 3179
e-mail: boo3@eircom.net
Open: By appointment and for annual open days. Contact for details.

Directions: In Camolin turn left after McDonald's Parkside Pub. Drive to a fork in the road and turn right. Drive uphill and take the left at two yield signs. The garden is 100m along and marked by a tall laurel hedge.

The garden around what was the old Ballymore schoolhouse is exceptionally good. It also comes as something of surprise, hiding as it does behind a tall laurel hedge on a country lane. The dropped-jaw effect is increased even more when, standing surrounded by something so beautiful, you are reminded that a few short years ago this was a scrubby field, the play area around the old school, with nothing more interesting than a boundary of aged, gnarled old Scots pines.

Then John Mulcahy arrived and the transformation began. These days, the two-acre hilly site is divided into a series of garden rooms, some of which can be glimpsed from each other and some of which come as a complete surprise, tucked away in sheltered corners.

It would be fair to say that there is an overall Japanese theme and feel to the garden. John is hugely taken with both Japanese plants and Japanese gardening practices. So in places the influence is overt and dominant: for instance there is a tea house, complete with rice-paper screen walls perched on the edge of an islanded pond. This little house sits at the top of the hill and the pond is fed by a pump from a water source sixty metres below. Elsewhere, raked gravel expanses wash around massive boulders. According to Sylvia, John is in love with stone and he has sought out some great examples for his garden. The bamboo hedges and two life-size statues of Japanese guards, called the 'Huffing and Sniffing Guards', further drive home the Japanese mood. John has even imported some gardening techniques from Japan – including tying fences and supporting plants with leather thongs, rather than lengths of plastic or rubber.

I first saw this garden in spring and it was full of flowering magnolias and acers with early unfurling colourful foliage, early alpine clematis, hellebores and snowflakes (*Leucojum vernum*). It was magical at that sparse time of year. As the year matures, so does the garden. One of the most memorable features is the laburnum walk and the little winding cobbled path under it. The patterned cobbles under the dripping yellow laburnum flowers lead up to a small red iron pig-gate in the distance. It is gorgeous. Later in the year roses, hydrangeas and clematis take over and splash the place with colour. The range of shrubs, trees and herbaceous plants used is wide and the ways in which John deploys them where they will look best illustrate his good design eye.

Along with John's love of boulders and rocks, he also loves stone work: the garden incorporates so many well placed sets of steps, raised stone beds, dry stone walls, walls built around circular moon windows, and decorative pebble paths. These are the stars of the garden in winter and they frame the plants in summer. In particular I love the herringbone-patterned wall. In spring, tufts of primrose and fern sprout from between its pencil-slim stones.

Apart from creating the pond on top of the hill, John has directed little streams through the garden, bridging them in places and damming them in others to create pools.

The final ingredient in the banquet is sculpture. In every direction you see pieces of art set about, complimenting the plants and creating focal points. From the overpowering Japanese guards to witty little metal birds and other creatures, there are works scattered everywhere. Even the shed is beautiful, clothed as it is in *Rosa* 'Compassion' and *R.* 'Bantry Bay'.

The garden is full of ideas that turn practicalities into features, such as the tiny wooden house at the top of the garden – it looks like a decorative folly but it was built to store tools. There are features here that stay in the memory long after a visit, like the laburnum tunnel or the white double flowering 'Shirote' cherry tree being trained as a sort of trellised roof over a little arbour.

THE BAY GARDEN | CAMOLIN, ENNISCORTHY, COUNTY WEXFORD

Contact: Frances and Iain MacDonald
Tel: (+353) 053 938 3349
e-mail: thebaygarden@eircom.net
www: www.thebaygarden.com
Open: May to September, Sunday 2pm-5pm / June to August, Friday and Sunday 2pm-5pm. Partially wheelchair accessible. Guide dogs. Groups welcome.
Special features: Plants for sale. Garden talks and teas by arrangement. **Directions:** Situated on the N11, just under 1km from Camolin (on the Ferns side), opposite the turn to Carnew.

Garden designers Frances and Iain MacDonald have spent the last two decades working together here in Wexford, creating and playing with what is both their garden and their shop window. They are nothing if not thorough people. When they first arrived they spent five years eradicating perennial weeds before ever beginning a garden. Five years spent killing weeds is a statement of intent and there are few of us who could put off the pleasure of planting up a garden for so long in order to make sure the place was weed-free. This place was built on patience and planning and it shows.

Arriving at the front of the house, one is met by a welcoming little old-fashioned garden surrounded by tall stone walls and the front of the MacDonalds' double-fronted Georgian home. It could be a garden straight out of a Jane Austin novel. Shrub roses, white anemone, sweet-smelling tobacco plants (*Nicotiana sylvestris*) and lengths of fat, clipped box melt together in a mix of strong, green foliage and white- and pale-coloured flowers. The upper parts of the house host a big wisteria, *Rosa* 'Cecile Brunner' and *R.* 'Mermaid'. The white-and-green foliage of *Euonymus* 'Silver Queen' does the same job at the lower levels. Bright gravel and stone paths divide the beds and draw light into this intimate little garden room. This is the sort of design that would look perfect in the small garden that fronts many period town houses.

Exit, however reluctantly, by a side gate into a bigger and completely different place. Out here there is a large open garden with big colour-matched beds swept through by expanses of grass. In one island, pink geranium knots through a pink variegated phormium with crinum lilies and pink-tinged goat's rue or *Galega officinalis* all together in a far-from-obvious combination that nevertheless works fantastically.

In another bed they have teamed reds, silvers and whites together. Reds and silvers work well but in gardens there is often a reluctance to trust an otherwise good sense of colour. Not so in the MacDonalds' garden.

It is said that good bone structure will never fail a beauty, and the bone structure here comes in the shape of small trees such as cornus, azara, acer and lilac, dotted through the beds.

The trail leads from this big open area, and steps down to a small, formal garden. This is a square divided by crossed paths into four smaller square beds, sharply colour divided. The first two beds are filled with white and shell-pink roses, white cosmos and anemone and a delicate pink- and white-tinged *Gaura lindheimeri*. I love the plum roses matched with plum-coloured penstemon and wine scabious. In the fourth bed, lemon-and-lime is the theme, with yellow roses, pale, butter-yellow *Anthemis tinctoria* 'EC Buxton' and lady's mantle or *Alchemilla mollis*.

The next treat is the red-hot border. Here there are exotic cannas, savage red dahlias, crocosmia, tiger lilies, kniphofia and mad orange rudbeckia. They work like an inferno in a bed.

And then, my favourite section is what Frances calls her 'funereal border'. This is full of serious and sombre-looking plants. There is black grass, *Ophiopogon planiscapus* 'Nigrescens', *Cercis canadensis* 'Forest Pansy', a shrub with dark purple, heart-shaped leaves, *Scabiosa atropurpurea* 'Ace of Spades', *Physocarpus opulifolius* 'Diablo' and black aeonium. There is something voluptuous about black flowers – but, apart from 'Queen of the Night' tulips, few of us use them enough. (I imagine there are plenty of these too in this stylish bed earlier in the year.)

New additions arrive in the garden on a regular basis. The path through the formal yew garden leads to the barn garden. This is a sort of mad spot where the meandering trail winds between beds of different grasses speckled with flowers. It is like a firework display on the ground, informal and dynamic. But for all its good looks, Frances told me that the only work that is ever needed here is one trip around with the strimmer in February. For that small amount of work she gets an ever-changing show for the rest of the year, particularly in July when the lychnis, geraniums, *Verbena bonariensis* and thistles are at their best. It looks great even in November when the first frosts hit the grasses and the planting of grasses and flowers is so dense that the weeds must look elsewhere to find a footing.

The wet garden is a new and developing feature. This was an expanse of wet flood-plain that they planted up a few years ago. Building a boardwalk to cross the damp ground over to a summerhouse was a great design idea. Crossing it between crowds of astilbes, arums, ranunculus and rodgersia feels like traversing a little jungle. The jungle atmosphere is enhanced further by the gigantic gunnera leaves that rise up like huge umbrellas behind the little summerhouse at the far end of the boardwalk.

The growth here is phenomenal: for instance, hunt out the huge *Pinus montezumae*, a giant at thirty years old, or the pretty *Cornus capitata* and *Cornus satomi* in the Japanese area.

Fern and container gardens close to the house show that the MacDonalds never cease conjuring up new gardens. Their favourite recent creation, according to Frances, is the small vegetable garden in the gravelled apron to the side of the house. Here, in raised beds, she grows a delightful fifty-fifty mix of flowers and vegetables. The whole area takes up the space of the average postage stamp-sized new house garden and shows just what can be achieved on a tiny plot.

There is also now a woodland garden, full of birches, chestnut and Spanish chestnut, beech and a host of other trees, under-planted with bluebells and narcissi.

'When everything else is gone the woods will be still here,' says Frances.

Coolaught Gardens |
Clonroche, Enniscorthy. County Wexford

Contact: Caroline and Harry Deacon
Tel: (+353) 053 924 4137 / 087 644 6882
e-mail: coolaughtgardens@eircom.net
Open: May to September, all week. Other times by appointment. No dogs.

Special Features: Plant nursery all year. Partially wheelchair accessible. Teas by arrangement.
Directions: On the N30, in the village of Clonroche turn at Greene's Supermarket. Drive 2.5k to the garden, which is well signposted.

Coolaught is something many help-strapped gardeners might envy – a family affair. Harry and Caroline Deacon and their family all work the garden together. As well as giving tours of the garden, the Deacons could probably clean up by giving advice on how to entice family members out to help with the digging and dunging to those gardeners who have failed to harness their own domestic workforces despite their best efforts. Once again, this is a sort of laboratory garden, where the Deacons experiment with as many plants as they can, so that when they sell a plant from their nursery, they can recommend it with full confidence.

There is a whole array of gardens here. The most memorable in spring must be the crocus lawn to the front of the house. The sprinkling of thousands of *Crocus tommasinianus* that has been developing here for the past century, makes quite a start to the year. This small square garden is surrounded by big billowing roses with names as romantic as their scents – *Rosa* 'Ferdinand Pichard', *Rosa de rescht*, and *R.* 'Blanc de Double de Coubert' over sheets of *Geranium* 'Hocus Pocus' with crinodendron above and behind them.

This little gem of a garden leads out through a small gate into a laneway, which in turn leads to the first of a whole series of long borders running the length of the garden; turning corners and leading into woodland gardens, past flower-draped arbours and into secret little sun rooms. The Deacons love plants and there are over eighty varieties of clematis alone, and if I began to count there must be just as many rose varieties.

Open, sunny gardens full of perennials lead to gravelled herb gardens, and from there to the shade of flowering shrubs and fruit trees. The barn garden is particularly good. This is built around an old stone barn, the home of a big family of swallows in the summer. It is a purely romantic flower garden full of scent and flowers throughout the summer.

Swallows apparently operate like dynasties, with a family seat to which they return, generation after generation, for the summer. They then leave for warmer climates when the Irish weather gets cold. So the swallows seen in a building several hundred years old such as this one could represent hundreds of generations of a single swallow family.

The Egyptian garden was discovered to be a corner planted up with blue, red and gold flowers. These are the colours Caroline and Harry associate with Egypt, as well as a smattering of plants with Egyptian names. So *Agapanthus* 'Lily of the Nile' and *Hemerocallis* 'Nefertiti' are planted in with hedychiums, red rhododendrons and verbenas.

At the outer edge of the garden, there is a growing acre-and-a-half arboretum. *Magnolia tripetala*, also called the umbrella magnolia, and *M. dentata*, the lily magnolia, rub in with golden larch, *Acer negundo* 'Kelly's Gold, a number of different species of cornus, camellias, Wollemi pines and tree ferns. It is a sort of trip around the world of trees where, with the space for big specimens, they are experimenting on a garden for the future.

JOHN F. KENNEDY ARBORETUM | NEW ROSS, COUNTY WEXFORD

Tel: (+353) 051 388 171
e-mail: jfkarboretum@opw.ie
www: www.heritageireland.ie
Open: May to August, daily 10am-8pm / April and September, daily 10am-6.30pm / October to March, daily 10am-5pm.
Dogs on leads.

Special features: Exhibition centre. Seasonal tea room. Picnic area. Play area. Self-guiding trail. Guided tours may be booked April to September.
Directions: Travelling south on the R733 from New Ross, turn right 12km south of New Ross at the sign for the arboretum and the John F. Kennedy Homestead.

The John F. Kennedy Arboretum was set up in the late 1960s in memory of the Irish-American president, appropriately close to the old Kennedy homestead and it would seem a shame to visit one without a trip to the other. The arboretum is huge, covering 250 acres, and is laid out in blocks and groves of trees joined by wide paths, runs of grass and lakes. Alongside the profusion of specimen trees, there are two hundred forest plots. These scientific experiments were laid out to study how trees from different parts of the world grow as forests in Irish conditions.

Over 4,500 species and cultivars of tree and shrub from all the temperate regions of the world can be found growing here. The plants are arranged in a well-signed grid system. The arboretum is an educational facility with ongoing research into such problems as Dutch elm disease.

But it is also a pleasant walk. The walks are divided into two main circuits, one of broad-leaved trees and one of conifers.

Apart from the vast array of trees, there are displays of different hedging plants, varieties of shrubs, conifer beds, rockeries, lakeside and marginal plantings around the different water features. If you want to see a dozen differing species and varieties of cotoneaster, this is the place to visit and the same applies to sorbus, ceanothus, spirea, berberis and a great number of other plant families. Wild flower areas have been encouraged in a number of places.

The arboretum displays a wealth of trees and plants. It is worth taking a whole day to explore and appreciate it fully, taking in a walk to the viewing point. Up here, on top of the windy hill, the surrounding geography of Wexford, Waterford, Tipperary, Carlow, Wicklow and Kilkenny can be studied on a bright day, as well as the view out to sea to the Saltee islands.

The gardens suffered a great deal in the winter of 2010 and this, in combination with meagre funds, tell a not altogether happy tale at the time of going to press. The arboretum needs a big hug.

KILMOKEA MANOR HOUSE AND GARDEN |
GREAT ISLAND, CAMPILE, COUNTY WEXFORD

Contact: Mark and Emma Hewlett
Tel: (+353) 051 388 109
e-mail: kilmokea@eircom.net
www: www.kilmokea.com
Open: March to October, 10am-5pm.
Supervised children welcome. Dogs on leads.
Special features: Partially wheelchair accessible.
Art and crafts for sale. Teas and light lunches.

Hotel. Guided tours by arrangement.
Directions: From New Ross take the R733,
signposted for Campile and the JFK Arboretum.
Pass the turn for the arboretum and continue for
1.5km. Turn right at the signpost for Great Island
ESB and Kilmokea Garden. Drive 2.5km and take
the left fork to the entrance.

Kilmokea is in the unusual situation of being sited on an historic site that was once an island in Waterford Harbour. In the early nineteenth century, land reclamation joined the little pocket of frost-free land to the mainland. Soon after, a pretty Georgian house was built on the site. The garden looks venerable laid out around the old house, but it was in fact started in 1947 when the Price family created a formal garden within the kitchen garden walls of the house. The enterprise was taken over by the enthusiastic Hewletts in the late nineties and they have faithfully minded and continued to develop Kilmokea since then. At the back of the garden there is a plaque commemorating Colonel David Price's gardening achievements.

Kilmokea is a romantic place, full of surprises, good plants and design. Low walls, impressive tall semi-mazed hedges as well as elaborate topiary deliver year-round structure. Many features in the well-divided garden would be perfect by themselves: for example the iris garden – all formal, straight lines with beautiful blue flowers over strappy leaves around big Chilstone urns full to brimming with flat-topped box. The precision of topiary bells, cones and mushrooms serves to make spreads of catmint, monarda and other loose herbaceous plants look even more flamboyant. I love the combination of formality and loose, easy planting.

The surprises are dotted around liberally. In one corner it will be an Italianate loggia with a formal pond. Chilean potato vine (*Solanum crispum*) and lobster's claw (*Clianthus puniceus*) clamber over the loggia in an unusual combination of colour and exotic-looking flowers. This is a delightful place to sit quietly if the sun is out.

Self-seeding is enthusiastically encouraged here. Desirable self-seeders, like echiums, for which the garden is well known, as well as love-in-a-mist (*Nigella damascene*), columbine or aquilegia and poppies, can be incorporated into most gardens by allowing them to germinate, and then deciding which little plants to keep or dump. Everyone loves the sight of opportunistic blooms emerging from seemingly impossible situations, like the tops of walls. Occasionally a plant will park itself beside another surprisingly complementary plant, for which the gardener can, of course, take all credit. The millions of seeds that an echium gives rise to should not scare novice gardeners, however. Like horticultural tadpoles, there may be countless seedlings, but by the time the Irish weather has taken its effect, there will be no more than two or three plants alive – with luck.

The big kitchen garden, reached by way of a cathedral of bamboo, is another one of the great surprises. This is a busy, working but presentable vegetable garden, worked organically and built to wander through as much as to raid for food. Tall beds of sunflowers vie with the beans and peas. Low, undulating and wobbly box walls enclose flower beds, and lines of lettuce enjoy equal billing with dahlias and delphiniums.

From the house, the view down the bordered lawn directs the eye to a gate in a wall. Behind the gate there is a second, secluded garden with a fernery, beds of geraniums and paths that run under big camellias and rhododendrons, past wooden summerhouses. Down here it is like a battle of the big leaves: huge rodgersia, three-metre-tall gunnera, skunk cabbage, acanthus and bamboo make the garden feel positively tropical. I almost expected to see a coconut fall from the sky.

Carry on through another gate and across a road to yet another garden. This is the *real* secret garden – a wild wood and 'horse pond' with a little boat moored picturesquely by the edge of the water. Once past the pond, the level of the land falls down to a glade of tree ferns, candelabra primulas and trachycarpus; it is damp, sheltered and warm. Little feeding ponds drip into each other, overhung with ferns and *Euonymus planipes* with pretty red-quartered fruits.

Walkways and bridges have been set into the trees; Mrs Hewlett built all of these. They give the feeling of walking on gangways through a giant greenhouse. 'It was heavy work making them, but it made a big difference,' she says. The Hewletts have definitely earned their stewardship of this extraordinary garden.

Tombrick Garden |
Tombrick, Ballycarney, Enniscorthy, County Wexford

Contact: Walter Kelly
Tel: (+353) 053 938 8863
Open: May to September, Friday to Sunday
2pm-6pm. Contact for annual dates. Other times
by appointment. Guide dogs only.

Special features: Partially wheelchair accessible.
Plants for sale. **Directions:** Situated on the N80
between Bunclody and Enniscorthy, 1.3km north
of Ballycarney Inn, signposted.

Walter Kelly built the house at Tombrick in a small rectangular field on an extremely windy hill back in 1988. The following year he began a garden and today it gives gardening visitors one of the most satisfying visiting experiences to be found in what is one of the best gardening counties in the country. Walter is something of a gardening magician. Walking through magnificent mixed borders full of wonders, it is hard to see how this could ever have been 'the windiest site on a wind-swept hill'. The first lesson of the visit is that there is wisdom in erecting good shelter belts.

The garden to the front of the house is made up of lawn surrounded by borders, but not so dense that the sweep downhill to the River Barrow and the valley beyond cannot be seen. It is pretty but it does nothing to prepare you for what is in store. The real garden is to the side and rear of the house. It begins with a series of impressive ledged rockeries. From there it moves out into woodland walks, sunny pond gardens, orchards and long serpentine paths through mixed borders filled with good and unusual plants.

The paths sweep up against massed, billowing ground cover plants, well pruned small trees and invisibly supported tall herbaceous plants. The range and number of plants is stunning, as is the upkeep. How he manages to run a full farm and still find the time to work this garden, which looks like a full time job in itself, is a mystery. One could be forgiven for thinking that night work using a Davy lamp must be involved.

Fancy fowl strut about the place, providing mobile entertainment and slug eradication along with a background of clucking and quacking. The fowl have their own pond, which of course doubles up as a water garden and home to collections of primulas, hostas and other damp-loving plants.

Walter has a talent for combining plants that has to be seen. He has a love for certain plants, hardy geraniums especially. From the gateway they seem to have been squeezed into every possible corner and between every second plant. Among the scores of species and varieties in one area alone I spotted *Geranium cashmeriana* 'Alba', a special little one called *G. oxonianum* 'Walter's Gift', *G. palmatum*, *G. magnificum* and *G.* 'Anne Thompson'.

Walter also uses stone well. In the wood garden and elsewhere, local granite has been pulled into service everywhere, in the shape of gate posts and standing stones, ledged beds, gravel paths and planting areas.

The gravel paths in particular give a sense of unity to the place, tying it together. They trail off in so many different directions, lighting up dark wooded areas and making sunny bright spots appear even brighter. They are more impressive because they are so well minded, swept clean and clear of leaves. This is a state of affairs that will leave lazy gardeners wanting to kick themselves.

COUNTY WICKLOW

JUNE BLAKE'S GARDEN | TINODE, BLESSINGTON, COUNTY WICKLOW

Contact: June Blake
Tel: (+353) 087 277 0399
e-mail: juneblakes_nursery@yahoo.ie
www: www.juneblake.ie
Open: April to September, Friday to Sunday 12pm-5.30pm. Other times by appointment.

Contact for exact annual dates.
Special features: Plant nursery. Part of the Dublin Garden Group. Refreshments. Guided tours.
Directions: Leave Blessington travelling towards Dublin on the N81. The garden is signposted on the left.

When we hear the words cottage garden, the picture that generally comes to mind is one of an old-fashioned, traditional flower garden, something along the lines of a Mildred Anne Butler watercolour. But June Blake has proved that the styles Cottage Garden and Contemporary, usually poles apart, can be melded together to create a garden that both looks good and makes sense.

June is, without doubt, one of the best plantswomen in Ireland. She has been selling fantastic plants from her nursery outside Blessington for years and her garden has been a favourite among visitors from all over. So the news that she was changing that garden a few years ago made no sense – until I saw the new creation. June's new garden is a rare treat, a modern garden that draws in the visitor and wraps them in flowers, welcoming yet stylish, and an example of virtuoso design and expert plantsmanship.

The garden is laid out in front of a house that similarly marries modern with cottage style. This is a gabled, granite Victorian cottage straight off the top of a chocolate box from one angle, but with a sharp modern extension of glass when viewed from another.

The open sunny flower garden is not far from the main road but it is protected and secluded from the carriageway by a grove of tall trees and a field of donkeys. Arriving from under the shade of the trees along the drive, you are confronted with a sea of bright colour ahead. Generous beds of every conceivable perennial seem to vie with each other for attention. Gorgeous mixes and combinations of flowers fill the place from early spring to the very end of the year. It is hard to know quite which direction to take first.

June has an enviable eye for putting plants together. In one area the flower mix will make visitors feel like they are walking through a seventeenth-century Dutch flower painting: dahlias in all sizes and shapes compete with lilies, agastache and persicaria for attention. The colour mixes vary from bold and brazen to subtle and cool. I think of pink sweeps of *Geranium* 'Ann Thompson' and black *Cosmos atrosanguineus* knotted together. Meanwhile, behind and between the flowers, tall grasses like *Carex morrowii*, different stipas and *Miscanthus sinensis* 'Gracillimus', provide handsome, swishing backup.

There are hot beds with aralias and ricinus, grown for their dramatic foliage, mixed with tall *Lilium lancifolium* var. 'Splendens', *Verbena hastata*, *Dahlia* 'Moonfire', *D.* ' Murdock', tall crocosmias and thalictrum. It is spectacular.

June grows most of the plants here from seeds and cuttings. The knowledge that this gives her means that her plants are both guaranteed to be interesting and unusual, well researched and understood. The fact that many of them can be bought here just adds to the attraction.

Her ability with and love of plants meant that it would always be plant-heavy garden, but well placed pieces of contemporary sculpture by some of her favourite artists add sparky punctuation to the plants. There are also pieces created by June herself, such as the weird warped sleeper staircase that rises up behind the flower beds through a meadow filled with fritillaries and species narcissi. It looks like an unhinged spiral staircase trying to break free. It is a beautiful, singular structure. A changing palette of wild flowers pops up throughout the summer in the grass between the steps adding an extra little zap of interest.

Up close there are other contemporary touches in the hard landscaping scheme: she has used wide metal edging to hold in runs of gravel and some of the borders. The rust-tinged metal looks smart and I think of its practicality every time I see rotting wooden edging in other gardens.

Hidden behind tall curtains of flowers and grasses we came upon a formal pond surrounded by granite and more metal edging. June uses the local Wicklow granite everywhere. It is a beautiful stone, glittery and bright with tiny bits of schist. Granite gravel is used in the paths that cut between the various beds. She employs large gobstopper chunks on wide shallow steps between different levels and there are all sorts of standing stones and small granite stone benches placed about.

She has left happy accidents in place when they improve the look of the garden, such as the big arching cedar, which seems as though it might topple over a path. Items like this add more quirky structure to the perennial-heavy garden. Another of these opportunistic features is the moss rock: it stands among the plants like a green *chaise longue* in the middle of one of the borders.

From secret paths set within and behind the borders to the obvious views up and down the paths and the panoramic view from on top of the hill, there is so much to drink in here. It is the sort of high-maintenance supermodel garden that looks as though it just tumbled out of bed, with tousled hair and looking naturally beautiful. You will not be able to do this at home.

Hunting Brook Gardens |
Lamb Hill, Blessington, County Wicklow

Contact: Jimi Blake
Tel: (+353) 01 458 3972 / 087 285 6601
e-mail: jimi@huntingbrook.com
www: www.huntingbrook.com
Open: See website for annual dates.
Groups welcome.

Special features: Garden courses and lectures.
Garden design and consultation.
Directions: Take the N81 out of Blessington in the direction of Dublin. 6km along, turn left and travel for 1km. The garden is on the left.

Jimi Blake has been a dynamic figure in Irish gardening for many years. At the time my last guide to Irish gardens came out, he was in charge of the gardens at Airfield in Dublin. He had carried out all sorts of interesting planting projects at that garden, and visiting it in his company was an education. In 2003, he moved home to where he grew up in Wicklow, and started a new garden from scratch in a field on the family farm. He built a wooden house in the middle of the site and began to garden. The resulting project has become one of the most highly regarded visits in the country, written up in a range of prestigious international gardening journals. Jimi uses his garden as a classroom and laboratory for the courses he runs and the whole enterprise is a pleasure to visit all year round.

This is a large-scale garden, covering almost twenty acres, if you include the wood and stream after which the farm was named. But the garden proper covers about five acres. And those acres are filled with plants grown from seed collected far and wide and propagated by Jimi. I think he is a true plantaholic and whenever he speaks there will be mention of some unusual plant he has just sourced on the net or found in an obscure catalogue.

His is such an individual's garden, not greatly influenced by anything other than his own interest in plants. The immediate impression is that of a place owned by a gardener who loves grasses. Massive stands of *Miscanthus sacchariflorus* and different cortaderias seem to have found themselves everywhere. Among the nearly eighty species of miscanthus here, one real stunner is *Miscanthus* 'Rotfuchs', which grows over three metres in a single year.

Big sweeps are another item Jimi is fond of – for example, *Rudbeckia* 'Goldstrum' is planted in drifts of up to 120 plants – as are the bee-magnets *Sedum* 'Autumn Joy' and *S.* 'Purple Emperor.' *Cortaderia richardii* is grown here in plantations of up to seventy plants. Using it at

the back of a bed, it creates a backdrop and hedge of sorts. Elsewhere, dierama is used in the same hedge-like way. Add thousands of *Veberena bonariensis* seedlings, masses of dahlias, and crocosmia, and the place is abuzz.

Jimi loves clashy colours. This is not a garden of pale lilacs and pinks. He will bind wine- and silver-coloured *Persicaria* 'Red Dragon' with rusty *Achillea* 'Terracotta' and *Kniphofia* 'Tawny King' together to produce the sort of look one sees in a *haute couture* fashion show. Elsewhere he mixes black kale with blood-red amaranthus, purple agastache and orange calendula. There are few plants as dramatic as aralias, particularly *Aralia echinacaulis*. The seed of this strange, fast-growing Dr Seuss-like plant was collected in China. In among the architectural stars like aralia and *Tetrapanax papyrifera* 'Rex', Jimi uses see-through plants like coreopsis, geraniums and alliums.

Between the mass of tall grasses, exotics, herbaceous perennials and bulbs, the paths are almost invisible and the house seems to stand in the middle of a large plantation of ligularias, inula, astrantia, coppiced and pillared eucalyptus and giant-leafed paulownias. One could have been dropped into a cabin in the middle of the jungle. On my last visit, the rain was coming down in monsoon proportions and we stood on the veranda looking out at what could have been a south-east Asian jungle.

A little way off, the wood garden is at its very best in the spring. In here, under the magnolias and large-leafed rhododendrons, the ground is littered with the lime-fresh foliage of hesperis, little violas and the beginnings of blue Himalayan poppies or meconopsis. The ground teems with arisaemas, trilliums, erythroniums, corydalis, ferns, moss, moss and more moss. A network of paths edged with the branches of fallen trees give the wood an even more verdant and untamed look and with mature trees way overhead, the wood floor, dappled with light, is a sight for sore eyes.

Jimi is today working on the outer wood, building more hilly paths through it, planting native and exotic ferns on the slopes to make hanging gardens down to the stream, and building wooden bridges across the little waterway.

I have described the garden as it was on my last visit. That description was different to my previous visit and no doubt it will be different to the garden as it will be in a year. Jimi Blake is experimenting constantly, changing what others would find perfect, adding in new features and different schemes. I suppose I should not try to describe it but just say: expect to be impressed.

KILLRUDDERY HOUSE AND GARDENS | BRAY, COUNTY WICKLOW

Contact: William Kinsella
Tel: (+353) 01 286 3405
e-mai: info@killruddery.com
www: www.killruddery.com **Open:** April, weekends 1pm-5pm / May to September, daily 1pm-5pm. Otherwise groups by appointment. Supervised children.

Special features: Tearoom. Occasional rare plant sales. Guided tours of the gardens and house can be arranged. Events. Movie tours. **Directions:** Travelling south on the M11, take the third Bray exit, marked Greystones/Bray. Killruddery is signposted from here.

Killruddery has been the home of the Brabazon family since 1618. The garden is unique – it is the only completely unchanged, classically French-designed, seventeenth-century garden on the island, partially designed by a student of the great André le Notre, designer of gardens to Louis XIV. A letter written in 1682 states that 'Captain Brabazon has and will make new great improvements there.' A few years later, William Petty, author of the Down Survey and owner of vast tracts of land in Kerry (see Derreen, County Kerry), complained bitterly that his French gardener of twelve years had decamped to Killruddery.

Work started back in the 1600s and continued for centuries and, as a result, today the garden's great size, austere formal beauty and mature planting make it a singular place that leaves a lasting impression. It is a garden that can be visited (with permission) at any time of year as it is not a place that depends heavily on flowers but on strong lines, mature trees, monumental and large-scale plantations.

Before setting off to look at the garden proper, stand at the house and look up the long sweep of lawn in the direction of the rough granite hill in the distance. The contrast between the manicured lawn and special trees with the wilderness from which it was wrought is striking and good to remember before seeing the rest of the gardens.

Killruddery's design is based on a number of large-scale features laid out along geometric lines, like an illustrated lecture on seventeenth-century garden design. The house stands on a wide terrace of granite softened with hummocks of arabis, rock rose and lavender. Running south from the house, the twin canals measure 187 metres. They lead down to a basin and beyond that to a long ride that runs for a great distance and imparts an air of grandeur. Le Notre pioneered this use of long avenues cut into woods, to give the impression, real or otherwise, that the garden owners' land extended for miles.

To the side of the canals is the 'wilderness'. This historic term today seems misleading, as the trees are grown in straight, ordered, almost military lines – not at all what we would think of as a wilderness. (See Royal Hospital Kilmainham, County Dublin.)

There is a beech-hedged pond, made up of two tall circles of beech, one inside the other like bracelets, with a circular walk in between. The inner hedge is cut with windows through which the lily pond in the centre can be glimpsed from the walk. This is a simple but exquisite design.

A little way off there is another unusual feature: an amphitheatre, or sylvan theatre, with steps of grass-covered seats that rise up above a stage, backed by more tall beech hedging. Live performances and recitals are still held in this little place during the summer. The day I visited, a quartet was practising and snatches of the music could be heard as it was picked up by the wind all around the garden.

The area called 'the angles' is the best of fun. This is a series of maze-like walks between 4.5-metre-high hedges of hornbeam, lime and beech. The walks meet at two points and radiate out from each other like an easy maze. Between the lines of hedging, taller, mature trees add height and some confusion to the otherwise straightforward 'maze'. Images of giggling aristocratic girls in ruffled skirts playing pretend hide-and-seek with suitors come to mind, especially when music can be heard drifting across the lawn from the sylvan theatre. There are occasional pieces of sculpture sited about and, these days, the area is sometimes used to hold temporary sculpture exhibitions.

The rose and lavender garden is a striking sight with charming, uneven box and yew hedges, just the answer for anyone who has ever tied themselves in a knot trying and failing to get a straight line on a hedge. The box surrounds fluffy, grey, scented lavender, roses and the big fried-egg flowers of *Romneya coulteri*.

This quirky garden is overlooked by the house and recently restored *orangerie* (statue gallery), a beautiful glass structure built by Richard Turner in the 1800s. It has been completely restored and its statues and tender plants of tibouchina and plumbago can now be viewed as part of a tour of the house. It too is used for small concerts.

From its windows you can see the ornamental dairy. This is a quaint, octagonal-shaped building with stained-glass windows, covered in roses and clematis. This was also part of a garden style that came from the continent in the late eighteenth century, when fine ladies would play at being milk maids and shepherdesses. (See Kilfane Glen, County Kilkenny.) Today it is used as a tearoom. Running out behind it there is a long colourful mixed border which overlooks a sunken bowling green bounded by little stone putti surrounded by agapanthus and penstemon.

KILMACURRAGH BOTANIC GARDENS |
KILBRIDE, COUNTY WICKLOW

Contact: Seamus O'Brien
Tel: (+353) 0404 48 411 / 01 857 0909
e-mail: seamus.obrien@opw.ie
www: www.botanicgardens.ie **Open:** November
to February, 9am-4.30pm/February to October,

9am-6pm. No entrance fee. Dogs on leads.
Special features: Partially wheelchair accessible.
Guided tours can be arranged. **Directions:**
Situated off the M11 at Rathdrum. Turn right at the
Beehive Pub.

Named a national botanic garden in 2010, Kilmacurragh is probably the most exciting large garden on the island. Started in the 1850s on the foundations of an older garden, Kilmacurragh arboretum was always particularly famed for its conifers. Thomas Acton planted it between the years 1850 and 1908 in conjunction with David Moore and his son, Sir Frederick Moore, both of whom were curators at the National Botanic Gardens in Glasnevin, Dublin. So the link between the National Botanic Gardens goes back to Kilmacurragh's creation. Frederick Moore in particular recognised that it was possible, in places like Kilmacurragh, to successfully plant many exotic trees that had recently arrived in Ireland from plant-hunting expeditions around the world. The slightly milder weather and higher rainfall in Wicklow meant that many specimens fared better and had a better chance of survival here than their relations in Glasnevin. Moore worked with Acton and other interested gardeners on gardens that had good microclimates around the country, sharing his rare and special plants with the Wicklow garden in the greater interest of Irish horticulture. He worked similarly with Mount Usher and in Rowallane, County Down.

But the garden fell into decline in the twentieth century, and for many years it looked like the neglect would never be repaired. Happily, Kilmacurragh is enjoying a renaissance and the current chapter of its history is going to read well. It is once again in the care of the National Botanic Gardens and under the expert eye and care of Seamus O'Brien. Under him, a programme of repair, restoration and development is galloping along and an extraordinary garden is being both uncovered and developed. Avenues of ghostly rhododendrons have been restored and turned back into the spectacular features they were once envisaged to be. The broad walk under some of these

rhododendrons was built wide enough to accommodate two ladies walking side by side in wide crinoline dresses. In May it looks like a crimson carpet of rhodo petals.

Glorious trees have been found throughout the wild garden: among them red-barked myrtle, different species of podocarpus, including the largest *Podocarpus nubigenus* on the island. Marvel also at a fine weeping Kashmir cypress (*Cupressus cashmeriana*) with silvery-fringed needles and a monster pink *Magnolia campbellii* escaping over the wall from the walled garden. This magnolia is like a one-tree example of how seed and plant exchange has evolved over the years. As a

A family gathering outside of Kilmacurragh House in 1932. The Queen Anne house was built to the designs of the noted Irish architect Sir William Robinson in 1697. Photograph © Seamus O'Brien

seedling, it was collected in Calcutta in 1830 and brought to Wicklow. Recently one of its seedlings was sent back to the Botanic Garden in Calcutta, to repay the favour – and so the horticultural world should spin.

There are countless numbers of the biggest, tallest, widest, first-to-flower-in-the-northern-hemisphere, rarest and most impressive specimens found all over Kilmacurragh.

Among the developments, there are a whole series of new gardens being created. These are strongly based on plants from South America, and in particular Chile. There are also great numbers of plants from China and the Himalayas gathered here. Some of these can be seen in the bog garden, where rare and special rhododendron splay and flower over blue Himalayan poppies. All these gardens incorporate plants brought in as seed from a whole series of seed-hunting expeditions, both modern and historic.

The shaded flower borders, unusual under the light cover of overhead trees and the linked tree fern walks must be seen. Along with the open sunny Regency border, these shaded beds are filled with special plants, unusual species and plants that have had to prove themselves to be included here. The Regency border close to the house was designed to be of interest from early spring to the end of the year.

In front of the old, ruined house, a young fossil lawn is in the process of being planted up with ginkgo, Wollemi pines, podocarpus and metasequoia as well as other ancients such as magnolia and drimys. These have been under-planted with species daffodils, fritillaries and crocus.

While these babies develop, the chief feature here is the eye-catching Japanese cedar or *Cryptomeria japonica* with its rusty-salmon foliage, coloured from the winter cold. And on the ground, painstaking restoration has brought a once-famous sea of blue *Crocus tommasinianus*, which had all but disappeared, back to life.

History is everywhere: the house is an unusual Dutch-style building, derelict yet still attractive. A wisteria over one of its side walls dates back to the 1830s. The remains of an older Dutch-style park garden can be seen in some of the vistas from the house, as well as a silver fir planted in the late 1700s. Meanwhile, there are memories of the great plant hunters scattered throughout, including William Lobb and his Monkey puzzles and giant redwoods, collected as seeds from Yosemite.

Down among the woods there is a pond fed by little trout-filled streams. Its design was such that it would overflow into a decorative run-off, but the design never quite worked.

The yew walk close by is a great ghostly cathedral-like feature, but it actually started life as simple yew hedging. In a period of neglect, this was left to run wild and so today we have an accidental wonder.

Along here there is a small stone building, which looks like it could have been a tool shed. It is nothing of the sort. This was the toll house along the original, cobbled road between Dublin and Wexford, used by Cromwell when he marched on that town. Part of it was planted up as an avenue of sessile oak. This is being restored now and will measure 1km long when finished.

Kilmacurragh Botanic Garden is gardened organically. Mown paths between the trees and a light hand make this garden feel as natural as William Robinson would have wanted. All over the gardens native hedges are being renewed, all propagated from plants grown in the locality. It will be three hundred years old in 2012, and by then the work will have advanced even further.

MOUNT USHER GARDENS | ASHFORD, COUNTY WICKLOW

Contact: Philomena O'Dowd
Tel: (+353) 0404 40 205 / 0404 40 116
e-mail: info@mountushergardens.ie
www: www.mountushergardens.ie
Open: March to October, daily 10.30am–5.20pm.

Supervised children welcome.
Special features: Partially wheelchair accessible. Tearoom. Craft shops. Guided tours may be arranged. **Directions:** Situated in the village of Ashford.

Mount Usher is one of a small number of Irish gardens with an international reputation, one it has enjoyed since the late nineteenth century. Although it started life as a modest acre under potatoes in front of the holiday home of a Mr Edward Walpole in 1868, under the stewardship of his son, E. Horace Walpole, it rose to become one of the places that the famous Irish garden

writer, William Robinson, championed as a perfect example of a fine garden. E. Horace improved it using the principles laid out by Robinson: in essence, to combine native and exotic plants in a naturalistic, seemingly artless way.

It has rightly been a favourite visit of garden lovers for generations. Today it covers twenty acres along the sheltered banks of the River Dartry, and is home to five thousand different species of plants.

The shaded and sheltered winding paths make it is easy to get lost. Just roam freely, perhaps using the tree trail to discover the names of some of the many exceptional specimen trees here. The river runs like an artery through the garden, with weirs, bridges and waterfalls spread along its length; it is the soul of the place and the views along it in each direction have been carefully constructed to maximise its beauty. Work has recently been put into clearing and repairing the different features to keep it perfect.

There are so many handsome arrangements that it requires a lot of visits to take it all in. Two-metre-tall Himalayan giant lilies (*Cardiocrinum giganteum*) set under the trees shine like visions from out of the shade. Spring meadows sprinkled with thousands of crocuses and miniature daffodils run up against groves of azaleas and other early-flowering shrubs.

'Layered' best describes the planting in Mount Usher. Graduated canopies made up of multi-coloured acers and magnolias, rhododendrons and eucryphias are breathtaking, particularly in autumn. Impressive trees and shrubs spread out every point, complementing each other in ways that look completely natural.

The collection includes stunning specimens such as a *Nothofagus moorei* (Sir Frederick Moore, the curator of the National Botanic Gardens in Dublin, assisted Mr Walpole in the early days of the garden). Look also for the *Osmanthus burkwoodii* and one of the largest New Zealand red beeches (*Nothofagus fusca*) in Ireland. *Eucryphia x. nymansensis* 'Mount Usher' is only one of many plants named for the garden, and indeed Mount Usher holds National Collections of both eucryphia and nothofagus. The eucryphias, covered in white flowers at the end of the summer and into September, are one of the great glories and are worth a special visit.

The groves of eucalyptus date back to 1911, when the Walpoles were given a gift of eucalyptus seedlings from Tasmania; the collection has been growing ever since. Their tall, regular peeling trunks are like sky dusters in army fatigues. The only impediment to Mount Usher holding the National Collection of these, however, is space. They take up a lot of it, and the garden is relatively short on that commodity. I was told, as we walked under some of the towering giants, that 'they have the ability to drop a branch at no notice whatsoever, as quick as a blink.' Suitably informed, we picked up the pace and made our way back to the open.

The path always seems to lead back to the water, and the noise of the river can be heard everywhere. Even in the pond garden, where the water is still, among the displays of primula and other wet loving plants, the roar of a nearby weir can be heard.

Meanwhile, back on dry land, the double herbaceous borders are a dream of colour and scent, full of old favourites like solidago or golden rod, rudbeckia, eupatorium, phlox and euphorbia.

Apart from the well known and renowned gardeners, for the people responsible for this great garden down through its existence, hunt out the series of plaques commemorating the gardeners who worked here. Many of them each gave almost half a century of service to the garden:

George Burns 50 years of dedicated service 1921–1971
Charles Fox 45 years as head gardener
Michael Giffney 44 years as gardener
Miles 'Miley' Manning 40 years

Today, the man minding the garden is the enthusiastic Sean Heffernan. He is working on new wild flower meadows, replacing tired old trees with new young specimens. His has the all-important task of bringing the garden well into the next century, extending the fabulous colourful maple walk, repairing the waterways, maintaining the weirs and walls, and adding new features. Like many of the great open gardens today, Mount Usher is being worked without chemicals. This might make the work hard, but it is all the more impressive.

Patthana Garden | Kiltegan Village, County Wicklow

Contact: TJ Maher and Simon Kirby
Tel: (+353) 086 194 4547 **Open:** August by appointment only. No Children. No dogs.
Directions: From the N81 in Baltinglass take the R747 for Hackettstown. The house is in the village, at the edge of the crossroads marked by an aubergine-coloured garage gate set into a granite wall.

I first came across TJ Maher in a different life. He was a young artist, nominated for an emerging artist's prize. An exhibition of nominated works was mounted in the gallery, where the winning artist would be announced. TJ was absent, travelling in India. To the chagrin of the PR people, he won. But it was impossible to be cross: the paintings were beautiful. Years later, word of a new garden on the Wicklow Gardens Trail came in. I arrived to see the garden and, by way of small talk, I mentioned to the owner, TJ Maher, that I had come across another TJ Maher years before. I should have known they were the same man – this was the garden of an artist.

Situated in Kiltegan village, Patthana is one of the best small secret gardens in the country. Standing outside the old granite house, one gets no indication at all of the magical courtyard garden that lies behind the wooden gates.

TJ arrived in the mid-nineties, taking over the house and tattered garden on what he explained was nothing more than a whim. He liked the fact that there were lots of birds about the wild garden. Without any previous experience, he took to gardening, and went through the place like a whirlwind.

The result is a delight. Close to the house, the space is dominated by a variety of paved, flagged and cobbled areas punctured with exotic shrubs, perennials, clipped box and flowers. Unlike more solid paved areas, this area feels very much part of the garden rather than an extension of the house looking out at the garden. Wooden pergolas covered in *Rosa* 'Madame Isaac Pereire' and a stylish summerhouse built by TJ deliver the backdrop and support for climbing jasmine, clematis and the rather exotic looking flowers of *Akeba quinata*. At the base of sunny walls tender plants like *Beschorneria yuccoides*, jasmine and *Fatsia polycarpa* from Crug in Wales bask in the warmth. Small lily ponds sunk into the stone run riot with frogs and newts.

He grows species dahlias and a fascinating collection of species pelargoniums, including *P. echinatum* 'Alba' in the summer house. 'I think species plants are better for nectar and pollen,' says TJ, who primarily grows plants to feed birds, bees and butterflies. As a result most of the garden is made up of species plants.

This is a great example of fine organic, chemical-free gardening. Well-tended ferns, arisaemas and the striking-looking *Pseudopanax ferox* and *P. laetus* melt together in little plantations around the courtyard. There is more than a hint of the jungle about the abundance of foliage and even the cobbles you walk on seem to float on a green sea of *Soleirolia soleirolii* or mind-your-own-business.

There are so many distractions here. Each time one looks in a certain direction something un-noticed only a little while before becomes apparent. The pond is both bounded by a waterwheel stairway and fed by a waterfall made of the same round stones. I missed this unusual feature among the dense foliage on first inspection.

Above the courtyard, there is a second garden. It is reached using those stone steps as they pick their way up between prostrate, draping rosemary and hostas. The top garden is TJ's personal take on a country garden. Here, his reworking of the hackneyed island bed is well worth studying: they are full of airy, light plants like stipas and *Verbena bonariensis*, *V. hastata* and *Persicaria amplexicaulis* 'Rosea'. These are almost see-through plants. A grass, *Molina* 'Red Pole', was being pulled over by the weight of tiny birds eating its seeds. Leaving these seed heads on a plant over winter is of great help to the birds. They will feed on them gratefully, if sporadically. Up here among the light grasses, hydrangeas of different types create the necessary solid presence. Lightness of touch allows TJ to fit more beds and more plants into a small space, and the place never feels claustrophobic.

The top garden is surrounded by hedges of native holly, hawthorn, and euonymus. These are spiked with imports like *Sorbus* 'Joseph Rock,' *Arbutus unedo*, the strawberry tree, *Buddleia* 'Blue Horizon', purple hazel and *Rosa* 'Kiftsgate'. TJ cut windows in the hedge to frame a view of an old church spire in the distance.

Meanwhile, the tapestry lawn underfoot is further proof that working with, rather than against nature can be the best and easiest route to take when dealing with the issue of a lawn. In this relaxed country garden this multi-species lawn is as beautiful as any perfect weeded and fed lawn. Patthana is a garden I wish I had created.

POWERSCOURT GARDENS | ENNISKERRY, COUNTY WICKLOW

Tel: (+353) 01 204 6000
e-mail: carmel.byrne@powerscourt.net
www: www.powerscourt.ie
Open: All year, daily 9.30am-5.30pm.
Closed 25 and 26 December. Check web for
winter times. **Special features:** Children's play
area. Garden centre. Irish crafts shop. Restaurant
with terrace. Multi-media exhibition on
Powerscourt's history. **Directions:** Leave the
M11 at the exit signposted for Enniskerry. The
gates to Powerscourt are a few hundred metres
outside the village on the road to Roundwood.

Powerscourt, set in the foothills of the
Wicklow Mountains, is one of the great
gardens of Europe, as well as one of the best-
known and most visited gardens in the
country. The lands here were given to the
Wingfield family in 1609 in an effort to have
them secure the area against the Irish lords
surrounding and encroaching on the Pale.
Houses were built and rebuilt on this site
until, in the eighteenth century, a grand
mansion and formal grounds were
commissioned by Sir Richard Wingfield, the
third Viscount Powerscourt. Unfortunately,
much of the house, and indeed all the
principle reception rooms, were lost in a fire
in 1974. Only a wing remains of the huge
building.

The grounds at Powerscourt include
forty-five acres of formal gardens, sweeping
and stepped lawns, flower gardens, lengthy
herbaceous borders, perfect clipped hedges,
shrubs and woodland walks. Added to these

there are walled gardens, statuary, follies, Japanese gardens, rambling trails, a monkey puzzle avenue, ornamental lakes and great variety of plants. There is also the largest pet cemetery in Europe and an arboretum. One day may just not be enough time to see it all.

For all its splendours, there is one feature that no one who has visited Powerscourt ever forgets, and that is the Italian garden. Designed by Daniel Robertson in the middle of the nineteenth century, what we see today took one hundred men twelve years to build. It was

planned as a series of flamboyant terraces modelled on the Villa Butera near Palermo. These would be filled with bronze and stone statues, among them Apollo and Diana, assorted cherubs and strange creatures, spread out like a gigantic stage set. The spectacle would look down over Triton's Lake, itself complete with a fountain modestly based on the waterworks in the Piazza Barberini in Rome.

But the work was cut short at a point when only the lake and the first terrace in Robertson's original design were complete. His benefactor, the sixth Viscount Powerscourt, died while on a Grand Tour and artefact-collecting trip in Italy. Years later, the work was continued by his son, in a modified way, yet the result is still one of the most lavish garden features possible. It is an elaborate confection of wide sweeps of steps, pebble mosaics in elaborate patterns, statuary, wrought iron work, topiary and stunning views. Beyond the lake, there are mature woods and the perfectly placed Sugar Loaf Mountain in the distance.

The lake is just the most dramatic of the water features: everywhere throughout the formal gardens there are spouting, spraying, dripping and spluttering watery attractions.

Each time I visit, I have a different favourite feature. My most recent visit was on a wet autumn day when the Japanese garden was luminous. Everything was glistening, from the water-falls, ponds and little streams to the moss-dripping, fern-sprouting stone grottos. The vivid scarlet acers and spreading cherries, also beginning to colour, were stunning. Greenery has never been as beautiful or as dramatic. Much as one might want to visit gardens in good weather, rain should always be laid on when visitors arrive in this big little corner of the garden. Be the person who comes prepared with raingear and umbrella and you will have the place to yourself in the rain.

LISSELAN ESTATE GARDENS

Munster

~∞~

County Clare

Bunratty Castle and Folk Park | Bunratty, County Clare

Tel: (+353) 061 360 788
e-mail: reservations@shannonheritage.com
www: www.shannonheritage.com
Open: All year daily, except Good Friday and 24-26 December. See website for seasonal hours.

Special features: Gift shops and restaurants. Medieval castle. Partially wheelchair accessible.
Directions: Signed from the N18 travelling west from Limerick City.

Bunratty is something of a guilty pleasure. It is a place of bells-and-whistles exuberance. And while I can live without harps and medieval-themed banquets, the gardens are utterly charming – with icing on the cake in the shape of farm animals, old fashioned farm and gardening implements and recreated historic dwelling houses with people in period costume carrying out tasks like making butter, bread and working little vegetable plots. It really should be visited, even if you might not be as scandalised by a pub called 'Durty Nellie's' as I was as a child in the seventies. Before heading to the gardens, lovers of old furniture will enjoy visiting the castle to see the unique collection of antique Irish furniture dating back as far as the sixteenth century.

The reconstructed village, where the various gardens are located, stands behind and in the shadow of the fifteenth-century castle. There is a main street lined with old cottages, school houses, a doctor's house and little hovels. Beyond this there are recreated farmhouses from various points around the country and even a Georgian manor house. Each of these, fascinating in themselves with their little settle beds, old kitchens, quaint and sometimes squalid living quarters, are accompanied by appropriate gardens. The prosperous landlord's impressive walled flower garden is the chief attraction, but the little vegetable plots, fenced in with old bedsteads are interesting and instructive on the mend-and-make-do ways people had to operate.

The houses and gardens have been faithfully reconstructed and together they illustrate the different social layers in nineteenth-century Ireland. The doctor's house is draped with a massive sweep of *Rosa* 'Souvenir de Claudius de Donegal'. Each of its big red blooms would fill a bowl.

This particular garden is almost too pretty with its white picket fence enclosing runs of Jacobs's ladder, Welsh poppies, wallflowers, wisteria, poppies and geraniums, lavender and Lady's mantle. Meanwhile, at the other end of the scale, the smoke from damp turf fires clings to the clothes as one walks past the potato and cabbage patches in front of a small hovel.

The country house walled garden is laid out on a sunny hill from the top of which the whole garden can be seen along with view of the distant hills beyond the wall. This is a place of mixed shrub and flower beds, rose displays and wall climbers. The iron semi-circular cages over which specimen roses are draped and wrapped are notable. They are like huge, upturned hanging baskets. The roses being grown are sweet-scented old-fashioned variety called *Rosa de rescht*. Seen in May with blue forget-me-nots underneath, they are unforgettable.

The long double borders below these are full of vibrant yellow inula, lysimachia and lupins. Along the south-facing side walls there are black, pink and white hollyhocks, soaking up the sun in between big spreads of jasmine, *Clematis tangutica* and figs. Hollyhocks are such easy plants, delivering much more than the little bit of care they require. The wall opposite this faces north, and its damp shaded soil suits hostas, ferns, Portuguese laurel and a fruiting Morello cherry. On the other side of that wall is a sort of maze through a big shrubbery, leading eventually out towards a stone slab-fenced paddock. This paddock belongs to the west Clare farmhouse. Slabs of stone from around the Cliffs of Moher were used for every job, from flooring a cottage and hemming-in animals to marking boundaries around fields. It also made an unusual and decorative fence.

The manor house, to which the larger garden belongs, is guarded by an impressive weeping ash, weeping beech and bounded by a ha-ha or sunken boundary.

Fields of fat sheep, goats, deer and geese, wild flower meadows, haggards of hay drying on top of stone mushrooms, all combine to make an extensive set of horticultural and historic displays.

The best thing about Bunratty is that the size is such that, even on a busy summer Sunday, you can still have a peaceful walk around the gardens and there are seldom more than one or two others in each garden. Finally, the examples of stone walls from around the country point to the almost lost skills and flair of stone wall builders. A revival in regional styles of wall building is unlikely but it is always possible as long as we still have good examples of the different styles preserved and recorded, as they are here.

CAHER BRIDGE GARDEN | FORMOYLE WEST, FANORE, COUNTY CLARE

Contact: Carl Wright
Tel: (+353) 065 707 6225 / 086 080 2748
e-mail: caherbridgegarden@gmail.com
Open: All year by appointment only.
Special features: Wildlife talks.

Directions: Drive south on the coast road from Fanore. Turn off the road at Fanor Bridge over the Caher River. Pass the church on the right. The garden is 1.5km along on the right, just before the stone bridge.

A certificate of competence should probably be required for anyone chancing to create a garden in a landscape as remarkable as the Burren. This is no place for suburban twee. I imagine Carl Wright would have no problem obtaining his certificate. With a background in ecology and countryside management, he arrived here several years ago and took on a hazel and blackthorn-filled field around a derelict farm cottage. With these ingredients, in a landscape generally thought to be inhospitable to cultivation, he conjured up a plantsman's garden that sits well into its tuck of the landscape.

Keeping many of the native trees, but lifting and moving them to strategic places along the boundary, lent instant structure to the new garden while still leaving it with a slightly wild feel. A depth of only two centimetres of soil meant that the two hundred different types of snowdrop and crocus now living here each had to be planted into individually excavated holes between the rocks. The scale of such a project would scare off even fairly dedicated gardeners.

Because he had no soil to speak of, Carl used the many stones and boulders dug up to make raised beds, importing soil from the locality to fill these. Using native stone immediately gave the beds the instant look of belonging. Apart from the raised stone beds, Carl also uses pots and troughs to grow plants that would not otherwise thrive here. Hostas in particular do much better in pots with a deep layer of gravel mulch covering the top of the compost to deter slugs. He marries big containers of hostas with little ones full of rhodohypoxis, sisyrinchium and saxifragas. These are all plants that thrive best in a regulated environment. Arranged in groups at the bases of walls and in sheltered places, the plants fare much better than they otherwise would in wild windy Clare.

The dominant feature to the side and front of the house is the pond. It is both unlined and fed from a stream, so it is just about natural. It certainly looks natural, colonized by native water plants including rare *Potamogeton lanceolatum*, hemlock, meadowsweet, bull rushes, yellow flag irises, comfrey and purple loosestrife.

The walls in this garden call for special admiration. They are all under ten years old and some are as young as two. But they were constructed with such craft that they look as though they might have been here forever. Largely rough, double dry-stone walls with a core of filler, they have been colonised by polypodium ferns, moss, saxifragas and fairy foxgloves.

Carl's is first and foremost a collector's garden and in the sunny area between house and pond there are 150 daylilies or hemerocallis and one hundred each of hostas, primulas and daffodils. All these are plants that we associate with soil, and if not good soil then at least plentiful. Carl brought every bit of soil in and then sieved it *by hand*. This is dedication above and beyond the call. Adding this sieved soil to his homemade compost provides a good living for colonies of drumstick and candelabra primulas as well as the daylilies and hostas.

As the stone was exposed, he studied the discoveries, and then harnessed it into the most appropriate features. So paths were put where the ground suggested it was amenable and steps were fashioned from existing stone formations that already looked like steps. This, of course, marries the garden further into its surroundings.

Earlier in the year, a collection of daffodils brightens up one area to the back of the house into which he imported loads of clay to raise the levels. In doing this he covered nearly seventy centimetres of the bottom of an ash tree trunk that he did not want to move. It was unorthodox but it worked, and the ash is now the dramatic centrepiece in a little lawn planted up with two thousand snowdrops, *Narcissus* 'Winston Churchill' and a double *N. poeticus* 'Plenus', crazy-looking salmon-coloured *N.* 'Cum Laude', pale *N.* 'Lemon Drops' and a multi-headed *N.* 'Tripartite'.

There are not many hydrangeas in the garden, as the ground doesn't stay moist enough for them, but *Hydrangea aspera* 'Villosa' performs well in this rich clay corner. What was to be a temporarily placed *Sambucus niger* 'Guincho Purple' is also managing quite nicely in the warmth of a sunny fence. It is one of many Irish plants grown here, from *Galanthus* 'Drummond's Giant' to *Prunus laurocerasus* 'Castlewellan', with white speckled leaves, a shrub that originated in the famous County Down arboretum.

There is one pocket of acid soil here, in a corner where the cottage's turf pile sat for decades. In an inspired move, Carl harnessed it as a home for his collection of ruscus. This corner backs onto another of the stone features, a moon window that visually links this area to the garden beyond its wall. That garden is a damper, darker, stream-dominated area full of rodgersias, epimediums, ferns and arisaemas.

In the centre of the garden, the ash tree is a feature not to be missed. As he began to unearth the garden, this tree was discovered, bolt upright, growing between the old hazel trees, trying to get at the sun and, almost incredibly, growing over bare rock. Today, standing in a clearing, the big roots can be seen snaking over the boulders. The dreams of Japanese gardeners are made of such things.

Vandeleur Walled Garden |
Killimer Road, Kilrush, County Clare

Tel: (+353) 065 905 1760

e-mail: info@vandeleurwalledgarden.ie

www: www.vandeleurwalledgarden.ie

Open: April to October, 10am-6pm / October to March, 10am-5pm

Special features: Café. Plants for sale. Gallery. Conference facilities. Wheelchair accessible.

Directions: Take the Killimer road out of Kilrush. Travel 1.5k and the garden is on the left.

'After we got the approval to buy the walled garden and stables, I walked through the garden and thought "Blast! They'll kill us." ' This was Jerry Sweeney's reaction to seeing the ruin of a garden just after he, as part of a committee of local people, had agreed to buy the walled garden and stable block of the Vandeleur estate just outside Kilrush. That was in 1997. The committee's aim was to take what was, after decades of neglect, in effect a walled field of self-seeded trees. They hoped to develop it, turning it back into the decorative and productive walled garden it had been a century before. Doing this would also provide some local employment and deliver the town a welcome tourist attraction.

The committee carried out research into the history of the Vandeleurs, who built Kilrush town as well as Kilrush House and this former garden. The important Lawrence Collection photos were studied to help with the garden restoration. Lawrence was a photographer who travelled the length and breadth of Ireland, recording every aspect of Irish life, between 1880 and 1910. His work has proved to be a hugely useful resource for scholars and anyone interested in the detail of life in late Victorian Ireland. Using these photos with the other information unearthed from the Vandeleur archives, the team then set to restoring the gardens. By the turn of the last century, the work was complete and the gardens opened to the public.

As it turned out, 'they' would have no call to kill the Vandeleur restoration team. Indeed, 'they' would have much to thank the team for. Following years of work, this is a garden well worth visiting. Having been brought back to life, it is worked enthusiastically by interested gardeners.

Today, in place of the many self-sown wild trees, large shrub borders encircle the walls. In the middle there are spreads of lawn, generous herbaceous borders, a small tree collection, fruit and vegetable gardens, a maze and a fruit walk, recently rebuilt glass houses, rockeries and gazebos. The Vandeleur gardeners have been busy.

On the sunny south-facing wall there are three-metre-tall exotic-looking echiums towering and flowering. Next to these, the informal display includes airy *Acacia baileyana* 'Purpurea', rampant hemerocallis or daylilies, figs and *Melianthus major*. They can fill the borders with tender and semi-tender perennials because the micro climate is benign. In fact, the conditions are so good that on my second visit, about eight years after I saw it as a new baby, the gardeners were in the middle of pruning and paring back many full-grown specimens, well ahead of schedule.

The curved design of this sunny wall came about in an effort to maximise the length of warm

wall space in order to accommodate the maximum number of sun-loving plants. A *Streptocarpus vandeleuri* is one notable plant found in the shelter here. This was introduced to Ireland by the Crofton family during the Boer War between 1899 and 1902, having been found on the rocky crevices of the Transvaal in South Africa. Today it basks in the sun that shines on this alpine bed in west Clare.

The beech maze in the middle of the garden has been fattening out nicely and the fruit tunnels of apples and pears are mature and gorgeous. They must be a sight at blossom time.

Outside the walls, the large courtyard dominated by a big bell tower has been restored and harnessed into useful life. Out here they planted a living willow for children to play in. There is also an old collection of puzzling farm machines, which should have even the most agriculturally knowledgeable people scratching their heads. Finally, plants grown from the garden are on sale in the middle of the courtyard.

Beyond the walls, there are about fifty acres of woodland walks. For anyone who feels that lost gardens are not worth reviving, the way the community has taken up this old ghost and resurrected it is a model worthy of study.

❦ County Cork

Annes Grove | Castletownroche, Mallow, County Cork

Contact: Jane and Patrick Annesley
Tel: (+353) 022 26 145
e-mail: annesgrove@eircom.net
www: www.annesgrovegardens.com
Open: April to September. Check website for annual dates. Other times by appointment. Groups welcome. Supervised children welcome. Dogs on leads. **Special features:** Accommodation. Partially wheelchair accessible. **Directions:** Located 1.6km from Castletownroche, on the Fermoy–Mallow–Killarney road (N72). Signposted from the village.

Annes Grove has been one of the best-loved gardens on the island for a very long time, and rightly so. Along with gardens such as Mount Usher (see County Wicklow), Derreen (see County Kerry) and Rowallane (see County Down), it is best known as one of the best Irish examples of a garden in the Robinsonian style. That style, championed by the nineteenth-century garden writer William Robinson, is the combination of native and exotic plants together in a naturalised fashion. Annes Grove also incorporates an older walled flower garden.

Blessed with pockets of both acid and alkaline soil, the garden accommodates an unusually wide range of plants. Richard Grove Annesley, creator of Annes Grove as it is today, was a co-sponsor of Frank Kingdom Ward's plant-hunting expeditions to Burma, Tibet and Yunan. He took full advantage of the bounty they delivered and filled his creation with the results of these and other expeditions.

First stop on the trail is the walled garden, thought to have originally been an eighteenth-century orchard. A well-maintained run of curved box hedges, called 'ribbon beds' due to their 'twisted ribbon' design, leads to an unusual, primitive-looking, three-legged stone sundial. The box ribbons are permanent. Variety is injected from year to year in the inner sections, which are planted up with different annuals such as cheery antirrhinums and impatiens. The path between these is so knobbly and uneven it could only be called a 'rocky road'.

A little distance away there are two long borders, where the dominant colours are blue and pink. They look like lava-flows of flower and foliage, and seem hell-bent on meeting each other in the middle of the stone-flag path. As silver and pink stachys tumble on to the flags, tall pink and white phlox, cannas and thalictrum bring up the rear and provide height. In the middle of summer they could be a painting of the perfect country garden border.

Pergolas knotted with wisteria, honeysuckle and roses stretch out from these double borders, leading in one direction through a shaded, woody walk under cherry and eucryphia, to a lily pond. Beyond the water, the path ducks into the shade of a Victorian stone fernery, an arrangement of natural-looking stone ledges and mounds built to hold a collection of ferns. Masses of mind-your-own-business (*Soleirolia soleirolii*) give the stone a look of being expertly covered with a very tight-tufted green carpet. This tiny, mat-forming plant has serious expansionist tendencies and consequently is loved and loathed in equal measure by gardeners. Like the ferns, it holds moisture and glistens satisfyingly after rain, giving the dark corner a romantic feel. I could live in this fernery.

The ruined Gothic summerhouse is one of the sad indicators of a place under the threat of age and lack of funds. Perched on a little hill at the centre of the garden, each visit there is a little less of it to see.

Outside the walls, the wood and wild garden spreads in all directions. This too is a fabulous place but one in

increasing need of care and intervention as it ages. Many people know it for its collection of rhododendrons, including *R. wardii* and *R. macabeanum*. A run of steps makes its way downhill under the rhodos, red flowering embothrium and myrtle (*Luma apiculata*). The pale, white splashed foliage of creeping nettle or lamium brightens up the wood floor.

At the bottom of the descent, having ducked under magnolias and podocarpus dripping with little ferns and strings of moss, it feels as though you could have wandered onto a different continent. Only a few hundred metres back up the hill, the garden was cosy and familiar. Down here at the bottom of the slope, one could be in a rain forest. The River Awbeg snakes along the bottom of the valley, overhung with gunnera leaves over two metres across. Beneath these monsters, rushes, skunk cabbage, naturalised candelabra primula and astilbe fight for space with dense groves of bamboo and six-and-a-half-metre-tall cordylines. No matter when I visit, the air always seems to be warm and humid down here. It feels like pith helmets and machetes should be issued at the gate.

The river was redirected, reshaped and bridged to allow access to the garden on both banks. This work was carried out by soldiers posted at the barracks in Mallow during World War I.

The path follows the course of the river, eventually emerging out of the jungle and into the open fields. The path wanders along, leading eventually to hydrangea rock, a gigantic open-air outcrop of stone rising way above the fields and covered in hydrangeas of every colour and shape. Another set of mossy, rough steps leads back into the woods to the top of the hill. I have never been able to follow the map provided, but it might be of some small use to those with a proper sense of direction.

But getting lost is probably a necessary pleasure in Annes Grove.

BALLYMALOE COOKERY SCHOOL GARDENS |
SHANAGARRY, MIDLETON, COUNTY CORK

Contact: Reception
Tel: (+353) 021 464 6785
e-mail: enquiries@cookingisfun.ie
www: www.cookingisfun.ie
Open: April to September, daily. Supervised children welcome. **Special features:** Garden shop. Cookery School. Groups can book meals in advance. **Directions:** Signed from Castlemartyr on the Cork–Waterford road (N25).

There have been gardens at Kinoith since the early 1800s, when the house belonged to the Strangman family. However, after 1952 they began to deteriorate. In the 1970s the Allen family moved in and work began on restoration of the wilderness in 1983. The gardens at Ballymaloe have been in development since then. Today they are mature, varied and very beautiful. If there is one emphasis it is that, being attached to a cookery school, a number of the gardens are productive in one way or another.

The different gardens are not altogether attached to each other, and I can never quite get the shape of the place in my mind despite the good-looking maps they provide. I love the fact that there are courtyards and little groups of houses and buildings dotted about, again adding to a comfortable confusion. A visit generally feels like something of a treasure hunt. I would start at the stream garden beside the restaurant, where a gang of wirework ducks and geese, along with a few live versions, congregate by the water. The planting scheme around the little stream is one of sedges, vinca or periwinkle, ivy and variegated *Sisyrinchium striatum*.

The well-known garden designer and writer, Jim Reynolds, created the fruit garden. It is not a large garden and its relatively compact dimensions mean it is well worth a visit by anyone with a modest-sized plot who dreams of an ornamental, productive garden. The arrangement is one of gravel paths between beds of fruit trees edged by collars of strawberries, rhubarb and pansies.

The bulk of the trees carry plums, pears, greengages, peaches and apricots. There are even almonds and olive trees. Old Irish apples trained over iron arched walks make good use of the paths. In the latter part of the year an under-planting of autumn crocuses cheers up the garden as operations wind down on the trees overhead.

From the fruit garden, a walk through a young beech wood leads to the *potager* – a French-style decorative vegetable garden. This is a confection of herringbone-patterned paths and *über*–smart symmetrical beds. This is not a place where you will find a messy gap: tidy parsnips, leeks and Florence fennel stand in measured lines. But marigolds and splashes of orange nasturtium soften the business-like look of the straight-laced vegetables. In here the scarecrows are made of willow that are so good-looking their efficacy must be doubted.

Out on the edge of the *potager*, a bench surrounded by an arch of golden hops makes a good place to sit and admire tomatoes interlaced with Devil-in-the-bush (*Nigella damascene*). This is a plant that single-handedly demonstrates the good sense of using Latin names for plants, because it is also called love-in-a-mist. Mop-head bay trees like green lollipops tower over the vegetables, and the whole garden is overseen by a raised beech-walled stage.

Lydia's garden was named for Lydia Strangman, whose watercolours provided a reference for the Allens when they began the restoration work. This is a beech hedge-enclosed garden with herbaceous beds. In one corner, a tree house overlooks this and several of the other gardens. On the ground underneath the wooden house is a delicate-looking mosaic, created in 1912 with a sign begging visitors not to walk on it. Do as you are told.

The pond garden can be seen from the tree house. This small field of rose-clad cherry trees leads to a Grecian folly and a pond, the des res to a sizable population of tadpoles. There is an air of cool restraint here, with a simple palette of reflecting water, wildflower meadow and trees.

After such restraint, the punch that the big double border next-door packs is knock-out. These two beds, each measuring eighty metres in length and separated by a wide grass path, are memorable to say the least. They carry all the usual herbaceous perennials from phlox, big red sunflowers and rudbeckia to yellow dahlias, cornflowers and bells of Ireland. In early summer there are coral-coloured lupins and bronze fennel. The colour combinations are bold and strong. This is no softly-softly mushy pastel affair.

The borders culminate on the shell house. Its inner walls were decorated by shell artist Blott Kerr-Wilson. A mix of the usual and unusual shells makes up the fantastical geometric patterns that cover both walls and ceiling inside the little hexagon-shaped house. The crowning glory is a delicate coral candelabra.

Beside the shell house is a Celtic design-inspired maze of hornbeam, beech and yew. It is still young but small children will by now find it hard to work their way out. In another few years bigger people may need to be fished out too.

BANTRY HOUSE AND GARDENS | BANTRY, COUNTY CORK

Contact: Sophie Shelswell-White

Tel: (+353) 027 50 047

e-mail: info@bantryhouse.com

www: www.bantryhouse.com

Open: March to October, daily 10am-6pm. Separate fee for house and garden. Children free.

Special features: Accommodation. Groups can book meals in advance. Gift shop. Spanish Armada exhibition centre. West Cork Music Festival venue.

Directions: Located on the N71 to Cork, 1km outside Bantry town, on the left.

Bantry House has been in the White family since the mid-1700s, when Richard White bought it from the Earl of Anglesey. In the 1940s it opened its gates to the curious and interested, becoming the first stately home in Ireland to do so. As a result, the Shelswell-Whites', as the family is now known, are well accustomed to welcoming visitors and they do it in an expert and informal way.

The garden was imaginatively restored about ten years ago after almost sixty years of neglect, and today it is one of the finer gardens in the country in one of the most extraordinary settings in the world. It is impossible not to be charmed by the place.

Bantry is quite unusual: handsome on a grand scale but also idiosyncratic and, despite its formality, a quirky sort of place. For a start, on my most recent visit, the job of distributing brochures and information was being carried out from the grand entrance hall filled with Pompeian mosaics and the accumulated treasures of generations, with Marian Finucane talking away on a transistor in the background. Bantry still has the feel of a home rather than a business enterprise.

The intricate Italian garden beside the house is such a perfect welcome to the garden. Within the box hedge boundary there is a fine circle of wisteria with knotty trunks that are every bit as good-looking as the dangling flowers and leaves. At over one hundred years old, the circle is made of two varieties of wisteria, one Japanese and one Chinese. A fact about Chinese and Japanese wisteria is that Chinese vines spiral clockwise while Japanese wisteria spirals anti-clockwise. This spooky, living trellis surrounds an eccentric-looking, fossil stone-encrusted water feature and pond. This was used as a *pêcherie*, in which fish were once kept, living decorously until their presence was required at the dinner table. Today they would presumably sit in the freezer until required.

The sunken flower garden to the side of the house is a busy mix of plants grown in circular beds. In one of these, bobbles of blue and white agapanthus grow under a multi-stemmed cordyline, itself like a series of bobbles on sticks. Around the circles, there are wide bands of *Alchemilla mollis* studded with *Stipa gigantea*, towering blue echiums and seas of scented phlox. Golden glass balls waving about on top of bamboo poles add glitter and sparkle to the pom-pom effect.

The yew-and-box garden next door provides a smart contrast to this frothy flowery garden. The two hedging plants are being trained in different shapes, some in cloud shapes, some in more regular, boxy lines. From these two garden rooms it is possible to look down over the sloped wildflower meadow, cut through with a mown path. This could be a short-cut to the walled garden – today used for allotments. A venerable old walled garden, built specifically to grow food, with protecting brick-lined walls and deep, rich soil worked for hundreds of years, is the most perfect place in the world to work an allotment.

On the north terrace at the front of the house there are fourteen circular beds in a line, all looking out over Bantry Bay. Phoenix date palm and yucca alternate with two varieties of box, one golden and one plain, between the circles. Additional weaving bands of coloured aggregates give the feature a final tweak of formality.

Continuing around to the other side of the house, the path leads to the rose garden, edged with cordylines and stone urns. Diana's bed, close by, could best be described as a circular riot. A little statue of Diana, goddess of the hunt, stands regal among explosions of blue-grey *Melianthus major*, silvery-blue thistles, tall alliums and *Hakonechloa macra* 'Aurea'. In the spring, before the real fireworks start, the ground around the statue is a mass of bulbs.

Leaving the garden, take note of the unusual hedge just below the house. It is made up of a combination of hornbeam, copper beech and evergreen Holm oak (*Quercus ilex*). Planted over a bank of aconites, cyclamen and snowdrops, almost unbelievably, this spot, right beside the house, was once the ash and rubbish tip. Over three tonnes of rubbish was cleared before the hedge and flower planting could begin.

For most visitors the glory of the garden is the stairway to the sky, which climbs up from the Italian garden like the stairs to heaven in the old David Niven film, *A Matter of Life and Death*. It is a monumental-scale staircase, cut into the steep hill above the house. The imposing formality of this massive feature is gently undermined by the encroachment of creeping green *Soleirolia solerolii*, alpine strawberries and quaking grass, and beyond them the woods that cover the hill. Lawned terraces run out from the stairs in ledges. The combination of architectural formality and exuberant wild growth is what makes this staircase so memorable.

As well as looking so imposing from beneath, it delivers a view over the house, garden, Bantry Bay and the headland beyond. This is a view not to be missed. To sit and take in the panoramic sights from the top of the steps on a clear day is a privilege. Yet for all its beauty, when on ground level, the garden is so full of distractions that one tends to forget how beautiful the surroundings are. That is an achievement.

BEECHWOOD | TEMPLEUSQUE, GLANMIRE, COUNTY CORK

Great gardens are sometimes serene and calm, sometimes arch and grand. The Kirbys' is another

Contact: Ned and Liz Kirby

Tel: (+353) 021 488 4489 / 086 315 7096

e-mail: lizkirby101@hotmail.com

www: www.beechwoodgarden.com

Open: Summer months by appointment to groups only.

Special features: Refreshments can be booked.

Directions: From Cork go through Glanmire and on to Sallybrook. Turn left at sign for Sarsfield Court. Pass the hospital and go straight through the crossroads. After 0.5km turn left. The garden is on the left, a further 0.5km on.

breed of great garden – a double espresso shot of a garden that leaves you feeling energised. There is the sort of busy, well orchestrated action here that sends you home wanting to dig up everything and start all over again.

Ned and Liz are part of an enthusiastic band of fine Cork gardeners that leave the rest of us wondering if there is fertiliser in the water down there. They have opened their garden to the public for many years, changing and adapting it in exciting ways since its first appearance on the scene. It is a great garden to visit.

Hidden from the road by a high beech hedge, it is firstly a plant-stuffed treat. A walk around should start on the garden side of that enclosing hedge. It shelters a sun-soaked bank of mixed shrubs knotted through with flowers, heathers and grasses. Among the flowers here, the splashes of pretty *Dahlia merckii* stand out. This is a delicate, pink-flowered specimen plant, more subtle than many of its cultivated relatives yet still eye-catching.

Close by is a nicely matched collection of stone pots set into gravel. Chives, grasses and catmint grow easily from the gravel and variegated white and green sage spills out over the path. The sense is one of controlled chaos in soft, powdery colours. Giving good-looking plants the leeway to sprawl and spread for as long as they look pleasing is a talent seen everywhere here. Arched, plant-strewn steps lead from one garden to another. The framed views back and forward between the gardens show a good design eye working on every aspect of the place. A bright *Cornus alternifolia* beckons in one direction while a stone-paved garden full of hosta, iris and Lady's mantle pull one in another.

In front of the house there are two beds facing one another with a circle of grass between and a central birdbath over a collar of more Lady's mantle (*Alchemilla mollis*) and horned violet or *Viola cornuta*. One of the two beds is low and herbaceous with lamb's ears or *Stachys byzantina*, more catmint, lobelia and striking blue agapanthus. Behind it the shrubs and small trees are layered up expertly in a display of variety and abundance.

The house is hidden under blankets of ivy, cotoneaster, climbing lobster claw or clianthus and golden yellow fremontodendron. The ground under all this is bright with a big run of variegated ground elder, *Aegopodium podagraria* 'Variegatum'. This is usually one of the worst thugs in a garden, spreading with terrifying enthusiasm. It will grow anywhere and even thrives in dry shade. The Kirbys fenced it in, so they can enjoy the cream and green leaves without subjecting the rest of the garden to the threat of invasion.

Walking past a beech hedge cut into by a small gate, you catch a glimpse of a neighbouring field full of cows in a good example of borrowing nearby landscape and supporting cast. A low, banked bed along the other side of the gravel path spills over with mounds and hummocks of creeping hardy geraniums. Among these, more rarefied celmisia shows that this is another sun-trap. Celmisia is a fussy plant, more often than not sickly and with a malingering look. Here, it looked positively beefy. Deep gravel paths by the side of the house hold back banquettes of clipped cotoneaster and golden privet cones.

So far so good, but follow your curiosity through another gateway in a tall hedge and the place changes radically. This is the wild garden, an exuberant and mad explosion of plants. A few years ago it was a relatively open lawn area that accommodated the younger, ball-playing Kirby generation. The footballers grew up and as soon as they evacuated the field, Ned and Liz moved in. That a kick-about area ever existed here is now impossible to imagine. Under the new design, even seeing the lie of the land is difficult: ponds, streams and waterfalls divide a dizzying maze of shrubs, exotic perennials and tall grasses on the hilly expanse. Much of the planting seems to grow straight out of beds of gravel or between mossy boulders. Quantities of stone make it feel like a bit of scorched Mediterranean earth in rural Cork. If the other side of the garden is manicured and well-mannered, this side is the wild child. The rising and falling path ducks under stands of bamboo, past waving plumes of cortaderia and flowering watsonias, geraniums of all sorts, exotic restios and euphorbias.

Standing back to look at the different gardens within these boundaries, it is clear that you *can* have it all – if you have a good eye for garden design and the willingness to work like a demon. It is that simple.

CEDAR LODGE | BANESHANE, MIDLETON, COUNTY CORK

Contact: Neil and Sonia Williams
Tel: (+353) 021 461 3379 / 086 836 7303
e-mail: cedarlodgegarden@eircom.net
www: www.irelandsgardens.com
Open: April to August, by appointment to groups. Supervised children welcome.
Special features: Teas by arrangement.
Directions: Driving from Cork city on the N25, take the Midleton exit. After 200m turn right over the bridge. Take the first left at the roundabout and pass a line of caravans. After about 2-3km take a narrow right turn. The garden is on the right. From Youghal take the left exit off the N25 after the fly-over bridge for Midleton. Take the second exit from the roundabout and follow the above directions.

Described as a 'plantsman's garden', Cedar Lodge is unsurprisingly full to brimming with remarkable and interesting plants. The retired former owner of the well-regarded Carewswood Garden Centre in Castlemartyr, Neil Williams is a man with a boundless wealth of knowledge, an understanding of plants and a photographic memory for plant names. His know-how is everywhere in evidence. A visit always feels like taking an advanced class in horticulture.

The garden covers almost two acres, divided into different areas that flow easily into each other and arranged in ways that show off his plant collection to best effect. Hard landscaping features are of course used, but the plants are the real stars here and all design is subservient to them. Everything is created to maximise the number of plants that can be shown to best advantage.

To the front of the garden, within the beech hedge boundary, there are a number of serpentine beds in a range of different sizes. Some are low and herbaceous, with small shrubs and evergreens providing a skeleton to hold up the fleeting displays of flowers. Some are taller; in these he pulls mixes of bamboo and cortaderia together and dots occasional flowers between them. All these beds are cut into a large expanse of lawn spread out in front of the house. They are arranged so that one will happily circle them again and again to fully study the mix of plants.

The pale pink house is complemented by pink-tinged gravel. Clouds of dusty-blue ceanothus and variegated vinca wash up against the base of the building, supplemented by seasonal pots of pink tulips. Growing tulips in pots is a useful way to enjoy the benefit of the flowers without having to look at bare stalks as the petals drop.

Standing at the house looking out, the stone-bound bank that the lawn stands on can be seen from this angle. It is a well-constructed low wall, studded with sprouts of rich purple aubrietia, butter-coloured primroses and low-growing *Cotoneaster* 'Gnom' in repeating alternate patterns.

The whole front boundary is marked by a massive, deep border, running in a sweeping arc. There is so much to see here: on first sight, brooms, peonies, delphiniums and echiums might stand out. On second inspection it will be euphorbia, roses and hemerocallis. As the bed changes direction, moving into the shade, it features hellebores, ferns, epimediums and *Dicksonia antarctica*. This long, deep bed weaves in and out so that it is necessary to walk its length both ways in order to discover smaller treats like dactylorhizas and *Myosotidium hortensia* or Chatham Island lilies. The bed turns a corner again and becomes a full-blown woodland garden before opening into an expansive area.

An elaborate figure-of-eight pond with a cascade, bog garden and raised rock bed is the central feature at the back of the house. The view of this from the terrace, through a well-placed window in a hedge, is particularly good but picking your way around it is the best way to see the little poppies, ferns and other plants it is home to.

An arched walk of roses and clematis runs the length of the garden and a walk under the tangles of *Clematis* 'Comtesse de Bouchaud', *Rosa* 'Étoile de Hollande' and wisteria is like a trip through a perfume shop.

On the other side of these scented climbers you can spy lines of onion, lettuce and beans between the tendrils and rustic poles. I like that the vegetables are both out in the open and yet partially disguised by the climbers and pergola. At the bottom of this walk, the paths branch off, leading between varied mixed borders full of perfectly maintained and unusual plants. Neil is a fascinating guide, full of information and small stories about different plants here. When I think of order and perfection in a garden, this is the place I think of.

COOSHEEN | 15 Johnstown Park, Glounthaune, County Cork

Contact: Hester and Patrick Forde
Tel: (+353) 021 435 3855 / 086 865 4972
e-mail: hesterforde@gmail.com
www: www.hesterfordegarden.com
Open: May to September to groups by appointment.

Special features: Rare and special plants for sale.
Directions: In Glounthaune, with the church on left, travel towards the train station. Turn left after the station. Turn right across the slip road and the garden is second last on the left. Park on the slip road near the trees.

Many of us only dream of achieving a glorious garden, idly and hopelessly. There are a small few who actually do it. Hester Forde belongs in the second, tiny category. Coosheen is nothing short of a *tour de force*.

Hester and Patrick came to their third-of-an-acre site many years ago when it was given over to gooseberries and apples. They quickly began to experiment on the rock-hard plot that had, they discovered, once been the site of a quarry. Crowbars rather than shovels were the tools of choice. As they struggled, they discovered the joys of raised beds, bringing in whatever soil they required as they went. Patrick is the hard landscaping expert: Hester picks the combinations of plants and Patrick provides them with interesting settings. The result is like the work of jewellers, a mixture of precision and elaborate display.

An obvious love of woodland plants can be seen everywhere: lovers of light shade carpet the ground under tree ferns, shrubs and small trees. Japanese acers feature strongly, from tall spreading varieties to smaller, recumbent types with dissected foliage. The number of trees accommodated in this small garden without it feeling either too shaded or crowded is a testament to their great skill as designers. Most people with small gardens run a mile from the thought of trees, either from fear of lack of space or the shade they cast. Anyone who thinks that trees should form an orderly line around the boundary would do well to visit this garden with a note book and camera.

Apart from small trees, if there is one unifying item in the place it is agapanthus. Their big and not-so-big royal blue, white, peacock and violet flowers seem to be everywhere, they even self-seed into the sides of paths. Such fecundity makes lesser gardeners feel even more envious than they might already be. I particularly love the *A.* 'Dark Star' growing over a low, cut-leaf Japanese acer.

Agapanthus aside, there are so many must-have plants here – from things like *Bessera elegans* which has strange square and hollow stems, to delicate little species *Gladiolus dalenii*. Contrasting-colour dahlias splash colours about the place liberally right through the summer up to autumn. There are always some roses in bloom, too.

Tucked in between the more robust plants, expect to spot a tender blue and black *Salvia patens* or an exotic-looking *Salvia guaranitica* in the shelter.

The house is on a ledge and overlooks the sloped front garden, which is surrounded by a dense boundary of shrubs. The front garden is in the path of some whipping winds being battled creatively. In farming terms, there are no 'plainer cattle' here but it seems that the sheer number of special shrubs packed together, permit fine specimens of *Cornus cotroversa*, young blue cedars and Japanese acers to act as a shelter both to each other and to the inner garden. Shoe-horned between the cedars and maples there are tall grasses, camellias, magnolias and smaller shrubs. There are clematis everywhere, from *C.* 'Vyvyan Pennell' to the green flowering *C. floraplena*. Look for them climbing shrubs, trees, poles, obelisks and walls.

The stepped area in front of the house is where the miniatures live; Hester has gathered quite a collection of perfect small specimens here. They include miniscule salvia, eucomis and geraniums. The little scree containers, with their tiny boulders, house fun-sized alpines – the sort of plants that might live around a doll's house. Baby hostas, miniature heucheras, leptospermums, minute cyclamen and geraniums are like Lilliputian delights, living the high life in well-presented tubs and troughs.

Hester could rightly be called a plant fashionista with an obvious love of the new and interesting. Be assured that she will be able to bring out some impossible-to-find treat and something, if not a number of things, you have never even heard of before. This is a garden that not only asks but demands multiple visits. Take a notebook and enjoy a master class.

DROMBOY | CARRIGNAVAR, COUNTY CORK

Contact: Maurice and Gertie O'Donoghue
Tel: (+353) 021 488 4555
e-mail: g.odonoghue@ucc.ie
Open: To groups by appointment and occasional annual open days. Contact for details.

Directions: At Rathduff on the main Cork-Mallow Rd (N20) take the Carrignavar exit. At the T-junction bear right, and take the next two left turns. The garden is the second entrance on the right.

The garden at Carrignavar comes upon visitors as a surprise. Set in a rough hilly spot about two hundred metres above sea level in north Cork, Gertie and Maurice O'Donoghue's virtuoso garden is as hard to find as real treasures always are. Even arriving at the gates and travelling up the long straight drive, there is little to declare this as the home of something special. Lined with well-clipped conifers, the drive is tidy and ordered but not especially indicative of the garden waiting to be seen. However, arriving at the top of the drive the magic becomes apparent.

A spread of perfect rolled, striped lawns sets the tone. It now is clear that you are in the midst of perfectionists. The grass is edged in a way that almost defies nature. They could probably write a textbook on keeping an old-fashioned lawn. Meanwhile, the house straight ahead can barely be seen under blankets of climbers, creepers and general growth, giving the impression that the O'Donoghues live inside a garden.

I could certainly live in their little hosta garden: this secluded corner is home to over 120 specimens and varieties, planted in big drifts around a little pond, under a grove of carved-out *Myrtus communis* and holly. Seeing so many different hostas together, all looking so healthy, is a treat. The variations possible within the strict confinement of a basic leaf shape that all hostas share, is fantastic: there are plants with plain green leaves, with blue-tinged foliage, as well as cream, yellow and white variegated types. Some have huge leaves, some small, some long and pointed like daggers, some corrugated. Gertie can grow them like champions.

The contrast between this calm dark corner and some of the bright flower borders a little way off is almost startling. The silver garden, with its artemisias, erigeron, astelias, white geraniums, dahlias and euphorbias, illustrates this perfectly. Next door the pink border is just as impressive, filled with every shade of pink geranium, campanula, lupin and a score of other herbaceous things.

Both O'Donoghues work the garden: Gertie is a plantswoman and Maurice has a talent for hard landscaping. Maurice also makes the fascinating sculptures placed around the garden. Together they have created a marvel of a place. The whole area covers about two acres but is divided successfully into a number of rooms, each with a different and definite style. If there is a common theme to be found here, it is impeccable upkeep. The standards set would put most of us to shame. If there is a stretch of gravel it will be free of weeds, loose leaves and any other debris. If something is clipped, it will be clipped perfectly. They must work all the hours God sent.

But for all its perfection, this is a personal garden and it is far from a predictable place. I loved the 'lollypop' garden, an area made up of clipped box, euonymus and ligustrum shrubs, all pruned into standard lollypops or mop-heads. It sounds a bit silly but it looks great.

Many of the best vignettes include Maurice's sculptures. In one corner there might be an arch of ligustrum around a little statue. Nearby a miniscule stone pyramid, home to some lucky insects, will draw the eye. Elsewhere a gallery of stone heads almost stopped me in my tracks. These works look almost pre-historic – they are fascinating. Maurice explained that he regularly unearths boulders out of the ground in the course of gardening. Sometimes the shape of the stone will suggest an idea. He then modifies it in small ways to further bring out that sense, and in so doing, he produces his powerful works. They add a strange, extra dimension to the garden.

The surprises are around every corner, from secret pond gardens, sunny dry riverbed and scree gardens, to shaded mossy corners, formal flower beds and big bulging shrub borders. At each turn, there will be another marvellous sight, from a beautiful specimen Japanese acer to an arch of fat roses. I love the collections of pots gathered together behind the house and the little topiary works tucked away in corners.

Such an amalgamation of features and plant combinations so meticulously minded calls for the sort of study one visit alone will not allow. Ten visits might not even do it. By your ninth visit you *might* have mastered the intricate directions.

Fota Arboretum and Garden |
Fota Island, Carrigtwohill, County Cork

Contact: David O'Regan
Tel: (+353) 021 481 2728
www: www.heritageireland.ie
Open: Arboretum: April to October, Monday to Saturday 9am-6pm, Sunday 11am-6pm / November to March, Monday to Saturday 9am-5pm, Sunday 11am-5pm. Walled garden: April to October, Monday to Friday and summer weekends. Contact for exact details. Car parking charge. Supervised children welcome. Dogs on leads. **Special features:** Tearoom. Shop. Picnic area. **Directions:** Take the Cobh exit off the N25 marked R624. The entrance is approximately 3km along.

Fota was formerly known as 'Foatey', from the Irish *fód te*, which means 'warm turf' or 'warm sod'. This is an appropriate name for a garden that basks in the mild Cork climate and is blessed with a type of fertile brown earth so conducive to healthy, rapid plant growth. Back in the late nineteenth century, William Robinson said that the bamboos grew as well and appeared as natural here as they did in their native China.

The garden covers twenty-seven acres and is attached to the grand house built by the Smith-Barry family in the early nineteenth century. They took full advantage of the favourable climate. Working well into the twentieth century, they planted the finest trees and plants from all over the world here. The result was an arboretum of remarkable proportions and a range of pleasure gardens, including a fernery, an Italian garden, a walled garden and a lake. The house and land left the hands of the family, moving through those of University College Cork and, after the college could no longer justify the cost of running the garden, through some uncertain years, ending up in the care of the Fota Trust. The Trust has since restored the gardens and house magnificently.

The walled garden carries a collection of 160 varieties of Irish-bred daffodils, making it an unbeatable early spring feature. Running the length of one of the walls there is a bed of monocots (plants that start life with only one seed leaf and later on bear narrow, often strappy leaves with parallel veins); arrangements of libertia, grasses, phormium, tradescantia, iris, crocosmia and hemerocallis make up much of the display. Plants from Central and South America and shade-loving plants fill another border. There are generous displays of primula, pulmonaria, hellebores, hosta and astilbe. The old roses above these include big showy pink *Rosa* 'Comte de Chambord', *Rosa de rescht* and *R.* 'Old Pink Moss', a dusty pink variety bred in 1700.

Beyond the walled garden are the pleasure garden and the old Italian garden. Lined along the outside of the wall there are beds full of banana plants, verbena and hardy plumbago. In the centre of the long bed are a classical folly and a massive *Magnolia grandiflora*. this overlooks stands of multi-trunked cordylines and yew hedging under restoration.

The paths lead out past plats of lawn that fill up with picnicking families and kissing couples in the summer. Pass the restored *orangerie* full of containerised citrus trees and make your way to the arboretum; advertising the location of it are two huge Canary Island date palms or *Phoenix canariensis*. One of these measured eight metres in 1984 and they are a source of pride at Fota. Close to them is a Camphor tree or *Cinnamomum camphora* from Japan and a Mexican Cyprus (*Cupressus lusitanica*). But these are just two among many distractions. The evergreen oak (*Quercus ilex*) has an awe-inspiring canopy and the Wellingtonia or *Sequioadendron giganteum* from California measured 31x4.8m in 1984. The spongy-barked tree continues to rise skyward. Walking between and under the Monterey pines (*Pinus radiata*) is an experience. (The cones on a Monterey pine can stay on the tree for up to thirty years.) It would be hard not to fall in love with trees walking around Fota, as the eye is pulled away from one fine specimen to something even better off in the distance.

No trip should be made to Fota without a visit to the fernery, a natural-looking maze-like rock formation smothered in deep, velvety moss sprouting all sorts of ferns. This secluded garden is shaded by sweet chestnut and umbrella-like *Dicksonia antarctica* tree ferns. Seeing a fernery on a dry day always feels wrong – visit them in or after rain. The leaves are at their best dripping water and in summer this place may even steam a little, giving an even more jungle-like feel to an already tropical place. Close by, and visible from the fernery, is the huge pond. This is almost as much lake as pond, a naturalistic expanse of water, with a scattering of lilies over its surface and wild flowers, gunnera, bamboo and grasses around the edge.

Every time I visit Fota I fall in love with a different plant. This time it was a tree near the pond – a *Cryptomeria japonica* 'Spiralis' or 'Granny's Ringlets'. This giant looks like a renegade from a willow pattern plate. Around here the air is so damp and the trees so huge and lush you can almost hear the parrots and monkeys squawk. All this for a paltry €3 car park charge. Well done, Fota Trust.

GLEBE GARDENS AND GALLERY |
THE GLEBE, BALTIMORE, COUNTY CORK

Contact: Jean and Peter Perry
Tel: (+353) 028 20 232
e-mail: glebegardens@gmail.com
www: www.glebegardens.com
Open: May to September, daily 10am-6pm. Groups by appointment. Supervised children welcome. Dogs on leads.

Special features: Restaurant. Produce for sale.
Directions: Approaching Baltimore on the N71, the garden is on the right-hand side opposite the 'Baltimore' signpost.

Negotiating the tight rope between productive and ornamental gardens is tough, particularly when you are trying to produce enough to provide a restaurant with its fruit and veg. But the family have the routine down pat. Theirs is a market garden that is also aesthetically pleasing, laid out around the restaurant it provides for. This is certainly no twee show garden. Jean grows a full range of fine produce, from vegetables and fruit to flowers and herbs, in a hard-worked five-and-a-half acre plot attached to her old house on the edge of Baltimore. But while the area around the seaside village is very beautiful, it is also wild, rugged and rocky. Driving up hills and down hollows toward the coast, the land does not suggest 'garden' as much as it does 'natural rockery'. So it comes as no surprise to hear that the garden at Glebe was hard won. 'We literally dug the herb garden out with a crowbar and even then some of the stone was just too tough to move. But herbs like the stony ground so it suits them,' Jean explains.

The flower garden is a beauty. Reached through the opening in one of the hedges, it is made up of double borders divided by grass paths. The mood is informal, with tall wigwams of sweet pea, lupins, amaranthus and euphorbia prettily twined around each other. On a ledge overlooking this is the hot garden, a sun trap, mixing gravel with trailing scented rosemary, lavender and borage. Its view over the flower garden is perfect.

In the little courtyard garden, where the restaurant is, the smell of lemon verbena wafts around and purple-flowered hyssop, rue, golden hops and echiums run wild. Black kale, dahlias and *Hydrangea* 'Annabelle' seem to fill every spare space. The rough stone arch in the wall has a big draped clematis over it and underneath there are pots of heaven-scented lilies. There are scores of other pots too, from pelargoniums and cosmos to ginger lilies and abutilon.

At the centre of the courtyard there is a fine olive tree. 'That olive deals with everything – wind, rain, cold, everything – and it even fruits in some years,' says Jean. The herb beds have been edged in slate, which creates extra warmth in the abutting soil. The canopy, like a large boat sail, flapping about over the café tables is perfect in maritime Baltimore.

The workings of the garden can be seen in lines of onions laying out, drying in the sun on top of a low galvanised roof. A set of steps fringed with white roses, white fox gloves, white anemones and ferns leads to the vegetable garden, where hard-worked salad crops are grown in a 'cut-and-come' way. Cut-and-come involves harvesting by pulling a small number of leaves from the plant as needed, rather than taking up the whole plant. The pruned plant then continues to renew itself through the season, delivering a great crop over its lifetime. It obviously works best with a long line of plants, so that not too many leaves need to be taken at one time.

I was taken by the ongoing experiments with outdoor varieties of tomatoes between purple-podded French beans, sweet corn, pumpkin, squash and 'Painted Lady' runner beans. Although most of us grub them up as annuals, the beans often survive the autumn and winter, coming through again the next year and cropping a second time. Espaliered fruit trees add both good looks and extra production power per metre of garden. Flowers around the edges of the beds encourage beneficial insects to live among the crops.

The garden faces northeast, a far from ideal aspect, so the beds have been divided by griselinia hedge clipped into waves. It saves the garden from the worst of the winds as well as providing something good to look at.

'All the beds in here are raised. It makes them much easier to mind,' Jean tells me. Timber edges allow her to use a no-dig method. With nobody walking on the beds, the earth never becomes compacted and so never requires digging or disturbance. She adds layers of mulch annually, building up deep piles of rich organic matter into which she can plant with ease.

Seaweed is piled on the potato beds and the spuds obviously respond well. But whether it is seaweed or compost or farmyard manure, Jean believes that keeping something on the soil all the time, even simply spreading out grass cuttings, is good because it keeps the worms active, the ground warm and insulated, and the weeds covered.

Jean is an informative gardener and generous with her knowledge, so it makes sense that she would organise classes and lectures. Talks are regularly given at the garden by various guest speakers.

POULNACURRA | CASTLE JANE ROAD, GLANMIRE, CORK

Contact: Mrs Mairead Harty
Tel: (+353) 086 602 5791
Open: For charity days. See local press for annual dates. Otherwise by appointment.

Directions: Driving from Cork city to Glanmire, turn left at the traffic lights. The road forks just after that. Take the right fork onto Castle Jane Road.

It is stating the obvious, but the most enjoyable gardens are the ones where the enthusiasm of the gardener is visible. I love gardens where you can tell that the gardener has fun with their 'baby'. Mairead Harty's garden sings of her enthusiasm. Every corner is busy, worked and loved. This three-and-half-acre garden set around a fine Queen Anne house is, despite its setting, a recently made garden. Ten years ago it was the site of a great number of trees and Mairead was busy doing other things. Then, as she says, the well-known garden designer Brian Cross happened along. Things were never the same again. The result of the collaboration between the two is a veritable spree of gardens. But a spree was not what Mairead initially envisaged. She says that all she wanted was an easy-to-mind, no-fuss garden. Brian Cross had other ideas. Those ideas would sweep her up, and fire her with an enthusiasm for plants and designs she didn't know she had. These days Mairead happily spends a great deal of her time lavishing her high-maintenance super-model garden with the care it demands.

The most memorable features are the mirroring borders of catmint or nepeta, shell-pink and fuchsia-coloured roses that run up the centre of the garden. These are backed by tall standard variegated euonymus. Taller again, behind these there are sentry-like acers. The path in the centre is made of rough-hewn slabs and suitable for only the most sensible walking shoes.

Up at the top of the garden, running at a right angle to the mirror borders, is the millwheel walk. This is a long path made from about a dozen big millwheels. They were all unearthed from under decades of fallen leaves and humus when the garden was being made. They make a dramatic feature, running down the centre of an avenue of hydrangeas, under the shade of more acers. At the end of this walk, one path forks off onto another millwheel walk – a millwheel should be the garden's logo.

A new garden room at the top of the main garden comes upon the visitor out of the blue. In through a gate we catch sight of a great explosion of flower, roses and herbaceous perennials. This is a much looser arrangement than the double border in the lower garden.

To one side of this flower fest, there is a strange-looking tall ash tree, standing on a mound of large round river stones. It might be strange but it is a dramatic-looking feature. The big stones gradually morph into an expanse of gravel spiked with *Verbena bonariensis* and clumps of grass.

The individual garden rooms are punctuated by large lawns and divided by groves of acers, camellias and roses, all placed in combinations that block off and open up interesting views of other corners of the garden.

The one linking feature between these gardens is their smart, well-kept look and to that end Mairead was proud to show me the ride-on mower that allows her keep the lawns impeccably trimmed and the leaf blower that keeps everything free of fallen leaves.

In stark contrast to the smart main garden, just across the drive there is a wild meadow garden, spiked with a mix of dog roses, weeping junipers, variegated azaras and embothriums, all planted in a more haphazard, natural-looking way. This spot is where Mairead takes the opportunity to play with a palette of plants in ways not possible in the formal areas. Her current project is a little cottage garden which she is creating beside the small lodge at the front of the garden. The horticultural playground just keeps expanding.

ILNACULLIN | Garinish Island, Glengarriff, County Cork

Tel: (+353) 027 63 040

e-mail garinishisland@opw.ie

www: www.heritageireland.ie

Open: 1 March to 31 October, Monday to
Saturday, 10am-4.30pm, Sunday 1pm-5pm /
April to June and Sep, Monday to Saturday
10am-6.30pm, Sunday 1pm-6.30pm /

July to August, Monday to Saturday
9.30am-6.30pm, Sunday 11am-6.30pm.
Note: Last landing on the island is one hour before
closing time. Supervised children welcome. Dogs
on leads. Partially wheelchair accessible.

Directions: situated 1.5km off the coast
from Glengarriff.

Ilnacullin sits in the harbour of Glengarriff in Bantry Bay, an island with views out
to sea and back to the mainland, reached by boat over a short stretch of water. It is
without doubt the best situated garden in Ireland. I rode Brendan O'Sullivan's
Harbour Queen out and he led us past basking seals draped over their warm rocks
as we journeyed over the water.

The thirty-seven-acre windswept, gorse-covered island was bought by Annan
Bryce in 1910. He employed the famous English landscaper and architect Harold
Peto to design a seven-storey house and garden for him on his island. The house
was never built, and heaven knows what a building of such height would have
looked like on the small rock, but today the garden stands as a reminder of that
wildly optimistic plan.

They had their work cut out for them from the start. While the warm Gulf
Stream and huge annual rainfall make it possible to grow exotic plants from
Australia, New Zealand and the tropics with success, Ilnacullin was not without
its difficulties. Based on solid rock, with a miserable sprinkling of poor quality,
rain-leached soil low in organic material and fertility, the island was no natural
paradise. It must have required enormous quantities of imagination for Mr Bryce
to believe he could create a garden on the rock in Bantry Bay. The struggle to cart
huge amounts of good soil over the water and fight salt-laden winds in the early
years can only be imagined. There are also stories of young trees regularly uprooted in bad
weather before they could anchor themselves properly.

But in 1928, the Scottish gardener Murdo Makenzie arrived on Ilnacullin and applied himself to erecting a substantial shelter belt within which the more tender plants would be able to grow.

The most famous feature is the Italian garden with its casita, or tea house, and pergola of golden Bath stone, inset with variously coloured marbles from prestigious Carrara to local Connemara stone. This formal garden is surrounded by huge pines, elegant and good-sized flowering leptospermum, myrtle, camellia and rhododendron. The edges of the sunken pool are lined with azure tiles and stone planters of venerable and famed bonsai. Exotic white datura or trumpet flowers, wisteria, lilies and sprawling clematis mix with fuchsias and bedding plants around the rectangular lily pool. This is the sort of feature that says, 'if less is more, think how much more, more would be.' To the southwest, the Sugarloaf Mountain rises up in an extraordinarily dramatic backdrop.

Away from the Italian garden, the trail leads in several directions. One path with wide, rough stone steps leads to a Grecian temple on top of a hill. Up here all the formality of the lower garden is cast off – the impression is of tempered wild growth. The temple, entered past big stands of blue agapanthus and a fine Chilean fire bush or *Embothrium coccineum*, has some fine views out over the sea.

Looking back into the garden, everywhere the rock, never far from the surface, peeps out, a reminder that this garden was gouged, using dynamite, from an unyielding foundation.

The paths lead on through the romantically named Happy Valley, past fragrant pines, hydrangeas and a tender *Dacrydium franklinii*. This is a tree from Tasmania, and proof of the manufactured micro-climate on the island, because it only grows in the most protected of positions. There are so many rare and unusual things in this garden, for example trees like *Phyllocladus trichomanoides* from New Zealand. The specimen in Ilnacullin is one of the biggest growing outdoors in these islands.

Up toward the Martello tower, built at a commanding point on the island, there are so many ferns and recumbent pines hugging and mimicking the rock. The track back down towards the garden goes by way of a rocky gorse-and-heather-strewn outcrop called the viewing point, and

down steps past evidence of storm devastation in the shape of fallen trees.

This leads into the walled garden, a feature only partially open on my last two visits. Stretches of it are penned-off and not well tended – evidence of staff and money shortages. Only the central herbaceous border is fully visible and it is handsome and generously planted with fine flowers, sometimes backed by espaliered fruit trees and specimen shrubs. Asters, roses, erysimum, hydrangea, cimicifuga, delphinium, *Cardiocrinum giganteum*, campanulas, verbascum and all the usual herbaceous plants stand cheek-by-jowl, holding each other up. But even this great border is a bit faded and in need of a bit of extra care. There are also collections of climbers within the walled garden, but it is not possible to see them close up because the paths leading to them are closed off.

Overall, Ilnacullin is a truly glorious garden, but it is in need of a good overhaul and in some respects it is looking tired. This is too important a garden to be neglected. Created by great gardeners, it now needs another great gardener, of which there are many in the country, to conserve and develop it to stop it from becoming an old ghost. Let a talented enthusiast loose on it.

INISH BEG GARDENS | BALTIMORE, COUNTY CORK

Contact: Paul and Georgiana Keane
Tel: (+353) 028 21745 **e-mail:** info@inishbeg.com
www: www.inishbeg.com **Open:** All year by
appointment, 10am-5pm. No dogs. Partially
wheelchair accessible.

Special features: Accommodation.
Directions: Situated on the R595 approx 6km
south of Skibbereen. Turn right just after the sign
for 'Canon Goodman's Grave' and travel over the
bridge to the island.

I couldn't find this garden. I drove up and down the R595 in and out of Baltimore twice and could see no sign of it anywhere. An exasperated phone call to the garden was answered with directions to 'turn off the road and drive over the bridge to the island'. Those words 'the island' have an extraordinary ability to make anything that bit more exciting. There is an extra dash of expectation that you hope the place can live up to. Inish Beg lives up to it. It feels like the sort of place where Agatha Christie could have had a wonderful time killing people off in a country house whodunit.

From the stone bridge over the water, the drive leads under some dramatic cedars of Lebanon onto a sunken avenue that rises up under lines of beech and oak. You feel dwarfed. Then there is a second stretch of avenue, with a lower storey of cherries under the oak and beech. Masses of bluebells and daffodils naturalising on the ground under these add yet another layer. This is promising.

The house looks out over lawns bounded by unusual stone walls, groves of myrtles and magnolias and some very old white cherries. Standing in the rough field beyond all this is a poignant famine burial ground.

The main body of the garden is taken up with walks through and under woods, between groves of ferns and tree ferns, and alongside sunken, quirky-looking stone-lined streams. One could be convinced that this is simply a case of nature untamed, wild and perfect. But it is a carefully tweaked, gently worked woodland garden of the best sort. This is one of the hardest styles to carry off successfully.

The older, mainly native woods have been spiked with specimen trees and shrubs. So for example Japanese acers have been planted under tall ash trees. Camellia and bamboo live in the shade of sky-scraping beeches. The place is a maze of little 'barely there' paths. Apart from the large area covered by woods, there are also newly planted orchards and walks out by the sea. Look out for the pond named for a deceased bulldog called Boadicea.

But the jewel of Inish Beg is the unusual walled garden. This is a recent creation surrounded by low walls that come just to eye level. This is a good height as it means the garden can be seen and enjoyed from outside as well as inside and it also feels more open and sunny. Within the walls, wide paths break up big square beds full of decoratively arranged vegetables and flowers. This is quite a different-looking example of a large and functional walled garden. Sturdy, permanent-looking obelisks and ornamental wigwams for beans and other clambering crops add height all year round, as does the good-looking decorative fruit cage.

The bone structure is good too: low stone walls with box hedging planted on top enclose the large beds; and rudbeckia, cosmos and black kale, sedum, asters and Florence fennel are all tidily tied in by the box walls. Growing on their mounded-up beds they look even more impressive.

The large beds contradict the idea that small beds are easier to work. Almost invisible mulch paths are secreted between lines of heleniums and verbena within the bigger beds. These invisible paths and kneeling spaces make the beds just as easy to work as narrower borders. The whole walled garden contains only one original plant – a big old gnarled apple tree that lords over the young garden and imparts an air of maturity to the enclosure.

The workings of the garden are everywhere visible. These are good to see, from the wire, wood and metal supports, to lines of ancient-looking rhubarb forcers. As a reminder that this is mild west Cork, there are healthy olive trees growing outside in the garden. I think the shelter provided by a great buffering encirclement of mature trees around the walled garden is the reason for this. They too are probably the reason the garden walls can be as low as they are.

Ask to see the auricula theatre before you leave. Whether full of pots of auriculas in late spring, or empty during the rest of the year, this is a little beauty.

Kilravock Garden | Durrus, County Cork

Contact: Malcolm and Phemie Rose
Tel: (+353) 027 61 111 / 087 816 1526
e-mail: kilravock1@eircom.net
www: www.kilravockgardens.com
Open: During the West Cork Garden Trail and for charity days. See website for details. Otherwise by appointment only. No dogs. Groups welcome. Supervised children over 12 welcome.
Directions: 1.6km from Durrus on the Kilcrohane Road. The garden is on the right and signposted.

Phemie and Malcolm Rose have been working this garden for over twenty years, and gaining a reputation in Cork and beyond during that time. I imagine they must be among the foremost experts on gardening on rock, although walking through the lush garden today it is hard to tell that it was hard-won from a stony, boulder-laden site.

Because rock was never far from the surface, and in the way wherever they wished to put the spade, the Roses learned to make the best of it. In so doing they wrested a fertile garden from the tough landscape without the breaking of backs. Although it is a hard place to work, Phemie told me that most plants do well 'once they establish'. Those three words illustrate the point that getting things to establish out here, on the edge of the Atlantic, is a difficult task.

She continued to tell me that, once establishment is achieved, 'not too much care is required from then on and they more or less take care of themselves.' This is because, along with the rocks, the garden gets a great deal of rain.

The place is full of unusual, rare and seldom-seen plants from all over the world and both of the Roses are avid collectors. There are thirty-two different restios alone here. Malcolm is fascinated by sorbus and has planted a collection of over seventy species and varieties, including a square fruited *Sorbus hostii*. He says the birds adore its exotic fruits.

Another love affair with ferns led him to build a special fern house and a raised platform from which to enjoy his favourite tree ferns from a bird's-eye view. Meanwhile, under the platform, the shade-loving ferns live beneath the fronds of their light-loving, taller relatives. As I visited he was still busy, this time building another fern house; this one to house more tender specimens. It will have a warm, controlled environment with misting systems for the little plants. This is no ordinary garden.

But Kilravock is not just made of the rare and exotic. Out in the open garden, collections of acacias and acers grow beside the more humble pheasant berry or *Leycesteria formosa*. If a plant is good-looking, it's good-looking.

The oriental area beside the house has been a long-time favourite of visitors. It features raked gravel, a stream, Japanese anemone and a spreading umbrella of *Acer palmatum* var. 'Dissectum' which, like many of the other acers here, is draped over a rock like a huge bonsai. The tall *Rhododendron sinogrande* by the water is also gorgeous. Above this area, the spring garden is made up of azalea and primula with a huge acacia overhead. Lobelia, salvia, hosta and ferns grow alongside a natural stream in the damp.

There are also hot areas with aeoniums, agave, eucomis and puya growing outside. The collection of cordylines includes an unusual prostrate species. Walking around the garden, it is clear that the Roses are keen on southern hemisphere plants, and Dunmanus Bay allows them to indulge their tastes fairly comprehensively. They germinate a number of these plants from seed, including various varieties of furry-flowered anigozanthos, more usually known as kangaroo paw, and a tibouchina that has survived outside for several years.

West Cork's frost-free climate is an advantage that midlanders envy. It is hampered somewhat by salt winds, so a tall hedge shelters the bottom part of the garden, protecting it from the spray that whips up from the bay. The hedge is not so tall that it prevents a good view of the water however. The two-acre garden is ice-cream-cone-shaped, with the narrow end reached through a tunnel of white wisteria, golden hops, including an unusual clematis with small, fat and spongy purple flowers. Finally, there is the Mediterranean tower. Yes, a Mediterranean tower.

LAKEMOUNT |
BARNAVARA HILL, GLANMIRE, COUNTY CORK

Contact: Brian and Rose Cross
Tel: (+353) 086 811 0241
e-mail: crosscork@gmail.com
www: www.irelandsgardens.com
/ www.lakemountgarden.com
Open: By appointment.
Not suitable for children.

Directions: Drive from Cork on the R639 to Glanmire to Riverstown Cross. Turn left at the lights and go up Barnavara Hill. The garden is on the left past the 50km sign and marked by a stone wall and black gate.

In a world where certainty is rare, a visit to Brian Cross's garden is a treat one can depend on to exceed expectation. Lakemount was started over half a century ago by Brian's mother on the site of a chicken and fruit farm. He joined her the age of eight, when he began to grow Sweet William seeds. Today, Lakemount is famous around the horticultural world – a sophisticated garden, beautiful, well groomed and in a constant state of development.

The house stands on a level above the garden on a low stone ledge that provide planting space for climbers while backing a bed of euphorbia, helichrysum, phormium and camellia. Below this, there is a formal pool. Its corners are guarded by four elegant, standard wisterias. From here one can catch sight of the gravel garden where white libertia and dierama self-seed into the stone. But even as a particular area is lovely, one also catches sight of a score of other corners to investigate and paths to follow.

The garden is cleverly divided into intimate, secluded rooms or compartments, each with a particular mood. In one, canna lilies form a two-and-a-half-metre-high wall over beds full of multi-shaded pink penstemon. Brian mixes colour like a master painter, and here rich purple *Verbena bonariensis* and reddish-black chocolate cosmos is only one luscious colour combination. Tree ferns, acers and camellias dripping in red tropaeolum all lead up to a variegated hosta and fern walk decorated with big granite mushrooms. A Brewer's weeping pine (*Picea breweriana*) looms over white lychnis, romneya and fuchsia.

Lakemount garden covers two acres but the shape and style is such that it seems even bigger, and walking back and forward one finds oneself revisiting rooms already seen from other paths and angles. Rough stone urns full of hardy geraniums and unusual sculptural pots by the artist Tim Goodman stand in the middle of beds, punctuating the plants. Labyrinthine trails wander in all directions, dividing rooms and leading from one to another with steps up and down and gates leading here and there. There are gates at every turn: low, wrought-iron, wooden and picket fence gates lead through arches of rose and honeysuckle. Sometimes they are set into hedges. Regardless of the style, they lend a tantalising feeling of something about to be discovered. Little summerhouses smothered in clematis sit secluded in quiet corners.

The rockery garden is a room set out in slabs of Doolin stone with mats of creeping mint, thyme and geranium between the flags. A scattering of raised beds are home to sharp, architectural red phormium, rich red berberis and lobelia. From here a set of steps – half stone, half creeping campanula – lead to another flagged area planted through with galtonia, anemone and troughs full of dianthus and hairy little pasque flowers. Ginger lilies add to the exotic feel. *Dahlia* 'The Bishop of Llandaff', alstroemeria and a tiny *Rhododendron impeditum* work off each other well and a tub of grass resembles a mad Muppet wig.

Over the years, Brian has carried out a lot of work pruning up trees and shrubs. This allows him to plant in layers, and use the maximum number of plants in a restricted space; he is a master of the art. The revealed trunks of sweet chestnuts, oak and acers are gorgeous. The way to do this successfully, he confided, is to do one branch a week and continuously stand back to study the results. Working like this he can successfully fit a ginkgo, variegated aralia, cercidiphyllum and various acers in one area together.

The greenhouse has been so densely covered in creepers that the building looks like it was constructed from leaves, flowers and glass. The bay hedge room, cut with niches and windows to display small pieces of sculpture, is a bit of fun. It is here that the combination of a *Cornus* 'Norman Hadden', which carries creamy white bracts, and a red rose climbing through it, can be seen. Rose's flower garden is in this area too: this is a busy border full of bulbs and herbaceous perennials like francoa and *Anemone rivularis*.

Brian Cross is one of the few gardeners happy for his garden to be inspected at times other than May and June, declaring it to be at its best in the autumn. This alone makes it a good visit, because Irish autumn weather is frequently better than that which the summer visits on us.

Lisselan Estate Gardens | Clonakilty, County Cork

Contact: Mark Coombes
Tel: (+353) 023 883 3249
e-mail: info@lisselan.com
www: www.lisselan.com
Open: All year daily, 8am-Dusk.
Groups must book. Supervised children welcome.

No dogs. **Special features:** Guided tours. Partially wheelchair accessible. Teas can be booked. Golf course. **Directions:** Located 3km from Clonakilty town, on the N71 travelling towards Cork city.

The gardens at Lisselan are set in a valley beside the River Argideen. Covering around twenty acres, they were laid out by the Bence-Jones family in the last century following the principles of William Robinson, the famous Irish garden designer and writer. They must be among the most romantic, peaceful and handsome gardens on the island, a perfect combination of water, flowers, wildlife, fine trees, tranquillity and taste.

Through the old blue-painted iron gates, the drive leads in through a mature wood. Fine specimens of huge trees, like podocarpus, eucalyptus and tulip tree or liriodendron, line the front driveway. From the car park, a leaf-strewn path leads past the house to the garden. A sign by the house entices the visitor to the gardens by a circuitous route through a series of old yards; there are also signs warning that only golfers should enter the rose-edged balustraded parterre. Upon entering and finding the sand bunkers dug into the lawn, gardeners will wince just as much as golfers will dance a jig. Bunkers aside, the place is a sheer delight.

The first view most visitors get of the garden is the rock garden at the foot of the house. The building is reminiscent of a French château, all turrets and gables draped in Virginia creeper. It stands on a cartoon-like precipice looking down on the garden. That precipice is laid out as a rock garden, steeply sloped from the base of the building down to the river valley floor. It is a bold, memorable feature. For visitors with the footing of mountain goats it is possible to climb up the rockery and through it. However, be careful not to step on the thousands of seedlings in

the paths – walking on these feels like committing plant infanticide. There are innumerable cyclamen, primulas and ferns, lysimachia and dianthus – the tiny progeny of healthy parents in the beds. The rockery is one of the most beautiful features in the county and worth a major detour in its own right.

Off to the west of the house is an impressive shrubbery with mature pines overhead and acacia, myrtle, robinia and vivid-coloured rhododendrons beneath. A meandering walk called the ladies' mile leads through this, along the river and though the rhododendron woods. A long, rough-paved set of steps covered by arched trees and edged with dahlias and other flowers leads down to this river walk.

At one point, the river is spanned by a white, wisteria-covered bridge leading to an island with a lily-stuffed pool and then out past weirs, sluice gates and more of the little waterway to a woody walk.

Snaking paths by the other riverbank are edged by flowering camellias and bamboo on one side, and primula, ferns and irises on the other. Hidden in the middle of the rampant growth is a quaint little bamboo summerhouse surrounded by great tufts of cream-flowered libertia.

The most recent development at Lisselan is the fuchsia garden. This has been developed in the old walled garden, at the far reaches of the main river walk. Fuchsia is almost the official flower of west Cork, used in much of its marketing and publicity, symbolic of the fact that most species of these often tender plants would not survive outdoors on the rest of the island. So filling the walled garden with over thirty species of fuchsia was thought to be a fitting use for this flower-filled garden. It was.

Contact: Jacky Ward, Head Gardener
Tel: (+353) 064 668 3588
www: www.derreengarden.com
Open: All year daily, 10am-6pm.
Supervised children welcome.

Dogs on leads. **Special features:** Teas can be booked in advance. Guided tours.
Directions: Derreen is 24km from Kenmare on the R571 travelling toward Castletownbere. Signposted.

Derreen is a singular garden, a place of such charm and beauty that it lodges in the memory in a way that much showier gardens generally cannot. A completely man-made garden, it nevertheless has an air of untamed nature about it. When lists of quintessentially Irish gardens are made, it is the always at the top of the list.

In the 1600s the lands at Derreen were among the massive tracts owned by the Cromwellian William Petty, the man who carried out the Down Survey. (This was first great land survey of the south and west of Ireland, carried out in order to redistribute lands confiscated from Irish landowners.) He was paid for his work with 270,000 acres in Kerry, of which he wrote, 'for a great man that would retire, this place would be the most absolute, and the most interessant place in the world, both for improvement and pleasure and healthfulness.' The lands moved through Petty's family and a series of tenants until the 1850s, when the Lansdowne family, as they were known by then, began to take an interest in the property at Derreen and its grounds.

Today, Derreen is a large woodland garden, created through the improvements carried out by the fifth Marquess of Lansdowne in the 1870s on the rock, scrub and what had been called 'unprofitable land' around his house on the Beara Peninsula. The house and garden have continued in the same family ever since. They are now in the care of the fifth Marquess's great grandson, David Bingham.

Back in 1870, the first job carried out was to plant a windbreak of trees, including recently introduced North American Western red cedar, *Thuja plicata* and Western hemlock or *Tsuga heterophylla*, on the rocky land that was to become a new garden. From these beginnings a lush, green jungle garden arose. It has matured into a place that is simply perfect, and today it is rightly known as one of the most beautiful gardens on the island.

The garden visit begins close to the house by the big rock. This is a massive, flat, smooth outcrop of stone, known since ancient times as a meeting place. Today it rises out of a sea of lawn, and gives the visitor some idea of the original quality of the land not far below the fine plants.

Between the sheltering trees are the tree ferns or *Dicksonia antarctica*, for which Derreen has become famous. They grow in such numbers and sizes that they only serve to highlight the difficulty of growing even fairly scrawny specimens elsewhere in the country. It is almost possible to become blasé about tree ferns in Kerry generally, and at Derreen in particular. They naturalise and self-seed here like refined weeds.

Within the woods, some of the individual gardens have strange descriptive names, like the 'King's oozy' and the 'little oozy'. On wet days, of which there are no shortages, the term oozy seems particularly apt as the slurp of boots through the ooze is a necessary part of a visit – the annual rainfall here can be as high as 200cm. One of the best areas in the garden is the Knockatee seat, perched to take in a view over the woods to Knockatee Hill. A knobbly path picks its way up towards it between rocks, trees and ferns. The wild feel of the garden is enhanced as you make your way over a bridge built to straddle and accommodate the exposed roots of a huge eucalyptus tree in the woods.

Another interesting sight is the largest *Cryptomeria japonica* 'Elegans' in the world. Even growing on its side, it still reaches over eighteen metres. The magic of Derreen lies in its being so wild, and huge barriers of bamboo cross the path. But the wildness is contrived; the garden has been tended for many years by Jacky Ward. We have to remind ourselves that if it was actually wild it would disappear under native weeds. Impression is everything.

In parts, the path takes a route that leads out towards the water, past a private island reached by bridge, mysterious and out of bounds. Even on a dull, rainy day and late in the evening it is a surprise to emerge into sunlight and be able to look across the sea to the Caha Mountains on the other side of Kilmackilloge harbour. But this is only an interlude, because the path ducks back in again under the woods and trees and turns into a carpet of moss, lichen and fern. A more romantic soul might be moved to lie down on the moss and commune with nature. Appropriately, the method of payment here is through a rarely seen honesty box.

Derrynane National Historic Park |
Caherdaniel, County Kerry

Contact: James O'Shea

Tel: (+353) 066 947 5387

e-mail: derrynanehouse@opw.ie

Open: All year during daylight hours.

Free admission. Supervised children welcome.

Dogs on leads.

Special features: Café, Historic house.

Partially wheelchair accessible.

Directions: 3.5km from Caherdaniel, off the N70. Signposted.

Memories of trips to Derrynane years ago involve sitting on the grass in front of the slate-sided house for picnics and guided tours of 'The Liberator' Daniel O'Connell's home. Today a trip to Derrynane conjures up pictures of Wellington-clad expeditions through a fascinating and growing plant collection.

A number of years ago the garden was allied to the Edinburgh Botanic Gardens and as such was chosen to trial a whole array of seeds and plants collected in far-flung places. Today the lands of the national park around the grand old house are home to an experimental and expanding wild garden, made up of plants from all over the world

The feature that makes this horticultural laboratory most remarkable is the way in which James O'Shea, the head gardener, and his team grow these plants. Once again, the magical fairy dust of wild-western Irish gardening is in evidence.

Entrance to the garden is through a stone arch under the drive, draped with variegated clerodendron and mulberry. Once inside, instead of finding sterile laboratory conditions and neat rows, the plants are arranged in ways that they might look in the wild. So we see rhodochiton clambering along a fallen tree trunk, a fasicularia growing from a stump in among a mass of native ferns and unusual *Salvia corrugata*, black *S. discolour* and *S. confertiflora* all growing in long grass. Seeing the Chilean bellflower, bomaria, growing like a wild flower allows us to imagine what they must look like in their native South America. A watsonia sprouting from a little crack in a boulder further enhances the wild jungle atmosphere.

James is a passionate plantsman who talks engagingly about the little and not-so-little plants in his care with an easy knowledge. Listening to him talk adds hugely to a walk around the garden. A conducted tour would be of particular use to 'tidy gardeners' who might otherwise

find Derrynane a bit on the scruffy side. But that loose hand is what actually cossets the plants best. Huge rainfall, the lush growth, sheltering neighbours and soft climate bestow the conditions that allow plants to grow with great vigour. Plants from Chile, Argentina, Brazil, Australia and New Zealand, usually seen snug and pampered in greenhouses, are all growing outside quite happily. So tender tree ferns like *Dicksonia squarrosa* and lophosoria thrive side-by-side here. James uses the shelter of old stone ruins to house some of the collections, adding further to the wild look as well as providing practical shelter. It was rare to see *Xanthoria australis* doing well outdoors, along with tender Norfolk Island pines or *Araucaria heterophylla*.

Much of the garden is taken up with expanses of sunny lawn studded with these wild island beds and protruding rocks. Meanwhile, groves of tall oak and English elm tower so far overhead that they cast very little shadow on the gardens below. Shaded spots like the fern and rock garden link the more open areas to unusual features, such as the field of tree ferns. This display can be seen from different vantage points, both from overhead and beneath, like so many inside-out green umbrellas. The experiment at Derrynane is in its infancy and it will be a great pleasure to watch it develop in years to come.

Hotel Dunloe Castle Gardens |
Beaufort, Killarney, County Kerry

....

Contact: Reception   **Tel:** (+353) 064 664 4111
e-mail: sales@kih.liebherr.com
www: www.thedunloe.com
Open: May to October, by appointment only.

Supervised children welcome. Dogs on leads.
Directions: 10km from Killarney on the Killarney-Beaufort road (R562).

So many of the gardens in Kerry and west Cork are blessed with spectacular natural surroundings. Bantry House sits on the edge of Bantry Bay, Ilnacullin basks in Glengarriff Harbour and Valentia Island shelters Glanleam. The Hotel Dunloe Castle Gardens, looking straight at the Gap of Dunloe, is another magnificently placed retreat.

The castle at Dunloe has a confused and disputed origin. It may have been built in 1213 by the MacThomas clan, but it is also reputed to have been built by O'Sullivan Mór. Then again, another source claims it as a Norman keep built by Meyler de Bermingham. Whatever the facts, the garden is built on what is clearly a favourable site, overlooking and commanding passages across two rivers, the Laune and the Loe. Presumably because of that enviable position, the castle has seen multiple onslaughts and plenty of fighting, including an attack by Cromwell's forces, who left it in ruins. Rebuilt after Cromwell's departure, it continued to be inhabited until the nineteenth century, when it was left to deteriorate.

Dunloe had to wait until the twentieth century to be rescued. It was bought by Howard Hamilton, a keen plant lover from America, who created the garden. Once he had bought the property, he set to work at a furious pace and, with his considerable means, within only sixteen years (1920-1936) he had produced a huge collection of trees and shrubs, many of them rare and unusual specimens.

The garden is set in a very exposed site, so he began with a windbreak of Monterey pines, elm, sycamore and beech. The choicer plants were then bedded within the shelter belt. These include a number of unusual trees, which have since been catalogued by the British plantsman Roy Lancaster. Lancaster began advising on planting at Dunloe in the 1980s, taking over from another renowned name in English horticulture, Sir Harold Hillier.

The shape of the garden is a bit amorphous and, to be honest, not that relevant. This is not a place of framed views (apart from the Gap of Dunloe) and smart features. This garden is about the plants, and they are arranged so that the maximum number of choice plants can be seen to best advantage as one walks around.

The tower house castle is set in the midst of the garden, overlooking the River Laune. A little stone path travels from here through newly planted camellia and hydrangea beds, down to a lower walk. Three-metre-high stone walls surround this area and mark the drop to the beech woods below. Close to the main hotel buildings there are several huge mixed beds of fuchsia, hebe, cistus and lavatera interspersed with herbaceous plants. Crinum lilies, erysimum, angel's fishing rod or dierama, penstemon, buddleia, hydrangea and yet more varieties of fuchsia form a low frame beneath the view of the Gap of Dunloe.

Paths lead from the buildings out to the arboretum and walled garden, both filled with specimen trees and flowering shrubs. There are varieties of camellia, athrotaxis and magnolia, including the most fabulous *Magnolia delavayi* and a *Cornus mas*, which looks as though it could collapse under the weight of its fruit. The Japanese banana (*Musa basjoo*) is as exotic as its looks suggest and there are dawn redwoods or *Metasequoia glyptostroboides*, rediscovered in the 1940s in China, having been thought extinct. The southwest's most famous trees, the strawberry tree or *Arbutus unedo* and myrtles, grow here in great numbers. Myrtle or *Luma apiculata* comes from Chile, but does so well in Kerry that it might as well be a native, self-seeding happily and decorating the garden year-round with glossy green leaves, tiny white fragrant flowers in August and little red fruits later in the year.

Illicium anisatum and a huge *Osmanthus yunnanensis* tower above the lower layers of magnolia and camellia, tree ferns, ginger lilies and crinum lilies. Rough stone paths lead through these groves of trees, shrubs and herbaceous things.

There is far too much in this large garden to take in on a single visit and for many the handy 'Around the World in Thirty Minutes' leaflet, which marks out thirty of the most remarkable trees, will be a lifeline from the sheer mind-boggling spectacle of so many wonderful plants.

GLANLEAM HOUSE AND GARDEN | VALENTIA ISLAND, COUNTY KERRY

Contact: Meta Kreissig
Tel: (+353) 066 947 6176
e-mail: mail@glanleam.com
Open: Easter to October, daily 11am-7pm by appointment. Supervised children welcome. Dogs on leads. **Special features:** Self-catering houses.

Catered accommodation and meals can be booked. **Directions:** Driving from Portmagee over the bridge to Valentia Island, follow the signs to Knightstown. In the village, turn left after the Church of Ireland. Travel along for a short distance. Glanleam is on the right, signposted.

Glanleam, like Derreen and Derrynane, is another of the great 'wild' gardens of Kerry. It was the creation of Peter Fitzgerald, the nineteenth Knight of Kerry. In 1830 he took the bare rock of Valentia Island and began to mould it into a garden. He used his many connections to fill the new garden with rare and unusual plants, many of which are still here today. It has been substantially well kept and today is being worked and added to by the present owners, Meta and Jessica Kreissig, who open the old house to visitors when they are not engaged in the massive task of preserving, restoring and developing the garden.

The ornamental garden is long and narrow, made up of walks through sheltering and lightly shading trees, with occasional openings and clearings. Close to the house there are lawns and a semicircular walled kitchen garden full of vegetables grown organically and ornamentally. There are also acres of woods to explore. This is a large and ongoing project worked creatively by Jessica and Meta. For example, the first feature I saw on my most recent visit were the 'lawn-mowers', a flock of Soy – self-shearing sheep, from the Hebrides, kept for grass-cutting purposes.

In the garden, the list of exotic and special plants is long. A lily-of-the valley tree (*Clethra arborea*) grows to twenty-three metres here. This is an extraordinary height, as they only reach about seven metres in their native Madeira. Embothriums, declared the finest specimens in Ireland, also reach heights here that they never manage in Chile, their original home. In the Knight's Garden there are special ferns growing wild, including the European chain fern (*Woodwardia radicans*) and the rare little Killarney fern (*Trichomanes speciosum*). Because of a craze among Victorians for ferns, this little plant was almost rendered extinct. Hordes of collectors would descend on woodlands like corseted and tweed-clad locusts, digging up everything ferny, with a particular enthusiasm for anything strange, rare or weird-looking. They would then bring these home where most promptly died. So it is heartening to see the native ferns doing well here. Regarding tree ferns, a group of New Zealand scientists recently did tests on one of the huge specimens in Glanleam and discovered that it was over 450 years old. The aged trunks were brought over in ships as ballast in the nineteenth century and then planted into the ground, where they started to grow.

The upper walk is the home of the camellia collection. They start flowering at the end of November and, like a tag team, continue in succession right through to summer.

The perfect blue water in the bay is reminiscent of the setting for a Bond movie and the mild climate adds further to that impression. Fuchsias thrive in the wet warmth but almost wilt under the weight of flowers. In an area called the dell, deep in the garden, there are tree ferns in such numbers and sizes that would make owners of single weakling ferns gnash their teeth. But one of the great sights is of massed myrtles (*Luma apiculata*). They have small glossy dark leaves, bark like smooth rust and sweet-smelling white blossoms. The fine variegated *Luma apiculata* 'Glanleam Gold', which carries green leaves edged in gold, originated in this garden.

The Spring Rice garden is a small grove created in memory of one Elizabeth Spring Rice, who died exiled in France as a consequence of smuggling IRA arms in 1916. It is filled with agave and ginger lilies or hedychium. A circular water feature with finely wrought stonework and little paths, steps and rills dominates this small garden. The Victorian decorative pebble drains are being unearthed and restored here, as they are all around the garden. The Kreissigs are also constantly finding and repairing little stone walls and sets of steps.

A fern walk overhung with fringed acacias leads onto another walk of dierama, or angel's fishing rod. In the spring this site fills with bluebells and libertia. To the front of the house, walk along the gunnera walk past more naturalised tree ferns and a thundering stream. There are streams everywhere around the garden. Many were lost under rhododendron. As they are uncovered, the Kreissigs are slowly restoring them too.

The results, good and bad, of storms and subsequent tree losses are remarkable: losses invariably reveal previously hidden features, like the thirty-metre-high monkey puzzle tree (*Araucaria araucana*). Meanwhile, a *Podocarpus andinus* from the Andes fell over in another storm and continues to grow on its side. The remains of a huge fallen cordyline gave rise to hundreds of seedlings and these have since been planted out as a young *allée*.

The Kreissigs are dedicated to cultivating and expanding the garden: more than 22,000 oak were planted in the early 1990s, along with 15,000 ash. These huge plantations have been greatly improved by being cut through with long, dark tunnelled paths that lead out to sunny openings. Within the woods, an ancient holy well was uncovered and an intriguing healing garden was created around it.

MUCKROSS GARDENS |
MUCKROSS HOUSE, KILLARNEY NATIONAL PARK, KILLARNEY, COUNTY KERRY

Tel: (+353) 064 667 0164
e-mail: killarneynationalpark@opw.ie
www: www.muckross-house.ie
Open: All year daily, 9am-6pm. Closed one week at Christmas. No entrance fee to park and garden. Supervised children welcome. Dogs on leads.
Special features: Partially wheelchair accessible.

Exhibition. Craft shop. Restaurant. Self-guiding trails, including a special trail for the visually impaired. Access to the restored greenhouse by appointment to groups only. Traditional farm, with Kerry cow herd. **Directions:** Situated 6km from Killarney on the N71 to Kenmare.

Set among the woods and lakes of Killarney, Muckross is a truly lovely garden. If possible, arrive in a jaunting carriage. Slowly driving toward the gardens in an open carriage, ducking under the branches of roadside trees and seeing the woods at close quarters is the perfect way to begin a visit. When gardens like Muckross were being made, movement was at the pace of the horse and travelling this way adds an extra sprinkle of authenticity.

The Tudor-style house was built in 1843 for Henry Arthur Herbert. It transferred to the Guinness family and then to the family of Senator Vincent Arthur, who presented it to the State in 1932. It stands deep in the park, surrounded by smart lawns that run smoothly down towards the famous lakes. Clipped hedges and topiary cones add a dash of formality and tidiness to these front and side lawns. Old shrub roses butt up against the building, along with an ancient wisteria. Its almost architectural trunk runs up and blends in with the grey limestone of the window arches. From the terrace there are views over the lakes to the mountains beyond and the beginnings of the arboretum, with groves of sculptural Scots pine, to the foreground.

A sunken garden to the back of the house contains beds of cannas, dahlias, roses, clematis and other herbaceous plants. The bedding borders, while not to everyone's liking, are part of the period planting.

A set of steps out of the sunken garden leads into the rockery, one of the great features in Muckross. Scramble up, down and around the rocks, which sprout cotoneaster, cornus, small Japanese acers and a vicious-looking *Rosa omeiensis* 'Pteracantha' with blood-red thorns and butter-coloured single flowers. This rock garden has a sort of tempered wildness about it. It is full of knotted heathers, native strawberry trees (*Arbutus unedo*), grey-shooted *Rubus thibetanus* 'Silver Fern' and blue-flowering *Teucrium fruticans*. There are many unusual, lesser-seen and interesting shrubs, creeping plants and trees growing on the big sprawling rock face, and the full extent or size of the rockery is difficult to see from most points within it. But on my last visit I was most smitten by the pure cherry-red foliage on a *Euonymus alatus* that also had gorgeous orange-and-pink berries.

Through shrubs and rocky outcrops deep within the rockery, one catches constant glimpses of the manicured parkland in one direction and the arboretum beyond. There are extensive plantations of rhododendrons, particularly *Rhododendron arboreum,* and azaleas throughout.

But before heading out to the far reaches of the woods and tree collections, the walled garden is worth a visit. It is all very smart and ordered. Lollypop viburnums punctuate box-enclosed beds of wallflowers, tulips, antirrhinums and forget-me-nots. There are perennial beds of kniphofias, rudbeckia and miscanthus backed by rustic fences. The gravel paths are perfectly swept and the tidy lawns are ruler-straight and manicured to a standard that will please even the most pernickety gardener. All this centres on a fine greenhouse filled with orchids and tender exotics. I discovered the hard way that it could only be visited *by groups and by appointment.* You might have to settle for a nose-pressed-against-the-window view of the treats. Another free-standing greenhouse in the centre of the lawn can similarly be visited only by appointment.

Continuing out past this and the shrub-studded lawns, there are walks through the water garden. This is a particularly attractive part of the garden, in contrast to the manicured walled and flower gardens. The paths trail alongside sunken stone-edged streams, sprouting ferns and moss and there are big clumps of crinum lilies and hostas growing by the water. The little stone walls and small slab bridges over the water are charming and the mature trees far overhead allow plenty of light through for plantations of hydrangeas and other shrubs beneath.

The arboretum melts off into the greater woods leading to the Torc waterfall. This is not a day's visit but a whole weekend's worth.

County Limerick

Ballynacourty | Ballysteen, County Limerick

Contact: George and Michelina Stacpoole
Tel: (+353) 061 393 626
e-mail: stacpoole@iol.ie
Open: May to September by appointment to groups only. Supervised children welcome.
Directions: Driving from Limerick to Foynes on the N69, turn right for Pallaskenry. In Pallaskenry village, turn left in the direction of Ballysteen. The garden is 3km along this road on the right-hand side. The gateway is marked by pillars topped with stone urns.

All-green gardens are quite rare. I am not sure why, but this stylish type of garden is not as widely seen as it should be. There are a great number of effects that can be achieved confining the palette to foliage, lawn, hedging, trees and shrubs. It might not be particularly low-maintenance, but neither is it high-maintenance.

Forty-two years ago, Ballynacourty was 'a plain, unadorned old farmhouse'. Today, the handsome garden has the appearance of a place that never knew a plain or unadorned day in its life. The years since moving to Ballynacourty have been well spent by the Stacpooles. They have turned the grounds into a sophisticated, handsome garden. The references to historic landscaping are strong: the lines of hedging are architectural and mostly green. Everywhere there are great big beech hedges, with the line of one tall hedge standing out against and above the contrasting

line and colour of a neighbouring hedge travelling in another direction. The garden has the feel of a maze, with little surprises found at the bottom of every cul-de-sac.

The house is draped voluptuously with a massive wisteria. Just visible under its trailing branches is a loggia-cum-conservatory; and it all feels as much Lombardy as Limerick.

A walk through the garden starts when you make your way through an arch in a big hornbeam hedge that runs out from the house. The path leads to the first of the garden rooms, where a substantial double curve of privet hedging, tall and expertly cut, dominates. Privet is a fast-growing evergreen bush that gives great height and width as a hedge. It is easy to shape and makes a good dense screen. It needs several cuts a year, however, making it the choice for those who don't mind work.

From this point, at the end of the privet hedge the garden meanders in several directions. 'One Christmas George thought we'd go this way,' explained Mrs Stacpoole, as she led the way into another garden in the six-acre plot. This route takes in a lavender walk that leads towards a wildflower area with grass paths cut through the buttercups, cowslips and meadowsweet. An arbour of privet stands perched on a bank overlooking a sea of daffodils and the River Shannon, which flows below the garden. Down from this there is a cherry walk, which George compared to 'paradise' in the late spring.

Ballynacourty is an easy garden to get lost in. Only at the top of a hill overlooking the garden can the shape and plan of the place, with its feature gates, pillars, statues and hedge walls, be seen in context.

Apart from the hedges, the other feature vital to the look of Ballynacourty is the statuary, and the place is filled with eclectic works that constantly surprise and divert. George is particularly proud of the effects they have achieved using surprising materials in these pieces. A guessing game as to what the materials are will add a bit of fun to a walk through the garden.

The Stacpooles also derive as much use from the natural features the land threw up as those brought in and built: old wells and huge natural stone outcrops peeping out of the well-kept lawns are used like stepping stones across a green lake. In addition to looking good, these huge expanses of stone give some idea of the sort of rocky limestone out of which the garden was hewn. Finally, there are some fine specimen trees. I love the mature walnuts and huge sweet chestnuts. 'Serene' might be the best word to describe the gardens at Ballynacourty.

Boyce Gardens | Mountrenchard, Foynes, County Limerick

Contact: Phil and Dick Boyce
Tel: (+353) 069 65 302
e-mail: dboyce.ias@eircom.net
www: www.boycesgardens.com
Open: May to October, daily 10am-6pm.

Other times by appointment. Groups welcome. Not suitable for children. **Special features:** Partially wheelchair accessible.
Directions: The garden is 1km from Loughill, travelling toward Glin, off the N69. Signposted.

The Boyces have been working this one-acre garden since 1983, and it has the look of a place on the receiving end of much love and dedication. The house and garden are built on the site of six labourers' cottages – a piece of history visible in the six varieties of hedging that run along the roadside in front of the present-day garden. It is a lovely thought that each short length is an historic reference to one of the old cottages.

Entering from the road through a door in the wall quickly shows you that this is far from the garden that might belong to a humble cottage. Instead, it is a maze of complicated garden rooms in different styles. Arched tunnels under blankets of climbers lead from one compartment to another. The look changes constantly, morphing from a perfect little alpine garden facing south and baking in the sun, to long double borders with delphiniums, phlox, irises and other blue flowers on one side of a path and yellow ligularia and rudbeckia, solidago and on the other.

There are small garden trees used extensively to draw attention upwards, from the elegant myrtle or *Luma apiculata* to a sambucus laced through by *Rosa* 'Nevada' flowers. The rose will cover the tree with its yellow-cupped, cream-coloured flowers in time. The double use of soil and space is something small-plot gardeners learn to master in order to get more bang for their buck. The flowers of the host tree and the roses burst into bloom one after another and are in turn followed by elderberries. It is an excellent example of a well-extended season of interest in a confined space.

A shrub of *Griselinia littoralis* 'Bantry Bay' overlooks the lily pond. Griselinia is a tender plant, as many people have discovered over recent hard winters. It does well here in the shelter,

however. Growing shrubs as standards is a favourite trick in this garden. They train-up small trees and shrubs throughout, pruning the lower branches and making a 'tree' shape, or lollipop, out of what would normally be a multi-stemmed, ground-sweeping shrub. It is also another route to expanding the number of plants that can be fitted into a small garden. Pruning out the bottom branches allows the insertion of shade-loving plants into the soil below, like spring bulbs, winter cyclamen, ferns and hellebores. Topiary is another feature in the Mountrenchard garden, and a golden myrtle trained as a perfect two-metre cone is the star among the trained box and lonicera plants in the garden.

Phil is a keen produce-grower and her tidy raised-bed vegetable garden to the rear of the garden shows what can be achieved in a compact space. She is a great lover of home-made compost and has been extolling its virtues for many years; the healthy vegetables in this garden are a testament to her compost. The brick wall behind the vegetable garden was built to house a little peach tree. It gives the tree shelter, catches the sun and holds the heat to help the peaches ripen. In the summer, lemons are grown in this area too, alongside cut-and-come salad crops.

The greenhouse is set in the middle of the garden but is not visible until one almost bumps into it, so abundant are the distractions around it. It is a small structure but it is like a treasure trove, full of grapes, succulents, an Australian *Todea barbara*, one of the rarer ferns, *Fuchsia* 'Annabel' with flowers like white ballet dresses, plum-coloured *Rhodochiton atrosanguineus* and a jam of other exotics. Outside the greenhouse, in a little shaded area, there is a lush little fern bed. The cool green foliage plants are in marked contrast to the mad colours inside.

At the lower end of the garden there is a boggy area with, among other things, a Japanese pagoda tree or sophora with zigzagging branches and miniscule sweet flowers. The garden is stuffed to capacity with plants. Being lovers of new things they constantly collect and everything is described and dated on big slate plant labels. This is an interesting place that will give novice gardeners a good idea of the size and spread different plants might reach.

Knockpatrick Gardens |
Knockpatrick, Foynes, County Limerick

Contact: Tim and Helen O'Brien
Tel: (+353) 069 65 256 / 087 948 5651
e-mail: hob68@eircom.net
Open: May to October by appointment only.
Charity day in May, contact for annual dates.
Supervised children welcome.

Special features: Plants for sale on charity days.
Directions: Take the N69 from Limerick for
34.5km. About 1.5km before Foynes village follow
the sign for Knockpatrick. The garden is 1.5km
from the cross and marked by an arched entrance.

The garden at Knockpatrick, started by the O'Brien family, has been in existence for over seventy years. Since then, three generations of Tim's family have worked and developed the plot, which enjoys an enviable situation overlooking the Shannon Estuary. Generations of O'Briens are to be thanked for Knockpatrick.

From the gateway, you are led enticingly under an arch of dripping gold laburnum, up a drive being slowly encroached upon by magnolias, liriodendrons and peeling barked Japanese acers. Tim is not too pleased with the bulging, colonising habits of these, but if one has to be bullied by plants, let it be by smart ones like liriodendrons and fine acers.

The drive runs below and parallel to the steep rock garden on top of which stands the house. This is a busy, plant-stuffed garden created using layers from ground to sky. Husband-and-wife team Tim and Helen are responsible for the extravagant show that today covers three acres.

When they arrived, Knockpatrick was a calmer garden, centred on a collection of rhododendrons, camellias and azaleas, shrubs that love the acid soil which predominates here. They maintained these treasures, including the big, eighty-year-old *Parrotia persica* or Persian iron wood tree. But they also set about adding to and varying the planting.

They are mad about plants, and brought in everything from bamboos and tree ferns to new trees like cercis, drimys and embothrium, hundreds of blue Himalayan poppies, thousands of candelabra primulas, hellebores, lilies and a range of climbers.

'We have the time to work the place and really we're at it all the time,' says Helen of their almost all-consuming project. Under their care this has become a truly varied garden, divided into different levels by pools and water features, streams and stone features like the moon gate.

This pretty circular gateway both joins and separates different garden rooms. A new developing arboretum is the most recently created garden. It is being constantly added to.

The whitewashed yard is a bright sun-trap and they take full advantage of the warmth it holds by growing tender echiums, shrubs like *Ribes speciosum*, actinidia and a whole range of different abutilons against its gleaming white walls. With the knobbly undulating lime-washed stone, gleaming bright in the sun with such a range of exotics against it, one could be forgiven for thinking they had been transported to some Greek island.

For all the new plants, the busiest and best time of the year in the O'Briens' garden is late May when most of the rhododendrons and azaleas bloom and they hold an annual charity day. Plants are potted up and teas and cakes are prepared for the crowds that arrive to enjoy the fleeting flowers and party atmosphere. Helen laughed at the thought of the crazy amount of work that goes into that open day: 'Every year we say this is the *last* year, and every year we do it all over again!' Such is the power of the gardening bug.

TERRA NOVA GARDEN |
DROMIN, ATHLACCA, KILMALLOCK, COUNTY LIMERICK

Contact: Deborah and Martin Begley
Tel: (+353) 063 90 744 / 086 065 8807
e-mail: terranovaplants@eircom.net
www: www.terranovaplants.com
Open: May to September by appointment only. Groups welcome. Not suitable for children.

Special features: Plants for sale. Self service tearoom. **Directions:** Travel to Bruff and leave by the Kilmallock Road (R512), follow it for just over 2km. Turn right at the crossroads and follow signs for Martin Begley Glass.

Terra Nova is a strange and wonderful garden. No matter how often I visit, it always feels like it has been given a complete overhaul since my last visit. It is a small garden, covering half an acre, but incorporates the sort of stunning use of space that even the Japanese would envy. It is almost impossible to describe how many plants in such wonderful combinations that Deborah and Martin Begley manage to shoe-horn into their garden. The Begleys are fanatical gardeners and a walk through Terra Nova almost brings on a bout of sensory overload. It is awash with treasures. The Begleys' garden is, for want of a better word, a laboratory. They subscribe to seed-collecting

expeditions to locate unusual plants, like African hemp (*Sparrmannia africana*) with its exquisite white flowers and big showy leaves. Deborah uses showy exotics like *Ricinus communis*, the castor oil plant, as annuals. Deborah also has a great fondness for arisaema, the strange-looking herbaceous perennial somewhat reminiscent of arum lilies.

The garden is not just a collection of plants, however; great thought has been given to the design. This is evident in the handsome betula-and-verbena circle and the unusually placed oak gate in the woods. The fun-sized fern garden at the shaded front of the house is one of my favourite items here – among the ferns is an unusual upside-down fern, *Arachnoides standishii*. The stained glass seen in various places around the garden comes courtesy of Martin and his glassworks.

A great love of trees and only a half-acre to play with means that small trees are the most practical. One of the favourites is a locally bred betula, known as *Betula* 'White Light', bred by Mr John Buckley of Birdhill in Tipperary. It has a great white peeling bark and good autumn colour. I loved the three *Acer dissectum*, which were planted together as seeds. They are all slightly different to each other in the way that seedlings often are. Among the huge number of plants there are some good grotesques too, like the memorable voodoo lily (*Sauromatum venosum*), which smells like a baby's bad nappy: 'The flies love it,' Deborah told me. I think they are alone in that.

Martin is the hard landscaping chief, maker of features like the little bridged frog pond, edged with canna lilies, golden gardener's garters and bulrushes. His most recent large scale addition has been the Thai house, surrounded by big tree ferns – including a *Dicksonia squarrosa*, which he says can be left out for winter in the shelter of the Thai house. When I first saw it, there were three women also seeing it for the first time. They were speechless, and obviously carried off, for a few moments, to the orient. It is quite a sight. The path away from it leads through a long snaking pergola walk, built to hold a number of roses, including a yellow cabbage rose called *Rosa* 'Teasing Georgia' and an unusual green *Rosa chinensis* 'Viridiflora'.

This is a truly inspiring garden, well worth visiting, especially for those who also work in restricted space. It is a testament to what flair, passion and back-breaking work can achieve. Don't miss the self-service tearoom.

 COUNTY TIPPERARY

KILLURNEY | BALLYPATRICK, CLONMEL, COUNTY TIPPERARY

Contact: Mildred Stokes
Tel: (+353) 052 613 3155 / 087 944 4662
e-mail: rowswork@eircom.net
Open: For selected open days in June. Contact for annual dates. By appointment at other times.
Special features: Partially wheelchair accessible.

Teas can be arranged. **Directions:** Driving from Kilkenny on the N76 turn right at Ormonde Stores. Take the third right at a sign for Killurney. Turn at the first turn on the left after the school and the house is first on the left.

Driving through the gates at Killurney, looking up the drive and through peep holes under the trees and between shrubs, it is clear that this is a garden worked by an assured talent. Everything spells expertise and flair. The source of that flair is Mildred Stokes, and this has been her domain for over a quarter of a century. When Mildred first arrived she was greeted by a congested one-acre site around a Georgian house. That acre was a dark, shaded place, hidden under and behind numerous heavy conifers. As she describes it, one could feel the oppression and gloom of those trees, and in all likelihood they must have been planted once upon a time as miniature decorative conifers in the front garden of the handsome farmhouse.

Once these were dispensed with, and the place was opened up to light, Mildred began to design and build her new garden. She did it all herself, from digging out beds and building

paths, to directing streams and creating ponds, with all the hard work those jobs entail. Mildred is a hands-on gardener. She also has a good eye. The garden was designed so that, standing at the front door, two generous flanks of shrubs, trees and flowers act like huge theatre curtains, framing a view of the Comeragh mountains in the distance, over the fields that sweep down in front of the garden.

While the view is an important part of its design, Killurney is principally the garden of a plant lover, with all the abundance and plant action that this involves. Mildred is a devotee of the layered garden, so everywhere there are multiple and constantly changing layers of herbaceous plants, shrubs and mature trees that melt together into fluid groupings. Between the plants, and within the beds, stone paths lead into, out of and around different compositions. They can be hard to make out until you are actually walking along them in summer, because so many well-fed plants seem hell-bent on spreading out to meet in the middle over the little tracks. Mildred knows how to keep order however. The paths also add a little mystery to the overall shape of the garden, and in winter they serve as bone structure in the more restrained, hibernating garden.

The idea of harnessing a natural sunken stream that ran along the boundary of the garden was an inspired one. Water was brought into the centre of the plot so that it could be directed to wander along between the vegetation and bridged with flat stone slabs. It looks completely natural. The path meanders back and forth over the little waterway, which at one point leads into a pond, heavily planted with waterside species like drumstick primula, astilbe and lilies. The sound of water, even when it is not always visible, is attractive in a garden and trickling water along can be heard everywhere here.

A feeling of privacy and intimacy is achieved by the strategic placement of taller plants, which then have to be skirted around in order to see more of the garden. The effect of this is to entice the visitor on to further investigation. The maze of paths delivers the walker in between runs of

Rosa 'Bonica', past tall stands of dahlias and under peeling *Acer griseum*, towards little groves of ferns in the woodland garden. The beautifully matched colour combinations come at you in waves as you move from one area to another.

From parts shaded by small trees like *Aralia elata*, *Acer palmatum* 'Senkaki' and *Cercis canadensis* 'Forest Pansy', to parts open and sunny, this garden is stuffed with a huge range of plants. But the real wow is the gravel garden to the side of the house. The sunken stream makes its way through this area too, side-planted by waving dierama. The gravel is studded by big boulders, which create natural-looking leaning posts and backdrops for creeping junipers and tufts of miniature alpines. The gravel garden is backed by a sun-soaked old stone wall, lightly covered with two rather poignantly named *Clematis* 'Prince Charles' and *C.* 'Princess Diana,' harking back to a long-gone time.

A classic country garden.

County Waterford

Cappoquin House | Cappoquin, County Waterford

Contact: Charles Keane
Tel: (+353) 058 54 290
e-mail: charleskeane@cappoquinestate.com
www: www.cappoquinhouseandgardens.com
Open: May to July, daily 9am-1pm, closed Sunday and bank holidays. Other times by appointment. See web for annual dates. Groups by appointment only. Supervised children welcome.
Special features: Castle ruins. Tours of house.
Directions: Entering Cappoquin from the N72, turn right at the T-junction in the centre of the town. The garden is 200m along on the left, with a stone gateway.

Cappoquin House is a fine Georgian house built on the site of, and incorporating, the walls of one of the FitzGeralds' Norman castles on the River Blackwater in west Waterford. Like Dromana upstream and Tourin, Salterbridge, Ballinatray and Lismore downstream, Cappoquin was built close to the river because the Blackwater was, in essence, the motorway of its day. It was easier to travel by boat than over land and the river cut its way up through the countryside, efficiently carrying goods and people inland from the port at Youghal for centuries.

The house has been the home of the Keane family for nearly three hundred years and the garden has the air of a place that has been tended and minded for all of that time. It is chiefly the result of the nineteenth-century inhabitants, however, with extra additions made in the 1970s. But there are also vestiges of even older gardens and buildings still to be found here, and work and development continue to this day.

It seems to be of indeterminate size, wandering off in all directions from the centrally placed house looking out over the town and down to the river. But the garden proper covers about five acres. Cappoquin is an easy, pleasing garden into which a great deal of care has been poured. Real thought has gone into stylish colour mixing, particularly with the many rhododendrons and azaleas scattered throughout the place. They have avoided the headache-inducing effect too often seen in rhododendron gardens, where glaring oranges scream at their fuchsia and bright yellow neighbours.

One of the gardens rises high above and behind the house. This is a maze of grass paths leading through meadows between groves of rhododendrons, shrubs and specimen trees, including a rarely seen specimen of *Grisselinia litoralis* grown as a tree and a huge Turkey oak or *Quercus cerris* with a girth of three-and-half-metres. From up here, Lismore Castle can be spotted in the distance.

Bamboo walks lead from one section of the garden to another, past runs of flowering magnolias and little ponds. Up toward the rhododendrons is a pear wall, where trained fruit trees grow on the outside of the old walled garden. The wall faces south, so the pears can soak up maximum sun. Paths along the hillside pass through damp beds full of meconopsis, euphorbia, more bamboo and hydrangea.

One route leads past a little rose garden, sheltered under an ancient-looking withholding wall. The mix of flowers is a lovely tangle of old, Gallica, modern and Damask roses, including *Rosa banksiae*, *R.* 'Dentelle de Malines', *R.* 'William Lobb' and *R.* 'Complicata'. At one end of the wall, a little stream emerges from underground, creating the conditions needed for a damp garden of big ligularia and gunnera. In the spring there is a collection of snowdrops here. Close by, set in between some other shrubs, a healthy little olive tree shows just how sheltered some of the planting pockets here are. One of the latest additions to the garden is an area of new varieties of rhododendron. They were the bounty of a seed-collecting trip by Thomas Pakenham to Tibet several years ago (see Tullynally Castle, County Westmeath).

The specimen trees at Cappoquin include a cropping walnut tree (*Juglans nigra*), weeping beech or *Fagus sylvatica* 'Pendula', pale-barked birches and groves of slim myrtles (*Luma apiculata*).

To the front of the house there is a beech hedge-enclosed garden. This is a mix of lawns, raised beds full of lamb's ears (*Stachys byzantina*), perennial wallflower or erysimum, wild strawberries and pink osteospermum twining through black grass. It is an intimate, domestic spot compared to the rest of the garden. This is overlooked by the elegant old conservatory to the front of the house. The conservatory is unheated but still holds a good range of tender specimens, like velvety-purple tibouchina, oleander, pelargonium and succulents in staged shelves. All these share the space with a big, scented, cabbagy *Rosa* 'Ophelia'.

The only formal spot in the garden is here, at the front of the house. This is a sundial garden. Stone paths, bleached white with lichen, divide mirroring beds of dianthus, penstemon, lupin and iris, lavender and white hydrangea. Beyond the balustrades surrounding this formal spot you can see the wilder-looking bog garden, hidden under the shade of a big Holm oak.

A run of acers, azara, witch hazels or hamemalis and a huge eucalyptus extend the garden out from the house to the spring garden, where daphne and winter sweet (*Chimonanthus praecox*) scent the air with perfume.

For all its individual charms, what is most memorable about Cappoquin is the creation of so many views and vistas back and forth between well-thought-out features, old ruins covered in white roses, aged stone gateways leading seemingly nowhere and little folly-like buildings under groves of trees.

FAIRBROOK HOUSE GARDENS | Kilmeaden, County Waterford

Contact: Clary Mastenbroek
Tel: (+353) 051 384 657 / 085 813 1448
e-mail: art@fairbrook-house.com
www: www.fairbrook-house.com
Open: May to September by appointment. No children under twelve. No dogs.
Special features: Contemporary art gallery. Teas by arrangement. Bric-a-brac shop.

Directions: From Waterford on the N25, take the Carrick roundabout in the direction of Cork (N25). After just over 1km take the first turn to the right. There is a sign at this corner for a low bridge. The garden is a few metres along on the right. The garden name is on the gateway.

Fairbrook House garden is a lock-me-in-and-throw-away-the-key type of place that took far too long to discover. This garden was built over the past sixteen years on a remarkable site by Dutch artists Clary Mastenbroek and Wout Muller.

I suppose it could be called a water garden, as water plays a huge part in this wild, hilly, woody place. There are streams, rills and ponds at every turn, an intriguing series of waterways that were once part of an old woollen mill built in 1776 on the little River Dawn. At different times of the year the river roars along and swells to great levels, and at other times it wanders, tamely and sedately, through the garden.

Along with the water, stone work features strongly, from walls to cobbled paths and little follies. These are divided into those that have been here for centuries and those that were made by Clary. This place is a fascinating mix of history, art, horticulture and nature.

Unusually for an Irish garden, Fairbrook features a great number of topiarised shrubs. Topiary is wonderful in all its guises, but this must be one of the best topiary gardens on the island, or indeed anywhere: a straight path runs between two lengths of alternating, clipped box. On one side the box plants are pointed, like green meringue peaks or pixie hats. Either way they are beautifully crafted. On the other side the box has been shaped into cushioned mounds of greenery like undulating, irregular waves. Caught in the morning sun with cobwebs draped over them, they are indescribably lovely.

Next door is another garden room, featuring walls of blue hazy lavender around rose beds full of white *Rosa* 'Winchester Cathedral'. Under-planting the roses with chives and black 'Queen of the Night' tulips transforms a good composition into a better one.

Different garden rooms lead from one to another in a beautiful series of individual gardens. An arch made out of weeping mulberry bushes leads to the dye house garden. This was the ruin of an old dye house which Clary used as a base for her reed bed and lily pond. It is both unusual and practical, as the reed bed acts as an organic water purifier.

Following your nose, you will come upon beech and hornbeam mazes, fern gardens and an all-green garden. This interesting corner is as exercise in working with only green flowers. So there is euphorbia, which, strictly speaking, carries bracts rather than flowers, but this is not a nit-picky place. There are lime green hellebores, and nasturtiums. Next, look for the rosemary-lined paths under a wisteria pergola walk, which vies with a crab apple pergola for the Best Pergola prize.

It is a toss-up over which is prettier between the knot garden and the bonsai garden. Throughout the place there are pieces of sculpture placed in niches, secreted around corners, in secluded spots and out in the open, to distract from and add to the picture. The exhibitions change regularly and the old buildings and planting schemes provide each piece with the perfect exhibition space. Walking about is an object lesson in placing art in a garden setting.

For all the cultivated plants here, there is also a great number of natives. At the edges of the garden in particular, the planting blends out into the surrounding countryside gently: Clary matches smart specimens of magnolia, acer and eucryphia with horse chestnut and wild hawthorn, hazel, ash and holly with great success.

LISMORE CASTLE GARDEN | LISMORE, COUNTY WATERFORD

Tel: (+353) 058 54 061
e-mail: gardens@lismorecastle.com
www: www.lismorecastle.com
Open: Mid-March to September, daily 11am-4.45pm. Groups by appointment at

other times. Supervised children welcome. Dogs on leads. **Special features:** Partially wheelchair accessible. Castle. Art gallery. Historic town. Contemporary sculpture in grounds.
Directions: Situated in the village of Lismore.

Giving directions to the castle and gardens in Lismore will seem daft to anyone who has ever approached the town from the main road from Cappoquin. The castle stands like something from a fairytale: on a height looking down over the river. Lismore is one of the most beautiful towns in Ireland. There has been a castle on this spectacular site since the twelfth century, with a colourful collection of past owners and inhabitants, including Sir Walter Raleigh, Robert Boyle (the father of chemistry) and Estelle Astaire, sister of Fred. The romantic castle seen today is largely a nineteenth-century creation for the sixth Duke of Devonshire, into whose family the castle passed in the 1750s.

The garden around the castle is divided cleanly into two areas: the upper and lower gardens. The upper garden, built on a slope, is reached by way of a rickety stairs up through a stone riding house that was built in 1620. This is an unusual, crooked little building that runs over the drive to the castle.

The walled garden is one of the oldest continuously cultivated gardens of its type in the country, laid out in the 1600s and worked since then. As a result, some of the plants are venerable to say the least. There are longs runs of old yew, beech and box hedges set about the large garden,

dividing it into smaller compartments and sheltered areas for herbaceous and mixed borders. Wide paths link the elements together and the steep slope is broken up with several sets of steps. The orchard is cut through with mown grass paths laid out symmetrically. This is the first part of the garden seen from the riding house entrance. Beyond it is a beech hedge which marks one side of a double mirroring border that climbs up the central axis. Eucalyptus and white hydrangea, abutilon and callistemon or bottlebrush shrubs reflect each other back and forth across the path. This bed opens onto the first set of steps. From here, a rose and lavender double border continues up to more steps covered in fairy foxgloves, santolina, snow-in-summer and thyme. In turn this becomes a more contemporary grass border of sharp black phormium, ophiopogon and trachycarpus, also looking at each other across the wide grass path.

At the top of this is a cross path which runs north-to-south, bordered on one side by shrubs and on the other by austere, formal nail-scissors-smart yew hedges incorporating topiarised pyramids and acorns. Seen from here, the views beyond the castle roofs to the town will lead you to want to visit the town after the garden. This is a good idea.

Below this walk, the unusual, accordion-shaped greenhouses designed by Sir William Paxton in the nineteenth century can be seen. The vegetable beds of artichokes, sprouts, leeks and a range of cut-flowers are laid out here and behind them trained fruit trees cover the walls. The upper garden is a model of its type, both good-looking and functional.

The lower garden, or pleasure ground, is linked to the upper by the riding house. It is made up of informal cobble-edged gravel paths that wind around magnolia, rhododendron and azalea in a landscape that includes a famous yew walk that was laid out in the early 1700s. Tree ferns and woodland bulbs, anemone and bluebells carpet the ground under the tree canopy. This part of the garden is also built on a slope and the top walk allows one to see the flowers on some of the blooming eucryphia and rhododendron from above. The wall bounding the top walk is lined with a variety of climbing roses, clematis, cottage garden herbaceous flowers and varieties of euphorbia.

Walking below the castle, it was strange to see rolls of Rockwool in one of the window bays – a reminder of the fact that even grand castles need to insulate themselves.

In this part of the garden there are a number of important contemporary sculptures, particularly a work by British artist Antony Gormley, which is set at the very end of the yew walk; it is a ghostly, powerful piece placed in a perfectly atmospheric spot. Close by, in the middle of some rhododendron, is a piece by Cork-born artist Eilís O'Connell: a blue, patinated, swirling flourish of metal. A second piece by her stands out in the open near a little round pond under the castle walls. The English artist David Nash also has a work here. These new works are perfectly placed in the old garden. The use of contemporary art at Lismore adds an additional layer of variety to the garden. It takes confidence and style to marry the history of a garden of this age with the raw, bare emotion that contemporary art at its best depicts. It shows a place with a future as well as a past to enjoy. The contemporary art gallery inside the castle adds another element to the visit of the garden.

MOUNT CONGREVE | KILMEADEN, COUNTY WATERFORD

Contact: Michael White
Tel: (+353) 051 384 115
e-mail: mountcongrevegarden@hotmail.com
www: www.mountcongreve.com
Open: March to September, Thursday 9am-4.30pm. At other times by appointment. Children under twelve not admitted.
Directions: Travel from Waterford on the N25 heading towards Cork. Pass the Holy Cross pub on the right and at the next crossroads, marked clearly for Tramore, take the right-hand turn on to a little road. Go through one crossroads and turn left at the next crossroads – be careful as both are dangerous junctions. Travel for about 500m and the gates are on the right-hand side. Follow the signs for the Estate Office.

Mount Congreve is an astounding place, built on a scale completely different to that of any other garden on the island. Created by Ambrose Congreve over the past 92 of his 103 years, it is more akin to one of the great estates of the nineteenth rather than the twenty-first century. It is a place that speaks of another age.

Boasting one of the biggest collections of rhododendrons in the world, and certainly the biggest in Europe, Mount Congreve is a place of superlatives. Think of 3,500 cultivars of

rhododendron, 650 named camellias and 350 named cultivars of Japanese maple. This is the world's largest plant collection, assembled in the last half of the twentieth century and started by a man of considerable wealth who decided, at the age of eleven, to begin planting and never stopped. The collections at Mount Congreve include one of lilac, due to be increased with the addition of cultivars from Poland, where much work has been carried out this century, and a collection of tree peonies, with many new varieties coming from China. Meanwhile, the rhododendron and camellia collections are being updated continuously. They have even improved the propagation process by inventing an ingenious new air layering system, made from a child's rubber ball, which means they can speed up the process as well as ensure a much improved success rate.

All that goes on in the greater garden. There are also four sloped acres of walled garden, arranged into May, June, July and August borders. Each of these is filled with usual and a lot of unusual herbaceous plants, including special iris beds and great runs of hydrangea in north-facing beds, as well as double borders of peoney, nepeta and roses bisecting the garden. These three, planted together, make the most luscious combination of flower and scent.

Every sort of vegetable that can be grown in Ireland is grown here, interspersed with beds of asters and chrysanthemums grown in great quantities for the house. Fruit trees fill the middle beds, while the surrounding walls home long runs of wisteria and the biggest *Clematis armandii* in these islands. The last marvel in the walled garden is a north-facing bed of Chilean bellflower

(*Lapageria rosea*), sheltered from the salt winds that sometimes bluster over the wall.

Of course, there is more. Wander through the extensive greenhouses past walls of nectarines, a mind-bending display of orchids and bromeliads, rare fuchsias and almost extinct varieties of cyclamen and clivia. Numerous pots of datura, streptocarpus, regal pelargoniums, hibiscus and gerbera grown from seed vie with masses of tall carnations, all grown for the house.

Separate to the greenhouses there are dedicated houses providing table grapes and peaches. A visitor could buckle under the sheer extravagance of it all, but stepping out into the garden proper only leads to yet more impressive sights.

The main body of the garden is woodland and its beauties are the flowering shrubs, runs of magnolia and camellia, rhododendron and azalea, cherry, acer, azara, eucryphia, michelia, pittosporum and prunus. The scents are heady, even at times of the year when very little is flowering; at the height of the late spring blossoming, 'overpowering' might better describe it. All of these flowering shrubs and trees are overlooked by eighteenth- and nineteenth-century plantations of oak and beech, many of them with big clematis and rambling roses winding up their massive trunks.

There are over sixteen miles of paths wandering in and around the plants. It is genuinely too easy to get lost and there are no maps or signs. And there are surprises: every so often the paths open onto a secret garden, a beech lawn with rolling turf planted through with spring bulbs, secluded dells and glades, a private garden room or a temple garden. One of my favourite parts is the Chinese dell, a sunken garden set within a twelve-metre drop, making use of the quarry from which stone was mined to build the house. At the bottom of the quarry walls, planted with oriental primula, ferns and meconopsis, there is a circular pond with a little pagoda standing on an island. Moving on from here, the path leads through a forest of *Magnolia campbellii* toward an eighteenth-century ice house, via a grove of tree ferns.

The garden hides masses of bulbs everywhere. During bluebell time the carpet of blue is so dense that much of the place looks like it's planted through water. The bluebells are joined by countless snowdrops, daffodils and fritillaries. There is an overall feeling of abundance everywhere. Plants are grouped not in the usual groups of threes and fives, but in groups of twenty-five, fifty and a hundred. One doesn't come across a single witch hazel but groves of them, not a single Japanese acer but an avenue; and as for the numbers of rhododendrons and camellias – get out the calculator. The varieties are invariably rare and unusual.

In one spot in the woods a huge natural outcrop of stone provided the opportunity for a cascade of water, which tumbles down toward the path finishing in two stone ponds. The damp provided by the spray makes this a great home for wet-loving meconopsis and primula. Another bank of rock provided the base for a football pitch-sized rock garden and a maze of little paths. The eight layered mature beech trees are unforgettable. Ask to see them. It is too easy to miss something among the thousands of features here.

The youth of the gardens is something one must remind oneself of continually. Mount Congreve has the feel of a garden much more mature than its double-digit age.

Tourin House and Gardens |
Cappoquin, County Waterford

Contact: Kristin Jameson **Tel:** (+353) 058 54 405 **e-mail:** tourin@eircom.net **www:** www.tourinhouseandgardens.com **Open:** April to September, Tuesday to Saturday 1pm-5pm. Other times by appointment. Groups by appointment only. **Special Features:** Teas can be arranged. Art classes held. Events.

Directions: 5km south of Cappoquin on the scenic road to Youghal. Signposted from both Cappoquin and Lismore.

There is a string of historic gardens dotted along the River Blackwater in and around the town of Cappoquin. This group includes Dromana, Salterbridge, Cappoquin House, Ballynatray and Tourin. In various ways they are all related country house gardens and for a whole host of reasons they make a wonderful trail. Seeing them together will give the visitor a fascinating insight into how related gardens built close to each other operate. They all share similar climates and soils and they have shared and swapped plants over generations. Yet there are differences, and the differences are part of what makes these gardens worth seeing.

Among the group, I think Tourin is particularly attractive because of its interesting mix of old and new. The garden, created around the old house and an even older castle dating back to 1560, was started as it is seen today by Kristen Jameson's parents. Kristen later took the baton and has been running the garden ever since. It is made up of a series of woodland gardens,

combining new and special trees with the older park trees and specimens that were here in the 1950s, when Kristen's mother arrived from Scandinavia and started to restore the gardens. She climbed among tangles of overgrown trees, unearthed old lost rockeries and replanted them with low-growing woodland plants and groves of camellias and rhododendrons.

Kristen continued the salvage work and today the result is a large woodland garden that meanders along in an informal way, taking in it goes *Magnolia grandiflora, M.* x *soulangeana* 'Speciosa' and *Rehderodendron macrocarpum,*an unusual Chinese tree. One of her favourite plants in here is an old unidentified red rose that thrives in the shade.

There are spring gardens made up of cherries, azaleas and camellias criss-crossed by a network of low dry stone walls. These too were made by Kristen's mother, and they add to the structure and charm of this area. Some of the best scents here come from winter-flowering *Camellia sasanqua,* which came from Chris Loder of the famed English rhododendron-collecting and -breeding family. Hostas and primulas, lily-of-the valley and fox gloves take over the show later in the year.

Kristen's own enthusiasm is for planting trees, and among her most favourite are the Japanese acers, which she can always find a spot for. She uses them a great deal in her layered plantations, which suit the style of the garden so well. But layered planting brings on problems when the layers include some much-loved evergreen oaks, under which it is hard for more special things like *Rhododendron arboreum* to thrive.

As well as planting, she spends a lot of time judiciously pruning. 'Gardens develop and you have to deal with that development,' is her philosophical outlook.

The Sitka spruce (*Picea sitchensis*), developing out at the edge of the garden, is a sight. Given the space it needs but rarely gets, this has grown to be a magnificent tree. As has the London plane or *Platanus* x *hispanica*, which Kristen has been told has the biggest girth in the country. (Although at Salterbridge, Mr Wingfield would argue that his London plane is the bigger of the two – another reason for visiting these lovely gardens together.)

The big walled garden is divided into pretty beds, fruit gardens, vegetable beds and greenhouses full of tomatoes. In the middle of all this action is a row of cherry trees, partially covered with a French tunnel, growing fruit for sale to the local shops. These trees carry the best cherries I have ever tasted.

Tara, Kristen's sister, is fond of irises and she grows over one hundred varieties of them in the walled garden. Some of the walls are given over to fruit, but there are also acacias and climbers doing well in the sun, including *Solanum crispum* 'Glasnevin' and, on the ground, pale blue *Agapanthus* 'Dublin'. The experimental bird seed bed, filled with plants like sunflowers and flax and designed to provide the local birds with seed-bearing plants, is an idea some people might like to bring home with them.

The courtyard is something of a hub. In it, a small collection of roses collected from derelict cottages around Ireland is being developed. Meanwhile, in the outbuildings, Kristen's other sister, artist Andrea Jameson, has her studio. There is a venue for garden talks and even cinema shows and the long refectory-style tables in here were all made from felled trees in the garden.

The old squash court is also worth mentioning: the Jamesons have lent it to the workers on a local FAS course who are in the middle of making a Blackwater cot, a traditional fishing boat once used widely on the river. When it is finished, they hope to launch it from Tourin Quay.

Appropriately, from here a cherry walk leads out to the river, where they planted sixty-five acres of hardwoods six years ago. The path toward the river and Tourin Quay passes the original sixteenth-century tower house that the Victorian house replaced.

Tourin is a fascinating place being utilised in so many unique ways by an enterprising family.

CONNAUGHT

KYLEMORE ABBEY

◈ COUNTY GALWAY

ARDCARRAIG | ORANSWELL, BUSHYPARK, COUNTY GALWAY

....

Contact: Lorna MacMahon
Tel: (+353) 091 524 336
e-mail: oranswell@eircom.net
Open: Contact for annual dates, otherwise strictly by appointment. **Directions:** Situated off the N59 about 5km out of Galway. Take second left turn after Glenloe Abbey Hotel. The garden is 250m up the road on the left, with a limestone entrance.

This is one of those special gardens that have an effect on people. Several times I have spoken to people from overseas who, when they hear mention of the words 'gardens' and 'Ireland', will ask if I know the garden belonging to 'the woman in Galway'. Invariably, they are thinking of Lorna MacMahon's garden, Ardcarraig.

Ardcarraig hugs the hilly land at the southern end of Lough Corrib. It has been here since 1971, when Lorna and her husband Harry arrived to take over a scrubby one-acre site around their new home. They took its humps and hollows and transformed them into one of the most innovative and beautiful private gardens on the island.

Following the contours of the land, the site is divided into separate garden rooms, each distinctive and linked by rising, falling and snaking paths.

As mentioned, the original garden surrounded the MacMahon home. Since my last visit, there have been changes, chiefly the arrival of Lorna's new home – a cool glass and steel structure which seems to have landed like a fabulous space ship among the plants without ruffling so much as a leaf. It gives the garden a completely new appearance; the coupling of hard-edged contemporary architecture and trained jungle is a great success. The sight, out of the corner of an eye, of a metal span or an expanse of clear glass contrasts brilliantly with the rampant plant life. If Tarzan and Jane lived in the twenty-first century, this might be their jungle home.

The first of the different garden rooms is a dry gravel garden, made up of low-growing heathers, tall grasses and evergreen shrubs such as *Chamaecyparis filifera*, with long, string-like leaves. Lorna has a passion for dwarf conifers – as well as a serious bone to pick with the nurseries that sell fast-growing giants to unsuspecting novice gardeners under the impression that they are buying dwarf trees.

From here, the garden quickly morphs into the hot stuff border, an exuberant flourish of kniphofia, plum-coloured opium poppies or *Papaver somniferum*, agapanthus, erigeron and South African plants that include watsonia and wine-coloured hemerocallis.

Running downhill from the building, there are umbrellas of azalea draped with red sheets of *Tropaeolum speciosum*. Catch the wonderful contrast between massive gunnera leaves and fine *Acer japonicum* 'Aconitifolium' leaves. This particular tree once lived elsewhere in the garden until Lorna decided that it would look better near the house. Uprooted with the help of an obliging man called Tommy, it is now known as 'Tommy's tree'.

The path runs past a chamaecyparis being scrambled over by a big *Rosa* 'Albertine', between layered shrubs and trees that gradually grow into a dark wooded canopy. Making its way through this, the trail emerges into the pond garden. Here, the damp earth encourages wild growth among giant hostas and astilbes as they fight for space with candelabra primulas. The primulas grow in what Lorna calls 'disease proportions'. All these plants combine to produce a lush abundance that is almost overwhelming. One remarkable small tree in an opening here is the *Rubus lineatus*, which carries singular, ridged foliage.

The path continues into the fern garden, a dark, wet spot, and from there out to a sunny opening full of prehistoric-looking restios and a weeping *Fitzroya cupressoides*, an unusual tree to see in Ireland.

'The whole idea here is to go from light to shade and back out into the light again,' explains Lorna. At this point the trail reaches a little stream that runs into the moss garden. Moss is a natural phenomenon which looks so beautiful that Lorna rightly wonders why so many people try to get rid of it, rather than encouraging it.

Next, we arrive at the stone lantern garden, inspired by the Japanese style, uninterrupted by flower. A small stone bridge links this with 'Harry's garden', which Lorna made in the late 1990s as a memorial to her late husband. The obliging landowner next door sold her an extra piece of rough land to create it. Lorna thinks he was intrigued by what might come of it. No doubt he is impressed. In the place of gorse, bramble and rough grass, there is now a collection of plants gifted from family and friends, from golden acers and blue Himalayan poppies to beautiful francoa and a large flowering stewartia. Meanwhile, around all this exoticism, birch and hawthorn provide a native plant border between the cultivated garden and the rough wilds that surround it.

Climbing up and down the formidable hills over which the garden is draped, on narrow little paths, the fact that Lorna, a tiny woman, manages to cart and carry, hump and tote plants, tools and wheelbarrows around the place, only makes it more impressive. Anyone else would want a staff of at least four.

CASHEL HOUSE | CASHEL, CONNEMARA, COUNTY GALWAY

Contact: Kay and Lucy McEvilly
Tel: (+353) 095 31 001
e-mail: info@cashel-house-hotel.com
www: www.cashel-house-hotel.com

Open: Contact for details.
Special features: Garden courses. Hotel.
Directions: South off the N59 between Oughterard and Clifden. Well signposted.

Driving from Oughterard to Cashel, passing Lough Corrib, a string of smaller lakes, the ever-changing Maumturk Mountains and the indented Atlantic coast, one might question the need to hunt out a cultivated garden in the middle of such overwhelming natural beauty. But, like the sheep that seem to own the pock-marked roads, the garden at Cashel House holds its own very nicely within a wooded boundary out on the bog.

Seen from the drive, the house looks as though it has flowers and shrubs climbing through its windows and doors. The paths are invisible behind plants, making the building appear to sit in the middle of a huge bed of flowers. This effect works from inside the building too: sitting in the conservatory, masses of white lychnis, red 'ladybird' poppies and lilies grow at eye level and a little bridged stream flows past beneath them.

These spreading borders reach out from the house towards the large mixed-shrub borders and, beyond these, a rising circle of woods. I wondered about such abundant growth in the middle of desolate Connemara.

'A good dose of Epsom salts in the winter counteracts what's missing in the soil,' Mrs Kay McEvilly, the lady of the garden, confided. 'We're on pure peat,' she added, as we made our way past ranks of eucryphia and a great number of other acid-loving flowering shrubs, under a venerable-looking bay arch into the vegetable garden. This arch is only six years old and proof of the fertility here.

In the vegetable garden, the number of lesser spotted crops is interesting. And, appropriately, these are hemmed-in not by the usual box, but by sharp-leafed *Euonymus japonicus* 'Microphyllus

Variegatus', more simply known as box leaf euonymus. It hems in lines of kohlrabi, lovage, red kale, Florence fennel and sorrel – all crops destined for the hotel kitchen. I admired a sweep of lavender and assumed it was being grown for cut flowers or potpourri. In fact they grow lavender to make ice-cream. A backing wall of *Rosa* 'Wedding Day' and *R.* 'Rambling Rector' encloses the space.

At the top of the vegetable garden, Kay put in an experimental fruit garden. In a 6x5x2-metre triangle she grows pears, apples, gooseberries, cranberries and strawberries, with space to spare. This is worth an inspection by anyone planning to grow a small fruit garden.

My great discovery here was the supersonic rabbit deterrent. This is a device which sends out a screeching sound that scares rabbits away while being inaudible to people.

'It's fabulous. Until I put it in the rabbits ploughed through and ate everything I sowed! There's one spot that the beams don't reach, so they still manage to devour the plants there!' she said.

Flanking the other side of the house is what looks like a dense wood. But stepping into it reveals an almost hollowed-out woodland garden, with camellias under-planted with hostas and primulas. The wooden benches by the path are all made from trees that fell during storms – they lost a hundred trees alone in one big storm in 1998.

'When we began clearing the felled trees and branches, we discovered a number of big tree ferns we didn't even know we had,' Kay told me.

This is a large garden that has been cultivated for more than a hundred years, the sort of place where a sizable grove of impressive tree ferns can conceivably be lost under vegetation and lie undisturbed for decades. Among the tall ferns there are loads of other precious items: take your pick from the tallest robinia on the island, a huge *Davidia involucrata*, an enchanting stream garden full of primulas or an old moss-covered well.

We made our way along, stepping out of the quiet shade and into the dazzle of a sunny area called Mary's garden. In the summer, this is a highlight – a special flower garden created at the edge of the woods – an explosion of delphiniums, lupins, phlox and roses all melting together to make a garden that almost blinds the visitor as they emerge out of the dark wood. It was made as a tribute to Kay's sister, Mary, herself a keen gardener, who died several years ago. This sort of mad flower garden was exactly the sort of place that Mary loved to work. It is as alive with bees and wildlife as it is with flowers. As we sat in the middle of all this flower and perfume, some American students walked by and congratulated Kay for the '*awesome* garden'.

KYLEMORE ABBEY | CONNEMARA, COUNTY GALWAY

Contact: Reception **Tel:** (+353) 095 41 146
e-mail: info@kylemoreabbey.ie
www: www.kylemoreabbey.com
Open: Grounds, daily all year 10am-5pm.
Garden, mid-March to October.

See web for annual dates. **Special features:**
Partially wheelchair accessible. Restaurant. Tea
rooms. Gift shops. Castle. **Directions:** On the
Leenane to Clifden road (N59), 9k from Leenane.

Knowing the romantic story of Mitchell Henry and his purchase of the lands at Kylemore Abbey for his wife Margaret adds something special to visiting this garden. In 1852, while they were honeymooning in Connemara, Margaret fell in love with the region – and so ten years later Mitchell Henry bought 9,000 acres and built her a castle on it. But this achievement involved more than dewy-eyed romanticism and deep pockets. Henry imposed an impressive demesne on the rough land at the foot of the Twelve Pins, employing hundreds of workers to realise his vision, which was completed in 1871. The story ended sadly, however. Margaret only lived to enjoy her extravagant gift until 1875 when, on a trip to Egypt, she died of Nile fever. Mitchell Henry sold the property and left.

At the beginning of World War I, the Irish Benedictine nuns, who had been in Ypres since the Reformation, fled their war-torn base in Belgium. They moved to Ireland, where they bought Kylemore and opened a boarding school for girls.

In the garden, a lack of manpower and money inevitably led to deterioration despite the best efforts of successive gardeners. In 1996, however, the rot was stopped. Studying some of the famous Lawrence Collection photographs taken at the turn of the twentieth century, and with money from the Great Gardens of Ireland Restoration Fund, the nuns set out to save the walled garden. Today it is perhaps as handsome as when it was created.

The first section is quite different from traditional walled gardens in that there are no tall, herbaceous borders. Instead, this is an example of Victorian formal bedding where annuals are grown in massive numbers to create borders that look rather like geometric floral carpets. Height is scarce and delivered by tall cordylines, phormiums, trachycarpus, tree ferns and in one area an unusual, large metal circular trellis festooned with hanging baskets. This seasonal garden is interesting from an historical perspective if it is not quite in keeping with current popular tastes.

Two of the original twenty greenhouses have been restored and house tender plants, not to mention cats asleep on the electric propagation heat mats. The footprints of most of the others are all that remain, with intriguing-looking bits of pipes and sumps and the remains of Victorian heating and watering systems.

Three features worth investigating are the restored gardener's house, a tool shed and the bothy. The gardener's house is a reproduction of the house the head gardener lived in, complete with its own little flower garden. It is fully furnished, true to period and illustrative of everyday life for a person of the head gardener's standing. The bothy, on the other hand, was home to the garden boys – who had to sleep close to the boilers they had to stoke twenty-four hours a day to keep the glasshouses constantly warm. And as for the tool shed, horticultural anoraks will always enjoy a display of old and obscure implements.

Walled and kitchen gardens are often placed a distance from the house. In the case of Kylemore, the garden is two kilometres away. Documentation does not explain the great distance, but one theory is that Mitchell Henry wanted it to have the best possible backdrop: he positioned it so that Diamond Hill could be seen in its full glory from the garden. Today, a shuttle bus brings visitors on the long road leading to it. More energetic visitors can walk to it through the woods if they wish.

History never stands still, and the day I revisited Kylemore, a celebratory dinner was being held for ex-pupils of the school. The Abbey has now ceased to function as a school, but as one chapter ends, another begins. Since 2001, the fruit and vegetable gardens have been fully restored; they are now among the best examples on the island. Healthy vegetables grown in handsome arrangements have become something of a highlight for many garden visitors. Kylemore's kitchen garden, laid out on a slope, is worth taking a serious detour to visit and the sight of a nun marching through with a trug full of carrots and onions reminds us that this garden still serves its original purpose – feeding the residents of the Abbey – along with being a huge tourist attraction. The adjacent water, woodland and fern gardens are also beautiful.

There are extensive woodland walks. Mitchell Henry planted a great oak wood, as well as plantations of lime and beech, Sitka spruce, alder, native wych elm (*Ulmus glabra*) and Monterey pine. The nuns continue the plantations to this day, concentrating on oak.

Portumna Castle Gardens | Portumna, County Galway

Contact: Reception or Ruth Carty
Tel: (+353) 0909 741 658 / 741 625
e-mail: portumnacastle@opw.ie
Open: April to October 10am-6pm daily.
Group tours can be arranged. Supervised children
welcome. Dogs on leads.

Special features: Working kitchen garden.
Castle. Craft gardening courses.
Directions: Situated in Portumna Castle Park on
the edge of Portumna town. Follow the signs from
Abbey Street.

Richard Burke, 4th Earl of Clanricarde, began to build Portumna Castle and its gardens in 1618 on an impressive site overlooking Lough Derg, bordering Galway and Tipperary. The castle is one of the finest surviving examples of an Irish semi-fortified house of this period. The grounds are thought to have been laid out in the most modern and fashionable style of the time, as his wife had come from the court of Elizabeth and as a result was *au fait* with court fashions.

The gardens are divided into two distinctive areas. The first is a re-creation of a formal Jacobean garden laid out to the front of the castle. It is a smart, substantial array of well proportioned paths and geometric beds of roses. Visited in the middle of a massive downpour, it was magnificent and the heavy scent of the roses, from the raspberry ripple-coloured *Rosa mundi* to *Rosa* 'Chapeau de Napoleon', filled the garden. Neatly raked gravel paths and smart lawns foil the exuberant rose beds perfectly. The house itself towers impressively over it all and standing on its steps, though it takes the house out of the picture, is the best ways to overlook this gorgeous garden.

The second area is a walled kitchen garden. It is sited through a gate in the wall of the formal garden. To say that the difference in style between the two is dramatic would be something of an understatement.

Walking into Portumna's kitchen garden is like entering into the middle of a riot after having just attended a deportment class. The explosion of foliage, flower, colour and sheer variety is a joy. Neglected for over a hundred years, restoration on the kitchen garden began back in 1996 under the care of a number of local organic enthusiasts. The aim was to produce, as much as possible, an authentic seventeenth-century kitchen garden and so period techniques and plants were used to a large degree. Archaeological research led to the discovery of ancient seed in the soil, and the Irish Seed Savers Association helped to source heritage seeds using that information. Meanwhile, many of the old paths, including a turning circle for a pony and cart, were uncovered and restored.

Today, following years of development, the kitchen garden is a delight – full of vegetables, fruit grown in little orchard areas, billowing herbaceous borders and arbours draped in sweet jasmine, roses and honeysuckle. Even on days when there are plenty of visitors around, the seclusion of each little part of the walled garden means that a visitor always feels as though they have the place to themselves. I adore this beautiful garden and its happy tangle of plants.

 COUNTY MAYO

TURLOUGH PARK MUSEUM OF COUNTRY LIFE |
TURLOUGH, CASTLEBAR, COUNTY MAYO

Contact: The manager **Tel:** (+353) 094 903 1755
e-mail: tpark@museum.ie
Open: Tuesday to Saturday 10am-5pm /
Sunday 2pm-5pm
Special Features: Museum of country life.

Galleries. Cafe. Shop. **Directions:** Take the N5 out of Castlebar for about 6 km. Follow the signs for Horkins. At Horkins, take the left turn and the museum is a little way down that road on the left. Signposted.

I came across Turlough Park for the first time about ten years ago. I pulled into the drive only to be chased away by earth movers and diggers busily working on some grand-scale landscaping venture. The results, now that they have matured, are, to say the least, well worth seeing.

The drive in, under mature park trees, runs past a little boating lake, which I recognised as the reason for the excavations back in 2000. The garden itself comes into view with a great flourish as one emerges from the car park through barriers of hedging and trees. The first sight is of an immaculately tended grand Victorian garden. The big house stands ahead, overlooking a long run of perfect, rolled and striped lawn and well maintained paths. There are smart island beds, full of bedding plants, cut into the lawn at regular intervals with all the attendant in-your-face colours we associate with old-fashioned Victorian municipal-style beds.

Overlooking these flower beds is a fine sized greenhouse, stuffed to capacity with a range of tender plants arranged beautifully on staging. Pelargoniums, chillies of all sorts, birds of paradise or *Strelitzia reginae* and waxy hoyas rub shoulders with ruby-coloured *Rhodochiton atrosanguineus*, strange-looking *Corokia virgata* and *Echium fatuosum*. When we dream of owning the perfect greenhouse, it usually looks like this. Unlike many of the better greenhouses around the country, this one is open to visitors without having to seek special permission and advance booking. The well maintained feature stands in front of some majestically tall sweet chestnut, oak and ash.

Walking in the direction of the house and museum, one path leads under a trellised arch into a completely concealed garden room. This enclosure is home to a flamboyant flower garden. Two mirroring borders full of all the usual herbaceous perennials run the length of the long rectangular space. There are lupins, monarda, acanthus, phlox, salvias and a host of other great border plants. One of the borders is backed by a beech hedge with towering park trees behind it. The other side holds an altogether more intriguing sight – the vine house. Inside, a massive climbing *Pelargonium* 'Lord Bute' takes up a great deal of space. It is like a plant of raspberry ripple. Beside it, almost fluorescent blue plumbago bracts contrast richly with the dark pink flowers and between them they fill an entire room in the house. The other room houses a big, healthy fruiting peach.

The lake takes up the other side of the grounds, led to by steeply terraced lawns. Beyond these there are views of the lake, a round tower in the distance and forty acres of wooded walks to explore. The garden is yet another that was lucky enough to receive help from the Great Gardens of Ireland Restoration Scheme, the European Development Fund and Bord Fáilte, while the house has become home to the Irish Museum of Country Life. Money well spent.

✺ COUNTY ROSCOMMON

STROKESTOWN HOUSE | STROKESTOWN, COUNTY ROSCOMMON

Contact: Head gardener
Tel: (+353) 071 963 3013
e-mail: info@strokestownpark.ie
www: www.strokestownpark.ie
Open: March to October. Check website for seasonal times. **Special features:** Wheelchair accessible. Museum. Plants for sale. Restaurant. Accommodation. **Directions:** Situated in the middle of the village of Strokestown on the N5.

The Pakenham family moved to Strokestown in the 1660s, when they were given huge tracts of land by King Charles II of England for services rendered to his father, Charles I. Over the centuries, the family built, improved and added to the impressive Strokestown House, a process that culminated in the nineteenth century when they decided that one of the tiniest villages in Ireland should have one of the widest boulevards in Europe. The street, forty-four-and-a-half metres wide, rivalling the Champs Élysées in Paris, was indicative of the grandeur the Pakenhams aspired to, living between Roscommon and London.

Strokestown House is an intriguing place that conjures up images of feast and famine. Once at the heart of some of the most dreadful suffering experienced during the Great Famine of the 1840s, today the outhouses and stable blocks – once known as 'equine cathedrals' – provide the venue for the country's most comprehensive Famine museum. This is slightly ironic, as the family's record during the Famine years was not exactly unblemished: Major Denis Mahon, responsible for clearing tenants from his estates, was assassinated in 1847 for his efforts.

The walled garden can be dated to the 1740s, when it was used to grow fruit and vegetables, with a smaller 'slip garden' of glasshouses growing peaches, melons and grapes. In 1890 it was converted into a fine pleasure garden. But by around 1940, lack of manpower and money led to the almost complete loss of its once impeccable croquet lawns, rose beds and ponds. Sheep and cattle moved in to graze where the immaculate flowerbeds once stood.

But Mrs Olive Pakenham-Mahon, born to Strokestown at the turn of the century, was still living in the decaying old house which was caught in a sort of time-bubble. She sold it, a fascinating piece of social history, to local business man Jim Callery. He then set about restoring Strokestown and as a result the house moved into the twenty-first century in good shape.

Apart from the restoration and preservation of the house, a huge restoration project was carried out on the four-acre walled garden in partnership with the Great Gardens of Ireland Restoration Scheme. This massive undertaking was well documented on television and attracted a great deal of interest in the late 1980s when it was carried out. We watched as decades of debris were scraped away to reveal the original garden paths and as the bones of the garden were pulled into place and set back together. The work continued after the cameras moved out and the matured results can be seen today.

The walled garden is entered through an ornamental gate, made in 1914, with the words 'EK Harmon' worked into the lacy ironwork. This was a gift to Olive Pakenham-Mahon from her fiancé, Edward Stafford-King-Harmon, who would die in the trenches at Ypres, Belgium shortly after their marriage. Its poignant presence sets the tone for a walk through the romantic old garden. The gate opens onto wide paths of gravel, lined with yews backed by beech hedges and leading down to a formal lily pond that dates to the 1780s.

The south-facing herbaceous border is the biggest in Ireland and Britain, according to the *Guinness Book of World Records*, and is based on the original 1890s border. As an advertisement for organic gardening, the border couldn't be more spectacular. It includes large stands of heavily scented nodding crinum lilies and plume poppies or macleaya. In August, yellows and oranges come into their own and the bed puts on a great late summer and autumn show. Huge fennel plants, ligularia with acid yellow flowers on top of black stems, red-hot pokers or kniphofia, golden rod, solidago, fringed inula flowers and red geum shout at each other for attention. It is a spectacular bed.

The summerhouse in the centre of the walled garden was copied faithfully from an old photograph of Olive Pakenham-Mahon as a small girl, sitting outside the original with her nanny. On the lawn, the old croquet hoops stand about, conjuring up a picture of genteel, turn-of-the-century summer garden parties. (Once upon a time it took eight men to tend this lawn.) A salvaged window from the house was turned into a folly that looks across the pond and yew walk.

The rose garden is made up of new hybrid teas, old roses climbing over obelisks and hanging in swags on ropes. The pergola is made of local stone and Irish oak.

The *allée* of beech trees, with two serpentine lengths of hedging spanning the width of the garden, is unusual. It contains a series of niches or bays, each of which was designed to take a piece of sculpture. Close by, the beech hedge maze is fun to wander through.

A gateway in the wall leads into the slip garden, where restoration work on the old glasshouses has now been completed. These had been in ruins since the 1930s; they needed a considerable amount of work and thankfully received it. Today, big runs of agapanthus grow outside, while inside there are vines and peaches. The substantial vegetable garden rounds off the garden and a collection of old garden tools will be of interest to many gardeners. The final feature is an unusual Georgian teahouse, the first-floor tearoom of which is reached by an outside staircase. As the saying goes, the urge to begin building follies is God's way of telling us that we have too much money. So restoring the follies must mean that every other job is complete.

 County Sligo

LISSADELL | BALLINFULL, COUNTY SLIGO

Contact: Isobel Cassidy **Tel:** (+353) 071 916 3150
e-mail: info@lissadellhouse.com
www: www.lissadellhouse.com
Open: On a restricted basis. See website for annual details. **Special features:** Museum.

Exhibition gallery. Café. Plants and produce for sale. Potato collection.

Directions: Drive 7km north from Sligo on the N15 (Bundoran Road). Go through the village of Carney and turn left at the sign for Lissadell.

For most Irish people, the name Lissadell conjures up pictures of the historic, literary and political worlds, W.B. Yeats, Maud Gonne, Lady Gregory and Countess Markievicz. But its horticultural history is just as compelling. Since the 1900s, Lissadell was home to a commercial seed potato, alpine and bulb growing business, a centre of general horticultural excellence as well as home to Lady Gore-Booth's School of Needlework. The plant lists were famous and the Lissadell method of growing rare alpines was particularly admired, as they were grown outside in the rock garden in specially built peat beds rather than under protected glass. The bulbs, particularly the daffodils, were equally famous, winning prizes at shows in Ireland and England.

Unfortunately, due to declining family fortunes, bad health and legal troubles, these enterprises dwindled away and the gardens went into serious decline from the mid-twentieth century. In 2003 the almost derelict house and garden were bought by Edward Walsh and Constance Cassidy. Working a brand of magic they should probably bottle, they have spent the years bringing the house and gardens back to life with the help of a small but busy team. In the garden, there was input from some of the country's best horticultural minds. The results have created one of the best garden visits on the island and a place worthy of the great horticultural heritage it stems from.

The drive from the village of Carney builds excitement in a way that would be unfair if the garden at the other end were not up to par. With the sea and Ben Bulben on one side and garden walls on the other, the way leads through the gate and onto a drive under an avenue of elegant trees, downhill to the house. The restored cobble drains along the drive's edge have to be seen – they are like little works of art.

Lissadell House is a strange, slightly forbidding, blocky house that feels like it must be overrun with ghosts. Overlooking the water and an expanse of lawn, there is no trace of fluff and flower around it.

For these, visit the walled kitchen garden and then, for a real fix, the alpine yard. The kitchen garden is surrounded by expansive yards and multiple ranges of greenhouses. One of these has been restored and there are plans for the others. Meanwhile, inside the walls, the decorous vegetable beds are, like the whole estate, worked organically. The two-and-a-half acres are divided by cross-paths and mature espaliered apple trees. They grow a broad range of vegetables, many of which are then sold to local restaurants and sold from the courtyard shop when the garden is open. The beds are laid out with military precision and home growers will learn a lot studying them.

The star of the walled garden, however, is the potato collection. It comprises over 180 varieties, grown along two of the walls. The collection runs chronologically, starting with varieties bred in 1798 and working up to the modern Irish cultivars bred in the past few years. Each variety is described in detail on plaques beside the beds. They are grown in buckets sunken into

the ground for ease of identification and so that the compost can be easily refreshed each year. In winter, the sunken empty buckets show fascinatingly how the high water table works on this damp sloped garden.

The path past the ha-ha, through the wildflower meadow on the way to the alpine yard, is a feature in itself, but there are enough distractions in the alpine yard to fascinate one indefinitely. It is terraced in places to accommodate the land as it slopes down towards the sea. At the top of the garden, a number of beds are held up on dry stone walls. These walls are themselves planted up with all sorts of vertical-growing plants, from dripping alpines and hummocks of saxifrages to miniature daphnes.

On the beds overhead there are David Austin roses and prairie-like wild loose plantings of grasses and herbaceous plants. The three-level stepped pond, made in the mid-eighteenth century, is a most unusual and pretty feature about which little is known.

Downhill from these is the alpine yard proper, including the crevice garden. There are very few examples of crevice gardens in Ireland. (See 17 Drumnamallaght Road, County Antrim.) A visit to Lissadell should be a priority for anyone interested in the art of creating these complicated features. The Lissadell crevice beds are intricate and fascinating, perfect for up-close inspection.

There are seas of good-looking alpines, like ramonda and oxalis, a score of different sedums and saxifrages and countless other small treasures ranged about. Meanwhile, the clambering rock beds are also delightful. Towering *Echium pininana* and helianthemums or rock roses and bulbs of all sorts fill these hilly beds. Early in the year there are examples of rare miniature narcissi.

The mounds of stone used to create these features were already present when the restoration work began. It just had to be dug out from under decades of debris and freed from under the huge trees that had sprouted throughout the place. Old photos of the features as they once looked were used in the reconstruction and re-planting.

Working this garden organically, it is particularly difficult to eradicate horsetail, and the gardeners are constantly digging at it, trying to wear it down.

Out in the wider estate, there have been so many restoration projects carried out: from the planting of 14,000 oak and Scots pine and the conservation of rare orchids to the restoration of a collection of heritage daffodils. Stone walls are being restored and rebuilt everywhere, and an old stone reservoir, filled by natural streams on the land, has even been re-activated. Lastly, a Victorian water ram, which drove water around the estate, has been pulled back into service.

It was planned that Lissadell would be open year-round as a preserved house, exhibition space and garden, providing the north west with a world-class tourist attraction. However, a dispute with Sligo County Council over rights of way has led to the family more or less closing the garden. This is a crying shame and it must be rectified. It is now only possible to see the garden on a very restricted basis. Contact Lissadell for information about how it might be visited.

Oakfield Park

ULSTER

∞∞∞

County Antrim

Benvarden Garden |

Dervock, Ballymoney, County Antrim, BT53 6NN

Tel: (+44) 048 2074 1331
Contact: Mr and Mrs Hugh Montgomery
Open: May, by appointment. June to August, Tuesday to Sunday and bank holidays 11am-5pm. Groups should book. Children should be supervised. No dogs. **Special features:** Farm implement museum. Plants for sale. **Directions:** From the main Belfast-Coleraine road, take the B62 ring road to Portrush. At Ballybogey turn right on to the B67. Drive 2.5km. Just before the bridge over the River Bush turn right. The garden is marked by iron gates.

There is an infectious air of endeavour at Benvarden, from Mike, who takes care of both the gate and vegetable sales with great enthusiasm, to Billy, the gardener, who had no more than a minute to chat between tying in delphiniums and heading off to tend a line of sweet corn in the kitchen garden. He mightn't have had much time to speak, but the beauty of his asparagus beds spoke volumes about his abilities as a gardener.

The estate on the banks of the River Bush had a colourful start. In the 1760s it belonged to a notorious man called John McNaughton, known in local history as 'Half-Hanged' McNaughton. A Trinity student, he eloped with a fifteen-year-old heiress, Ann Knox, whom he then killed by mistake. Because of a botched execution, he was twice hanged for his crime. Benvarden was subsequently sold to the Montgomery family and they have been here ever since.

Benvarden's walled garden is one of the oldest continuously cultivated gardens on the island: the two-and-a-quarter-acre feature appears on a 1788 map drawn up by James Williamson of Dublin. Over 220 years later, it still is being worked and is a model of its type.

You enter by way of the vegetable garden, which is unusually surrounded by a fairly low wall topped with railings, so it feels quite open and airy. A greenhouses full of tender plants doubles as the ticket shop and all around it there are neat crops and plants raised in the garden for sale.

With a promise to come back and pore over the bounty, and maybe fill the boot of the car with some delphiniums, carrots, onions or apples, you can then set out to see the main attraction.

This is the ornamental walled garden. In here, the first sights that stand out are the unusual double rows of box hedging around the herb borders and flowerbeds. The outer hedges, which are clipped higher, enclose lower inner hedges like green subsets. All around the tall brick walls are deep herbaceous borders crammed with delphinium spires, spiky irises and clouds of blue and pink campanula. I love the radiating rose garden. If it was a bicycle wheel, the beds would form the triangles between the spokes and the paths would make up the knobbly stone spokes, all converging on a central fish pond and small fountain.

There are scented rose arches and walks scattered throughout, leading between busy shrub borders stuffed with hydrangea, abutilon, fuchsia and rhododendron. A pergola, laden down under wisteria, leads away from the peach and grape house. One arch dripping *Rosa* 'Paul's Scarlet Climber' is particularly pretty.

The old tennis court, built in 1920, stands in one corner, surrounded by a fence being colonised by a big *Rosa* 'Albertine'. Mr Montgomery told me that this was one of two built by his father at what was then the outrageous cost of £300. At the other end of the social scale, you can walk into the restored garden bothy. This is the little hut where the garden boy in charge of stoking the hothouse boilers would have slept.

Within the walls the space has been divided into well-defined plots. Separated from the leisured world of tennis parties, the vegetable garden is made up of industrial-sized beds. Regiments of strawberries line out along the outside of tidy lettuce beds; to pick something from these sumptuous rows would feel like a crime. The fat tomatoes, guarded by straight rows of marigolds in the greenhouse, are almost as perfectly arrayed. There are apples on the walls and a lichen-covered sundial that has been telling the time on sunny days since 1705.

Leaving the walled garden by a little gate in the wall, you find yourself out in the pleasure grounds. These include a grass path walk down through yew, copper beech, pine, rhododendron and willow. It leads to a woodland pond festooned with ferns, primulas and other moisture-loving plants. This is a peaceful, quiet place made up of glittery water, dappled light and wildlife. The path then trails along towards the River Bush and an elegant iron bridge with a thirty-metre span. This was built in 1878, a testament to splendid Victorian engineering and design.

Brocklamont House |
2 Old Galgorm Road, Ballymena, County Antrim

··

Contact: Mrs Margaret Glynn
Tel: (+44) 048 2564 1459 / 079 775 11579
Open: May to September by appointment. Groups welcome. Children must be supervised. Dogs on leads. Occasional plants for sale.

Directions: Leaving Ballymena on the A42 to Portglenone, the garden is 0.75km outside the town on the right and marked by black iron gates, opposite the Ballymena Academy.

The house on Old Galgorm Road is a classic Victorian villa overlooking a two-and-a-half-acre garden. This is Margaret Glynn's creation. She is a talented gardener with a feel for both plants and design.

Enter through big old gates, past a small gravel garden, carpeted with *Viola labradorica*, Corsican mint, campanula, sedums and cushions of hepatica. From here, one's attention is drawn up and off towards tall stands of trees and sloped lawns punctuated by shrub borders and flowers. It is a very inviting garden.

Mrs Glynn's favourite plants are, in order, irises, hellebores and geraniums. She grows scores of each. She also grows a breathtaking three hundred types of galanthus. Ferns are favourites too and, as well as fitting them into corners throughout the garden, she has built a fernery at the bottom of one of the slopes. This is a damp area under an umbrella-shaped canopy of Japanese acer and magnolia. The ferns, like so many green shuttlecocks, are beautiful.

Overhead, sky-dusting pines lead the eye back upwards. These trees have been busily growing since my last visit ten years ago. As they grew, Mrs Glynn regularly pruned them to create more scope for under-storey planting. Pruning-up also permits the creation of a whole network of views and vistas through the trees, back and forth across the garden. Through one opening, the view will be of a bridged pool and a wedding cake tree or *Cornus controversa* 'Variegata' teamed up with white hydrangea. Through another, there might be the view of open lawns falling down and away, edged by low-clipped lonicera hedges. In yet another direction the picture will be of a little wood run riot with primulas, trilliums and aquilegias.

There is a giddy abundance of troughs around the house. Troughs done well are always a pleasure to see and there are so many perfect examples here, like rows of miniature gardens, filled with fun-sized alpines. Cleverly used chunky pots and gravel beds accommodate even more pint-sized plants. Mrs Glynn is a keen member of the Alpine Plants Society; it is clear that she knows her stuff and it is a joy to see that knowledge at work.

The old walled garden has been converted and part of it is now a patio and terrace garden aimed to catch every bit of available sun. On either side of the patio are two borders, herbaceous on one side and annual on the other. Someone called this the Botticelli garden – the two flower-filled expanses are simply voluptuous, with mixed poppies, cosmos, periwinkles and osteospermum elbowing for attention.

One last thing: remember to ask to see the compost system. This is the smartest and most tidy-looking set-up I have ever encountered, made of long, deep galvanised metal bins. One bin is filled with newly composted material beginning the process of rotting down, while the other bay is the home of the mature, sweet-smelling, dark-brown compost ready to go to work in the garden.

Ballyrobert Cottage Garden and Nursery |
154 Ballyrobert Road, Ballyclare, County Antrim, BT39 9RT

Contact: Joy and Maurice Parkinson
Tel: (+44) 048 9332 2952
e-mail: maurice@ballyrobertcottagegarden.co.uk
www: www.ballyrobertcottagegarden.co.uk
Open: March to September daily. Other times by appointment. Groups welcome.

Children must be supervised. Dogs on leads.
Special features: Plant nursery. Teas by arrangement. **Directions:** Just under 1km from the centre of Ballyrobert village on the Ballyclare Road, opposite the golf club entrance.

Marrying a garden of cultivated flowers to the wild countryside that surrounds it is not easy. If planted up without care, it can jar badly with its surroundings and even look garish. Ideally, it should blend in, almost unnoticed, from the outer boundary. But this is unusual. The Parkinsons could give lessons on the practice of blending a garden into the countryside.

Maurice and Joy Parkinson have been working here since the early 1990s. The venture started out as a cottage garden attached, appropriately enough, to a traditional old farm cottage and series of old outhouses Maurice located on the Ordnance Survey map of 1833. Close to the house, the style is still one of a classic cottage garden. Walking through it is like walking through a sea of old-fashioned flowers. The abundance of bloom and colour, scent and foliage, busy with butterflies and bees, is intoxicating. It is the very picture of a chocolate box garden. But as it travels out from the house, the garden becomes more native, wild and loose, until it finally meets with and melts into the rough Ballyclare landscape. This knitting of the two appears seamless and natural, but the work that produced that seemingly easy transition from cultivation to wilds was considerable.

The area in front of the house is called the field garden. This is made up of large mixed beds divided by grass paths so perfect they could be used as putting greens. The beds are chock-full of herbaceous favourites, like lupins, asters and irises, hollyhocks and violas. The individual beds are divided by colour and the most striking is the 'hot' bed, full of reds and wines, from plum-coloured hemerocallis and red crocosmia to chocolate cosmos (*Cosmos atrosanguineus*), a plant that smells like a big bar of the very best dark chocolate.

Tucked behind the house, there is a box garden full of more old favourite flowers, a dovecote, the beautifully restored old barn and some well made examples of cobbled paths. Apart from the old house and barn, the garden features some interesting antique iron farm gates with distinctive gate pillars peculiar to this part of Antrim.

At the outer edge of each of these gardens, the cultivated plants begin to butt up against wilder natives to dramatic effect. The contrast between bowling-green lawns and loose meadows full of buttercups and wild grass is as sharp as a knife. In the formal garden, the fronts of the beds are edged in clipped box while the backs are marked by undulating old field-stone walls, behind which a native wood trails off into a meadow and on out to the rough fields.

The flowerbeds are backed by a mix of exotic and native small trees. The balance between import and native shifts gradually from the cultivated to the wild: Japanese acers and magnolias marry with, and then are replaced by, hawthorn, blackthorn, ash and native birch.

The orchard is the sort of unusual feature that the lazy gardener would delight in. Maurice planted apple trees into raised mounds of compost simply laid down on the soil in a rough field out at the edge of the garden. Keeping the mounds weed-free is all that needs to be done while the young trees romp along, growing strong in the rich soil before their roots hit the surrounding field. This seems like the opposite to back-breaking, labour-intensive gardening.

Out by the lake garden, the feel is very much more native. There are expansive wildflower meadows and the views over little stiles, beyond the boundary, are of the rushes and wild grass from which the Parkinsons' wrested their garden. The feel they have for their surroundings is impressive.

17 DRUMNAMALLAGHT ROAD | BALLYMONEY, COUNTY ANTRIM

Contact: Mrs Dorothy Brown
Tel: (+44) 048 2766 2923
www: www.ulstergardensscheme.org.uk
Open: All year by appointment only. Groups preferred. Not suitable for children. No dogs.
Special features: Alpine plants for sale.
Directions: On appointment.

Mrs Brown has been tending her small suburban garden, growing and minding some very hard-to-mind plants, since the late 1990s. Like a small diamond, it gleams. Despite its size, I think I could discover something new here no matter how many times I visited.

We stood in the front garden looking at an arrangement of troughs overflowing with alpines and miniature plants, ancient-looking gnarled, tiny shrubs, rockery arrangements I could cheerfully kill for and just an occasional flower. Mrs Brown introduced it by explaining that the initial idea had been to create a scree garden, planting everything directly into the ground. But the soil proved too wet for that plan. The garden is on the boundary of the Leslie Hill estate and enjoys the shelter of its mature trees. But it also lies at the bottom of a hill and is, as a result, soggy and damp. The answer to the problem lay in planting the alpines, which crave free-draining soil, in troughs and raised beds, pots and other containers.

She propagates a lot of her plants. Many of them are hard to come by in the first place, so talent with seed is vital for a gardener who wants to specialise. Among some of the more beautiful small plants we studied, there were gorgeous green pillows of *Azorella trifurcata*. They grow like little jade hills in the gravel.

Given that so many of the plants are hard to grow, anything that sets seed is welcome and allowed to do so freely. Only then does she take out those plants that have grown in unsuitable spots. The effect of this is that everything *looks* natural, even in troughs.

The main garden to the back of the house includes a perfect small lawn surrounded by shrubs, small trees and an overstuffed lily-and-iris pond. But good as these are, they are really only the backdrop to the cabinet of curiosities that is her collection of pots, troughs and planters.

Mrs Brown has a particular talent for arranging containers – an underestimated skill that most of us discover we do not possess until we try. I was particularly taken by a collection of small acers in pots gathered on a set of steps. The combination of differing shapes, spreads, leaf-colours and textures put together, makes one study each plant individually more than one would an isolated

specimen. The conservatory, a calm place to sit in summer, cannot be accessed in the winter because of all the migrants. This is because many of the plants are exotic and tender and need to take sanctuary in winter.

But at the same time, many are simply exotic and *tender-looking*. We bent down to inspect the crevice garden. Crevice gardening is widely practised in eastern Europe, but not seen often in Ireland. Slates are laid on end and inter-filled with gritty compost to create crevices into which tiny alpines, miniature bonsai and other fun-sized plants can be insinuated. I suspect that it is very hard to get the look right, but Mrs Brown has the knack. The small pans of plants are like self-contained miniature worlds. In these she grows exquisite fuchsias the size of teacups and tiny willows with a 30cm spread. Elsewhere an arrangement of succulents on a series of ledges looks like a sweet-shop display. Dorothy Brown works in her garden from first thing in the morning to nightfall, nipping, tweaking and keeping it perfect. It shows.

GLENARM CASTLE | GLENARM, COUNTY ANTRIM

Contact: Jane Jenkins **Tel:** (+44) 048 2884 1203
e-mail: jane@glenarmcastle.com
www: www.glenarmcastle.com
Open: May to September, Monday to Saturday 10am-5pm. Groups welcome. Children must be supervised. Dogs on leads.

Special features: Tearoom. Gift shop. Plants for sale. Highland games. Tulip Festival. Food weekend. **Directions:** Glenarm is on the A2, north of Larne. The castle is in the village. Special parking facilities for disabled drivers.

Glenarm Castle is set at the foot of one of the Glens of Antrim in one of the most stunning settings on the island. The drive around the coast along the A2 is a rare pleasure, devoid of ribbon development and glaring new houses. The peace only needs to be shared with a few stray sheep and the occasional boy racer. This drive would be reason enough to make a visit to Glenarm even if the gardens weren't there.

Thankfully, that is not the case. The first time I visited, I approached from the wrong direction, and drove up a little road in the village, arriving at a bridge over what looked like a moat. (It is in fact a river.) At the other side of the bridge is the most wonderfully elaborate castellated gate lodge. This not-so-little building was erected in the 1820s in a rich Gothic style complete with arrow slits, battlements and a portcullis. This was clearly created with more than the needs of a humble gatekeeper in mind. It was also designed as a place of entertainment, possibly a banqueting room. Make a point of detouring in the village to see it before heading for the main entrance to the castle gardens.

In a *Top of the Pops*-style countdown of the best gardens on the island, the walled garden at Glenarm would certainly be in the toss-up for the Number One slot. Dating back to the mid-eighteenth century and covering four acres, this is a true *tour de force*. You enter via the former mushroom house, today set up to serve teas. This white-washed building, along with the gardener's cottage and a line of potting sheds, overlooks the first small walled garden, an area largely devoted to perfect vegetable beds. Sitting with a cup of tea and a big slice of cake, before setting off to oversee lines of Swiss chard, artichokes, strawberries, fat carrots and lettuce, is always a good plan. The wall-

trained roses can be inspected from this vantage point too; these are deep, quartered, plum-coloured flowers, and so pretty they look artificial. They look even more beautiful married with same-colour annual sweet pea. At the top of the garden there is a huge fig in place of a long-dismantled old greenhouse. A modest lip of glass on top of the wall protects the fig from the weather and probably contributes to the good crops it delivers.

In the big garden over the wall there are still long lengths of intact greenhouse. Pacing them out, they measure almost 100 metres in length. Those 100 metres hold vines, spectacularly good apricots, peaches, climbers and iridescent blue plumbago. Outside the glass, a long ribbon of blue nepeta or catmint runs the length of the building. I was told that they cut the nepeta back in July to encourage it to throw up a second flush of flowers in September. On the other side of the path that borders this are tall pleached limes, lined out like a hedge on stilts.

From here we begin to explore the rest of the walled garden, beginning with some mixed beds of well-matched colours. In one of these there are big clumps of pink love-lies-bleeding or amaranthus, pink everlasting sweet pea and ruby cosmos, as well as red pheasant berry or leycesteria and aubergine-coloured cotinus. Large flowering buddleia and tree peonies are used in repeat patterns over the length of the wide beds, to create continuity. Then there are beds full of purple, with *Papaver orientale* 'Patty's Plum', purple pansies, blood-red roses, purple salvia, toned down a little by more hazy-blue nepeta and pink geraniums.

The surprises are everywhere: a mirroring double border of silvers, blues, yellows and variegated foliage shrubs lines the path to a central sundial, surrounded by a tall yew circle. The circle is reputed to be the oldest in Ireland. The sundial seems to float over clumps of fennel, borage and creeping golden thyme. The trick to making this really work is that the inner planting scheme cannot be seen from outside the yew circle and it comes upon the visitor as a little bonus.

The centre of each yew section opens onto another garden room. One of these is a clever serpentine *allée* of beech hedging which leads on to a beech circle with a raised pond and fountain. That gives onto another short beech avenue. Every time the visitor thinks they have seen the full extent of this garden, another flourish appears from around a corner.

Since my last visit in 2000, there has been no let up in Glenarm's expansion. One addition is the formal stream that flows downhill between lines of gleaming white and jet black cobbles (these stones can be found in greater numbers on the beach outside the castle gates).

The next new attraction is a feature usually found in eighteenth-century landscape gardens: a viewing mound. It is climbed by means of a spiral path up to a sometimes windy point from where the whole tremendous garden can be taken in. From here, lines of newly planted box and beech walls can be seen clearly. Each of these walls encloses a fruit garden: there are individual crab apple gardens, quince gardens, mulberry gardens, and a pear garden with a circular pergola on which they are training two popular varieties, 'Conference' and 'Chanticlear'. The most remarkable of the fruit enclosures is the medlar garden, where the trees have been trained as supported two-metre standards. They would not be able to grow to this height unaided. Nearby, there is another unusual feature: box-enclosed squares of kniphofia, stipa and alliums, with one flower type per square. These are quite formal, modern and handsome.

In another direction, the mood loosens out with a wild flower meadow dissected by mown paths. Along with the native flowers, they grow vivid blue camassias in the grass. The mown paths can be seen best from the top of the viewing mound, as can the views beyond the walled garden, out to sea in one direction and onto parkland in the other. This meadow is cut to about 5cm from the ground once a year in August. The grass is left to lie and dry and drop its seed before being raked up. Yellow rattle is planted in the meadow to inhibit the grass from growing too healthily. It reduces the fertility of the soil, making it a better environment for wild grass.

Down on the ground, 8,500 tulip bulbs are planted each autumn for a tulip festival held in May. In September, they celebrate the end of the growing season with a big open food weekend, when dishes prepared from the organic produce grown in the gardens are made and sold.

Glenarm is a singular garden: ambitious, clever and attractive. Yet it is maintained by just two men. These are the remarkable Whally brothers, Billy and James, working to the designs of designer Catherine Fitzgerald and Lady Dunluce. The gardens were previously very good. Today they are stunning.

Sir Thomas and Lady Dixon Park |
Upper Malone Road, Belfast, County Antrim

· ·

Contact: Stephen Stockman
Tel: (+44) 048 9091 8768
www: www.belfastcity.gov.uk/parks
Open: All year during daylight. No entrance fee.

Children must be supervised. Dogs on leads.
Special features: Annual Rose Festival.
Directions: Located south of the city on the Upper Malone Road, signposted.

On my most recent visit to this garden, on a sunny 12 July, I was met by the sight of a dozen people gathered in the car park wearing running gear, carrying ski poles and skis. Winters have been bad recently and I could well see how a bit of cross-country skiing might be the order of the day in December. But were they planning on skiing on the grass in sunny July? It seemed that this city park finds itself called on to provide some strange facilities. It is nothing if not versatile.

The grounds and garden that make up this park were given to the city of Belfast by Lady Dixon in 1959. They were part of a demesne founded in the eighteenth century, attached to a house which is now gone. The main body of the park is made up of mature trees in rolling wood- and parkland along the banks of the River Lagan. The park is best known, however, for its rose gardens and as the home to the International Rose Trial grounds, which were set up in 1964.

For many people, rose gardens are not the easiest of gardens to love. Roses are beautiful and the scent and variety of the flowers cannot be denied, but beds full of hybrid tea roses with bare, stumpy or gangly legs are not to many people's tastes these days. The words 'beautiful' and 'rose bush' do not always sit happily together. Old shrub roses do have a more attractive shape and can look well even out of bloom, but in general we grow roses for the flowers rather than the look of the whole plant.

That said, the long runs and large beds of roses in the Sir Thomas and Lady Dixon Park work well and look good. I think it is the sheer scale of planting in the displays that is the key. The 130-acre park is an attractive and hilly place with great sweeps of lawn rising and falling in hills and hollows between groves of park trees. The rose beds, containing over 25,000 plants, run in long swathes of single colours and they roll out, up and over the hills like coloured streamers across the grass. The climbers, shrub, patio, floribunda, heritage and Irish heritage roses are all grown like with like in spirals, over festive-looking tent-supports and along pergolas.

There is a rose here for everyone, every situation and occasion. The long arched walks, dripping scented climbers and ramblers are a dream at the height of summer. Among the displays, the Dickson and McGredy rose beds take pride of place. These celebrate the enormous achievements of two famed Northern Ireland rose-breeding families. Both families have been working with roses since the 1870s and both are now in their fifth generation.

Every July the park is transformed into the buzzing home of the annual City of Belfast International Rose Trial, a huge event in the life of Northern Ireland horticulture. There are master classes in rose growing given by experts from all over, and a huge range of events, talks and walks arranged throughout the festival. It is a must for anyone with an interest in the most popularly loved flower of them all.

But the park has more to offer than roses. There are extensive camellia gardens with over one hundred varieties to be seen. (Camellia trials are held here too.) The yew walk is another notable feature and there are long sauntering trails through exotic trees and a smaller series of gardens around Malone House at the edge of the park.

My favourite feature is the Japanese garden. This was added to the park in the 1990s. It is a green valley dotted with acers, mature specimens of cornus, cryptomeria and picea planted between boulders. I wasn't the only one impressed by the little bridged lily pond. Two spaniels came tearing down the hill and leaped straight in for a swim. The uses a city park can be put to...

THE LEDSHAM GARDEN |

11 SALLAGH ROAD, CAIRNCASTLE, BALLYGALLY, LARNE, COUNTY ANTRIM

Contact: David and Janet Ledsham
Tel: (+44) 048 2858 3003
e-mail: ledshamd@aol.com
Open: Mid-April to mid-October by appointment.
Small groups preferred.
Special features: Unusual plants for sale.

Directions: From the A8 turn left onto the B148 sign posted for Cairncastle. After 6km, leave the road at the 'Old Dairy Cottage' and fork left onto Sallagh Road. The house just under 1km along, below the road on the right.

The Ledshams came to this spot in Larne, with its view over the sea to Scotland, in the mid-1990s. They bought an exposed two-acre sheep field surrounded by more sheep fields. Today, the whole area is a spectacular jungle garden. I studied an almost impossible-to-believe picture of the original site as I stood in the middle of the herb garden behind the house, surrounded by a sea of containers filled with cacti, bulbs, dramatic-looking proteas and small shrubs.

Looking up from this sun trap, the view is of masses of *Rosa* 'Alice Estelle Grey', cherries, Japanese acers, evergreen oak and a rare curry-scented escallonia. Planted up on a height, they seem like an impenetrable wall of flower and foliage. However, it is through these that the entrance to the garden proper can be found.

So began an enticing climb up into and under a canopy of hoherias, between phlomis, cistus and roses. There are plant in every direction: overhead, underfoot, in front and behind. As we went we breathed in the rich smell of cloves from an unusual spidery *Dianthus superbus*. David pointed to a line of willows in the middle of the knot of plants. These were originally sticks, stuck into the ground to mark an old boundary. Nearby there is an apple tree grown from a pip, growing alongside rather more refined *Acer griseum* and nothofagus. This is a garden with room for all comers. Making it all the more remarkable is the fact that everything has been grown from seed and cuttings. It is a gardener's garden first and foremost.

I commented on the natural rocky outcrop we were scrambling around as we made our way between plants and boulders. David explained that it was nothing of the sort. This is no more than a mound of stones, the remains of some old, broken field wall, dusted with a thin layer of soil. This impressive illusion is only one of many: the ground here is very wet. Because of this, much of the planting has been achieved using improvised, disguised, raised beds. The fact that it was also once a windswept hill can be seen deep in the undergrowth where David left the remains of the old shelter barrier to remind himself that this was not always a deeply sheltered woodland garden.

One could learn a great deal about how to make an exceptional garden from an unpromising site in this place. The once hostile site now houses little treats of plant, like hepatica and gentian, in such numbers that they need to be culled to keep them in check. These need to be given the best of protection; they will not live well if the conditions are hard. Overhead, pruned-up acers and pittosporums deliver the dappled light the ground-dwellers love.

The sound of water can be heard at this point coming from a stream. Over the course of its way through the garden, it is banked into ponds three times. We cross it over a little bridge leading to what David calls the 'Donegal garden', where all the plants hail from that county. They include an aspen, which came as a sucker from an ancient multi-trunked tree in Carnlough. The ferns, of which there are many, are all native, yet they sit perfectly beside exotics and rarities like erythroniums, *Anemonopsis macrophylla* and *Glaucidium palmatum*.

We emerge, blinking, into the sun and another garden of Japanese *Hydrangea serrata* lilac-flowered strobilanthes. Seeing a big clump of *Saxifraga stolonifera* outside was remarkable. This is normally a house plant known to most people as mother-of-thousands.

At this point the sheer variety of the garden becomes apparent. Out in the full sun the path now runs between

wild-looking hilly flower borders full of irises, echiums, more proteas and campanulas, planted on free-draining scree as they might be in the wild.

Farther along, the dry riverbed garden might be something of a horticultural joke, although it was no joke making it, according to David. The bleached stony look, like everything in this garden, looks as though it just happened.

Staggering out, under sensory overload, it was amazing to discover that this is David's first garden. A trained artist, at the age of fifty he bought the place 'knowing a bit about botany' and started to garden. Working with Janet, who had always gardened, he took to planting with gusto and found that he had a talent. Together they have created a remarkable garden.

 COUNTY DERRY

BROOK HALL ARBORETUM | 65 CULMORE ROAD, DERRY, COUNTY DERRY

· ·

Contact: David Gilliland
Tel: (+44) 048 7135 1297
e-mail: candr@iol.ie
Open: All year by appointment only. Groups welcome. Supervised children welcome.

Dogs on leads.

Directions: Take the A2 out of the city in the direction of Culmore and Greencastle. After two roundabouts, two giant anchors on the right mark the entrance.

In the late eighteenth century, successful Derry merchants erected a string of handsome villas along the banks of the River Foyle. Brook Hall is considered by some to be the finest of these, standing in a landscaped park with views of the river. History is draped across the garden like a creeping vine. There is even a yew tree that is said to stand over the remains of a French officer who died during the Siege of Derry in 1689.

The grounds cover thirty-five acres across a slope down to the river, and are part of a garden that dates back to 1780, although some parts of the walled garden were being cultivated in the 1600s. In *Notes of a Journey in the North of Ireland in the Summer of 1827*, Thomas Mitchell wrote of Brook Hall that, 'upon the grounds, evidently neither expense nor skill has been spared in furnishing and maturing one of the most luxuriant collections of shrubs I ever beheld.' Much of that original planting still remains, including parkland oak, beech and chestnut. But it is the modern arboretum for which Brook Hall is renowned. This was started in 1929 by Commander Frank Gilliland. Today, it is worked by David Gilliland, an enthusiastic tree expert.

When Mr Gilliland first began to manage the arboretum in 1959, the first task was to begin thinning out what was becoming a congested collection. Improving the spaces between each tree benefits growth, allowing each specimen to achieve full size and the best possible shape. It also allows the visitor to walk around the individual plants and fully enjoy them from all angles. This is a garden that will reward the visitor who wears wellies or waterproof footwear. You will want to walk through the long grass between the trees.

The collection of trees in the arboretum is extensive and the catalogued collection records over nine hundred varieties of trees and shrubs. The ideal way to approach it is to visit at different seasons to fully appreciate the trees and the huge changes they undergo through the year. Some have one season of interest, while others, like the Chinese red birch or *Betula albosinensis* var. *septentrionalis*, can boast everything: an unusual shape, decorative catkins, autumn colour and a rich copper bark. The specimen at Brook Hall was planted in 1937 and it is quite a sight. Mr Gilliland reckons that the huge dawn redwood or *Metasequoia glyptostroboides* at Brook Hall could be the first in Ireland, which would mean it was planted in 1949. However, Birr Castle's specimen came to Ireland around the same time and so the matter of the oldest dawn redwood joins a whole series of gentlemanly disputes that endearingly rumble on in gardens all over the island about the tallest, widest, oldest and biggest champion trees.

In autumn, look for the rare pink flowering eucryphias and the most impressive tall, straight Corsican pine that towers above the house.

Grass paths meander through the trees, allowing one to wander between southern beech or nothofagus, past *Dacrydium franklinii* from Tasmania and pink-flowering *Rhododendron arboreum*. This particular plant unfurls its first buds inside the tree, so this necessitates a hunt in among the branches to find the flowers. Another beauty close by is the *Rhododendron fictolacteum*, which has luxurious, furry orange under-leaves and white-and-yellow flowers. There are quite a large number of rhododendrons growing in the garden, including *Rhododendron basilicum* planted in numbers, despite that fact that its 'flowers are vulgar, like cabbages,' to Mr Gilliland's thinking.

Walking along, a tree that surprised me was the *Cupressocyparis leylandii*, grown as a specimen. Leylandii is not a bad tree, but one maligned because of the way it has been used by poor gardeners as fast-growing hedging, becoming known as 'the bane of suburbia'. The story behind this particular specimen is that it was smuggled to Ireland in 1937 in a tooth mug by an aspiring plant hunter. The man thought he had discovered something special, only to find that his discovery was no discovery at all – the tree was already in the country and growing at a pace.

Further along the walk is a Chinese dogwood (*Cornus kousa* var. *chinensis*), whose creamy bracts are replaced with ripening, strawberry-like fruits. In the autumn its leaves turn vivid red. This is another candidate for the tree-that-has-it-all award.

Apart from work in the arboretum, the walled garden was totally congested when Mr Gilliland started work here. In recent years he has cleared it out and has filled it with collections of camellia, magnolia and bamboo. The walls have been used to accommodate varieties of clematis, wisteria, ceanothus and cotoneaster, including *C. frigidus*. Out of the walled garden, the track leads on to the pond and a growing escallonia collection. Down here, a eucalyptus levelled by Hurricane Debbie fell over the brook after which the house is named. Today, it is still a beautiful tree – despite the fact that it is now growing on its side.

Gardeners have always shared stock, and here a Lebanese oak (*Quercus libani*) given to the garden by Thomas Pakenham (see Tullynally Castle, County Westmeath) is putting on great growth.

Brook Hall is not a garden of striped, rolled lawns and primped flower borders. Do not come hoping to see nail-scissors tidiness. Brook Hall is first and foremost a place to interest anyone who loves trees and shrubs and wants to study the rare and unusual.

Buchanan Garden |
28 Killyfaddy Road, Magherafelt, County Derry, BT45 6EX

Contact: Mrs Ann Buchanan

Tel: (+44) 048 7963 2180

Open: All year, Tuesday to Saturday. Book during the winter months. Groups welcome. Supervised children welcome.

Special features: Refreshments can be booked.

Directions: Leaving Magherafelt on the Moneymore Road, turn left opposite the petrol station and travel 1.6km. The garden is signposted.

The last time I visited the Buchanan garden I guessed that they would continue to expand into the surrounding fields. It was not a serious prediction, but it turned out to be accurate: this garden, like Topsy, just keeps growing.

The Buchanans moved here in 1971 and started gardening immediately. By the mid-1980s they had been so busy that expansion to a plot across the road was necessary. 'We never intended to grow on that spot,' Mrs Buchanan explains with the puzzlement of the truly addicted. But the rate at which they work the garden meant that expansion was inevitable.

The second garden, across the road, is mostly made up of herbaceous plants. Its overall style is dictated by the plants the Buchanans wanted to grow. Yet the garden is no untidy jumble. It is a nicely arranged series of borders full of well tended, well matched flowering plants. In a place with so much herbaceous planting, the dreaded task of staking could be a big job and an even bigger headache.

Not so at Killyfaddy Road. Ann Buchanan says that she has done away with the need to stake by planting everything cheek-by-jowl. It this way 'everything holds everything else up,' she smiles, as though it were that simple. For lesser mortals, it could be a case of everything knocking everything else over. But here, monarda, larkspur, agapanthus and foxgloves, still flowering like mad at the end of August, looked wonderful, planted *en masse* in one stuffed bed, where they did indeed all hold one another upright – and looked very good doing it. There are paths everywhere, but most cannot be used in the summer because the plants just spread out and take over.

If something looks good, the Buchanans leave it as it is. 'A variegated tropaeolum appeared a few years ago in the garden and it self-seeds around like anything,' said Ann. This was not a

problem because, as she continued, 'It's a bit of a weed but it's a good weed.' Close by we looked at a shoving match between a *Hoheria sexstylosa* and a pittosporum. They were grown from seed and the principle of survival of the fittest will decide the outcome. The plant-cram is impressive, even in the woody area where apple trees are under-planted with so many hellebores, hosta, cautleya and primulas.

In the middle of this part of the garden is a pond, or 'puddle', full of water snails and sticklebacks, with waterside planting of iris and *Potentilla palustris*. One of the prettiest sights here is the contrast between deep purple-blue willow gentian and airy white gypsophila.

In the main garden, back on the other side of the road, an island of *Pratia pedunculata*, is like a sea of pale blue stars in the grass. This side of the garden has more shaded areas, but it also has its own 'sunset strip', with a view of the west-facing fields beyond. A path leading up to the sunset seat is blocked at several points by clumps of herbaceous plants to make the space more interesting. There are more hellebores and wildflowers under the trees, including a spread of pyramidal and marsh orchids as well as fritillaries. And it all looks out over a field of Shetland ponies. Teasingly just out of their reach through the fence, there are drifts of scabious, borage, Shasta daisy, snake's head fritillaries (*Fritillaria meleagris*) and rose campion (*Lychnis coronaria*).

The barley sugar tree (*Cercidiphyllum japonicum*) is one of the best trees to plant in a garden, as at certain times of year its leaves smell of barley sugar. My experience is that it is not always reliable in this respect, but when it happens it is a delight. It reliably scents up in this garden.

The Buchanans never stop working their plot. Even as she stops to talk, Ann was deadheading day lilies. We looked out at the neighbour's field next door. A while back he admired her garden and in return she jumped the ditch and planted up the boundary of his field with a variety of woodland plants. Now they both have something lovely to look at. The expansion continues . . .

HAMPSTEAD HALL | 40 CULMORE ROAD, DERRY, COUNTY DERRY, BT48 7RS

Contact: Liam Greene
Tel: (+44) 048 7135 4807
e-mail: nora.greene@ntlworld.com
www: www.ulstergardensscheme.org.uk
Open: May to September by appointment and for occasional open days. Contact for annual dates.

Directions: Travelling out of the city in the direction of Culmore and Greencastle, turn left at the sign for Baron's Court. The garden is on the right marked by a stone wall and new gateposts.

There are few things we love as much as a surprise, and over the past thirty years Liam Greene has created a garden of full of horticultural surprises around his home overlooking the city of Derry. On arrival, it appears to be a decent garden, largely made up of raised mixed beds on top of newly made dry-stone walls, small formal lawns with sentries of clipped yew and Portuguese laurel planted in straight lines leading to the front door of the old house. There are some strong shrub and tree combinations with mixes of arbutus, embothrium and trachycarpus together. It is all ordered and smart and it complements the Georgian house. However, this is not the garden proper – for that, swing around the side of the house to where it really starts to strut its stuff.

This is where Liam created his Japanese garden. Much of the space here is taken up by a pond, side planted by miniature trees and creeping greenery. Wisteria-covered bridges and sets of stepping stones span the pond and the view across is it of a wooden Japanese summerhouse and some well shaped acers. The plants that really get the tone right are two podocarpus. One is a rare shrub, *Podocarpus salignus*, which carries shiny, waxy foliage that begs to be stroked. The other is *Podocarpus nivalis*, a rarely seen shrub with a memorable splayed habit. Liam planted it beside the water with a weathered stone lantern and some close-cropped junipers. On the ground,

under these perfect shrubs, there is a moss carpet and spreads of *Soleirolia soleirolii*. This is a compact but richly planted little garden room.

But this is not the whole show either. The path turns a corner into a completely different garden: a courtyard behind the house where soft brown sandstone outhouses, along with an unusual bow-backed house between them, enclose a sunny sheltered area. There are big camellias, a *Magnolia grandiflora* 'Exmouth' and *M. campbellii* and *Clematis armandii* all planted against the sunniest of the walls. These are then knotted through with jasmine and roses, which double the use of space and effectively extend the flowering season.

A rather grand-looking one-eyed white dove potters between big terracotta pots of clipped bay and frothy pelargoniums. This is his home.

Stepping through a stone gateway, there is another garden room. This is reminiscent of a perfect, manicured, enclosed garden, which looks like it might be spotted through an open gate down a side street in the old quarter of a southern European city. It is a formal walled garden with a box square in the middle. At each corner there is a five-metre-tall Italian cypress. Centred on the back wall, a spouting lion provides the sound of trickling water. And on the side walls there are well maintained box balls, a few white flowering magnolias and a fruiting fig. Everything is clipped, preened and gorgeous.

It then leads down another set of steps to yet another formal topiary garden with more clipped box around a square pond with fatsia, thuja and 'Castlewellan Gold' cypress. This garden looks good from above, but it is meant to be seen from the basement windows of the house and it works best from that angle, bringing the garden into the house.

Unusually, and for no reason I can put my finger on, for all its formality this feels like a garden that Liam has real fun with. There is a warm and relaxed atmosphere as well as an enormous amount of style. Liam has been playing with it since 1979. It is obvious that he loves it and he certainly knows how to do surprises.

STREEVE HILL |
25 DOWNLAND ROAD, LIMAVADY, COUNTY DERRY, BT49 OHP

Contact: June and Peter Welsh
Tel: (+44) 028 7776 6563
www: www.ulstergardensscheme.org.uk
Open: Easter to October by appointment. Groups

welcome. Supervised children welcome.
Directions: Streeve is next door to Drenagh, on the Limavady to Coleraine road (A37).

When they arrived in 1986 to restore it, Streeve Hill, the Welshs' fine redbrick home near Limavady, was enjoying life as a range of barns, a forge and a tractor shed. Having transformed these into a lovely house, the garden project began. That started when garden historian Patrick Bowe drew up a plan. Mrs Welsh has been working the garden ever since.

This is a charming country garden spreading out from the house to a surrounding of wheat fields and groves of mature trees. Close to the buildings, the style is that of a formal flower garden, divided into small outdoor rooms by neat, waist-high box hedges. There are not too many tall plants here apart from those grown over pergolas and arches. There are trees too, but these are held at bay in the outer, less formal garden, where they frame views of the landscape beyond it.

One of the first pictures is a dramatic line of irises sunbathing under a sun-trapping, south-facing wall. They make one imagine heat even when there is none – something of an advantage in a cool Irish summer. The box hedges around the flowerbeds have matured beautifully and one box cone rising proud in the middle of each bed adds an extra oomph of vertical structure and formality to the colour-blocks.

Each bed was planned to hold single-colour herbaceous perennials. Pink, white, yellow and bronze were the base colours. But June Welsh is in the middle of modifying this scheme a little, relaxing the rule and allowing occasional extra shades into the tight divisions. The result is both ordered and pretty and yet not too smarty-smarty. The ideas of a designer, it should be remembered, are there to be customised and personalised by the owner who knows the space intimately, dealing with it every day as they do.

Also warming themselves on the redbrick walls of the house are big runs of honeysuckle, jasmine, actinidia and old roses. These reach right up to the top of the building from feet tucked into flounces of lavender and pineapple sage at the base of the wall. Planting like this side-steps the ugly sight of bare-legged roses and deprives weeds of breathing space. Further along the path is a small rose garden with obelisks and arches for the roses to climb through. Again, not to be too purist, a *Clematis* 'Jackmanii' adds variety. *Rosa* 'Blush Noisette', with the scent of cloves, is the star plant here. It is an old rose, first bred in France in 1817. Mrs Welsh told me that it is her favourite. It deserves that status. Creamy and strong-scented *Rosa* 'Yvonne Rabier', grown through a crab apple in the centre, must also claim to be a favourite.

One path runs along the length of the west-facing wall bed. Here, the ground is damp and perfect for hostas, white hydrangeas including *Hydrangea aspera* 'Villosa' and rich blue *Ceanothus* 'Gloire de Versailles'. Green, white and blue are smart and stylish together. The path continues past these shrubs to the kitchen garden, where a good deal of imagination went into creating cropping walls of step-over apples and artichokes. These are immovable. Everything else rotates within the beds to keep the vegetables – including thirty different varieties of onion – healthy and vigorous. Mr Welsh is the onion enthusiast.

Away from the house, the structure of the garden shakes loose into wildflower meadows with mown grass paths. They lead out to the cut-flower garden under a grove of mature maple, cornus, camellia and a number of different hollies. This area, a distance from the house, was once a rubbish dump from which enormous quantities of old bottles and scrap are still being dug. Bergenia is used here to choking out the weeds. Mrs Welsh is a great believer in hiding the weeds with plants, and plenty of them.

In every garden there is room for a bit of the wild stuff and Streeve is no exception. There is one final flowerbed of wild reds out beyond the trees, well away from the house. The colour red travels and draws itself in toward the viewer, which is why many people find it best to plant it at a distance. Out here on the edge of the garden, the mad-coloured dahlias, ruby *Nicotiana sylvestris*, flamboyant varieties of hemerocallis and *Crocosmia* 'Lucifer' all sport happily.

With one final flourish, Mrs Welsh adds to the borrowed landscape, which in this case is made up of waving wheat fields, by planting roses like 'Wedding Day' along the boundary wire fence. As they grow, they are trained like swags along the wire. It is such a simple yet stylish idea, only one among many in this relaxed, old-fashioned country garden.

County Donegal

Glenveagh Castle Gardens |
Churchill, Letterkenny, County Donegal

. . . .

Contact: Sean O'Gaoithin

Tel: (+353) 074 913 7090 / 074 913 7391

e-mail: glenveagh@environ.ie / seanogaoithin@eircom.net

www: www.glenveaghnationalpark.ie

Open: All year 10am-6pm. Last admission at 5pm. Guided tours available. Groups welcome.

Supervised children welcome.

Special features: Interpretive centre. National park. Restaurant. Castle.

Directions: Take the N56 north out of Letterkenny. Turn left on Termon onto the R251 and follow the signs for Glenveagh National Park.

The nineteenth-century castle at Glenveagh sits in the middle of a 36,000-acre demesne of mountains, lakes and woods. It is the biggest single protected area of land in Ireland. As befits such a place, huge gardens were laid out in the 1850s and since then a succession of great design and gardening talents have combined to make Glenveagh arguably the best garden on the island.

Although it is not something generally associated with north Donegal in the way that it is with Kerry and west Cork, the Gulf Stream is largely responsible for the soft microclimate in Glenveagh. A deep shelter belt of Scots pine (*Pinus sylvestris*) around the castle and lake further improve the local climate. In addition, the northerly aspect tends to lead to sturdier and hardier growth in plants here than further south in Munster. As a result, alpines, Chinese and Himalayan plants all thrive in the garden. But it's not all good news. The garden faces northwest, and in winter there are many parts that receive no sun at all during the day. It is hard to believe, but in one of those dark spots is found in the beautiful walled garden – the *jardin potager*.

The *potager*, which covers one acre, is an important laboratory dedicated to Irish horticulture. 'In here we grow everything from seed,' Sean O'Gaoithin, the head gardener, explained. They use traditional practices and grow old cultivars and the sort of rare and unusual plants and vegetables that are losing ground in the wider world. Among the important items here is a small collection of old Donegal roses collected by Sean over the past ten years from cottages and ruins

around the county and planted in the walled garden among the other, more refined herbaceous plants and clipped yew hedges.

The *potager* is at its best between July and August, when the double borders and rows of perfect vegetables compete for attention. Among the masses of flowers, Sean pointed out a pretty single red *Dahlia* 'Matt Armour' – a lasting memorial to the great gardener who worked here for fifty years and from whom Sean learned much about the garden.

There are so many distractions, including the gardener's cottage garden, a confection of zigzagged box walls enclosing lilies, alliums, chives and marjoram. The special touch of adding a ribbon of primulas and alpine strawberries along the border is just one of many examples where the gardening team at Glenveagh always seem to deliver just that bit more.

Standing at the bottom of the sloped garden in front of the Gothic greenhouse, the whole layout should be inspected as a piece, after a session studying the close-ups. After that, take the route out through a lead urn-capped gate and along a camellia and rhododendron 'corridor'. This has the feel of a cool hallway out of an impressive reception room in a grand house.

The pleasure grounds are tropical in feel and brimming with remarkable plants. In quick succession we pass tree ferns, eucryphia, hoheria and the fragrant, magnolia-like flowers of *Michelia doltsopa*, a Chinese relative of magnolia.

Glenveagh receives a substantial annual rainfall, and this gives the place a steamy, damp, glistening look. It also promotes great growth. Everywhere there are impressive plants like the *Nothofagus dombeyi* and *Davidia involucrata*. This specimen was planted by the famous plantsman Roy Lancaster.

In 1996, a seed-collecting expedition was made to China's Yunan province. It resulted in a whole range of new plants coming to Ireland. Glenveagh's share of the treasure was planted in 1999 in a special new Chinese garden beside the lake. Among the young plants is a two-metre-tall *Cornus capitata*.

The list of special rhododendrons in Glenveagh is a long one. It includes a variegated specimen called *Rhododendron* 'Mulroy's Variety' unique to the garden. But this is only one of many unique plants here. The layered planting that delivers several storeys of trees and shrubs in one spot is a style that has been brought to perfection at Glenveagh. Everywhere, one gets a three-plants-for-the-price-of-one deal: under a hill of Scots pine you will see a layer of *Prunus sargentii* and under these a bottom storey of *Rhododendron sinogrande*. This is *tour de force* gardening and it means that no matter what time of year you visit, the range of plants putting on their best show will be wide.

On the edge of an opening in the canopy, we walked past a recently built gazebo. As we inspected it, Sean explained that it was built without nails, using huge larch planks, in another example of traditional work methods.

An impressive set of sixty-seven steps leads up through the woods to a Belvedere, or viewing garden, set out with large Italian terracotta pots. It was laid out in front of the upper glen and Lough Veagh and the view out over the castle, gardens and lake from here is unforgettable. At the moment the steps cannot be climbed as they are in a somewhat unsafe state and in need of restoration.

The other features within easy walk of the castle are the rose garden and the Swiss walk, so named because of its apparent resemblance to Switzerland. The Belgian walk was more obviously so named as it was created by recuperating Belgian soldiers during World War I. The Italian garden is intimate, full of eighteenth-century statuary, paved with Donegal slate and planted around with rhododendron and pieris. The Tuscan garden is planted with griselinia hedging and decorated with busts of Roman emperors and their wives. Interestingly, none of these look as incongruous as one might think in wet, northern Donegal.

OAKFIELD PARK | RAPHOE, COUNTY DONEGAL

Contact: Estate Manager
Tel: (+353) 074 917 3068
e-mail: info@oakfieldpark.com
www: www.oakfieldpark.com
Open: May to August, Wednesday to Sunday 10am-4pm (Closed Monday and Tuesday). Large groups by appointment.
Special features: 4km narrow gauge railway open Saturday and Sunday in summer. Picnic facilities. Toilets. Free car parking. Partially wheelchair accessible. **Directions:** Take the Letterkenny to Lifford road (N14). Pass the exit for Raphoe and continue for 1.5km. Take the next right at the crossroads by the burnt out Cross Pub. Travel 1.5k to the car park which is on the left. The garden is on the right.

We are not accustomed to new, large-scale garden creation in this day and age; making huge gardens has been out of fashion for well over a century. So arriving to Oakfield Park for a first visit can be something of an overwhelming experience. Take one hundred acres, insert several brand-new man-made lakes, huge walled gardens, follies, scores of acres of woods, several huge

spring flower meadows, parterres and large scale formal gardens, complete with all the usual glass houses, sunken gardens, Japanese gardens, kitchen gardens, tennis courts and ponds – and you have Oakfield Park.

Sir Gerry Robinson and his wife Heather created all this – not in the eighteenth or nineteenth centuries, but in the last fourteen years. It is a remarkable achievement. The garden at Oakfield Park is extensive, exuberant, good-looking and fun. It is all the more wonderful because, after creating it, the Robinsons then threw open the gates to welcome in the public.

It all started when they bought a derelict Georgian deanery in Raphoe and fifty-five acres. Once the house was restored, they found themselves taking up gardening – with what seem like bottomless reserves of energy.

The garden is built on blue marl. This is a difficult, heavy soil type that holds onto water. That may account for the numerous pond building projects here based on the 'if God gives you lemons, make lemonade' philosophy. The ponds naturally hold their water, but this heavy soil means that the husbandry of the rest of the garden needs to be thorough. The impressive growth seen throughout the gardens is a testament to the work and care invested in both feeding and lightening the soil.

A decade in, there is as much an emphasis on pruning and thinning as on planting. In the walled garden, lines of yew pyramids flank one path and look like they have been here for decades. The pergola over a little pool looks to be laden down under the weight of roses and clematis. And a swagged wall, quite lovely as it is, can barely be seen behind great skyward-bound cotonesters, tall betulas and acers.

The distractions are everywhere and come in every shape. In one corner we came across a secret garden planted up with aralias, white-barked betulas and paulownias. On the ground under these, bright white anemones contributed another layer of interest.

The dizzying route leads between pagoda gardens, pool gardens, white gardens and stream gardens. The kitchen garden is naturally substantial and filled with large expanses of well-tended vegetables, cold frames and trained fruit trees. I think that even the filling of the bird feeders must be a full-time job for someone.

This is a high-maintenance place and, as no garden is without its problems, neither is this. The box parterre to the side of the house is an impressive feature but it is suffering from box blight which they are trying, with great difficulty, to eradicate organically. But leaving the problems of box blight behind us, we took a mown path to the wild flower meadow – an expanse of orchids, ox-eyed daisies and knapweed.

Flax was once grown widely around here and used to produce linen, so its luminous blue flowers were at one time a common sight. Today, flax flowers are rarely seen. The Robinsons

have recently given a field over to the crop, inviting in a man from Raphoe, one of the few left in the country with knowledge of flax, to grow it. The field, surrounded by a stone wall, is as sweet a field as ever existed. Come in June to see it in bloom. In another field, running down a hill, they planted the September wild flower meadow. This one is filled with yellow corn marigolds, wild rape and poppies. A four-acre expanse of these waving in the breeze on a sunny day was enough to make me want to move in.

A huge area of the ground is given over to woods and, in keeping with its name and history, the Robinsons are trying to build up the collection of oaks here. At the moment they have sixty-five species.

Creating views and vistas is another ongoing project. The most ambitious example of this is the view from the house, downhill, over and beyond the pond and its little classical summerhouse, and on through an *allée* between the trees, to a mound planted up with 15,000 box plants. Opportunities to create such large-scale features are rare.

Eventually, you are bound to arrive at the train station. This is home to two trains, one diesel and one steam. The trains travel through newly planted mixed bluebell woods, past an even bigger lake than the summerhouse lake, through acres of reed beds and alongside a sham castle/viewing tower. All bells and whistles? Absolutely, and all the better for it.

SALTHILL | MOUNTCHARLES, COUNTY DONEGAL

Contact: Elizabeth Temple
Tel: (+353) 074 973 5387
e-mail: etemple@eircom.net
www: www.donegalgardens.com
Open: May to September, Monday to Thursday 2pm-6pm / May to July, Saturday 2pm-6pm.

Other times by appointment.
Special Features: Garden talks. Groups welcome.
Directions: In Mountcharles village, take the downhill road past the church. Turn right at the churchyard and continue to the T-junction. The garden is on the left.

Salthill is a classic country garden brought back from the brink of extinction. It covers about 1.2 acres enclosed within tall walls behind a Georgian house on the edge of Donegal Bay. When Elizabeth Temple arrived here, she saw drawings of the garden on old maps. It seemed to date to about 1820. But it was wildly overgrown and the original garden was well gone. So she began to redraw a new garden within the walls.

The entrance leads through a byre and into a courtyard surrounded by old farm buildings. This is like the starter in a substantial meal. It is a courtyard garden that could in all honesty have been lifted by spaceship from somewhere hot and dry, and then beamed into the wilds of Donegal. Visiting it on a sunny day certainly added to the sensation. Giant eucomis or pineapple lilies looked so healthy and bustling they could have been natives. Tall pink echiums, waves of phormiums, miscanthus with white agapanthus flowers dotted through them, look right at home

although they come from backgrounds quite different to these Donegal yards. The rampant self-seeding in the granite gravel drives home the exotics-turned-native impression even further.

The fun of this garden is that, having accustomed oneself to the idea of a Mediterranean garden in chilly Ireland, we wander like Alice through a gateway to find ourselves in a completely different world.

This is the main walled garden, a place that had been used as a dump for many years before Elizabeth arrived. That lamentable fact turned out to be a blessing in disguise. Life as a dump rendered the garden extremely fertile. Add a sheltered aspect and a talented gardener to the fertile ground and the result is a great bustle of a garden made up of beds full of good and some unusual plants.

The design is very much centred of the plants. I imagine the idea of curtailing her plants to fit in with a hemmed-in design would not meet with Elizabeth's approval. This is a plant-lovers heaven. We wandered past heavily flowering *Cornus mas* competing with a *Buddleja alternifolia* for attention, only to be side-tracked by *Euonymus cornutus*, a great flowering shrub with seed heads like extravagant crowns.

The seaside location means that there is always a plentiful supply of seaweed to keep the place topped up. The roses thrive on this. *Rosa* 'Ferdinand Pichard', *R.* 'Californica plena' and the thornless *R.* 'Zephirine Drouhin' all bore heavy cargoes of flower, and wafted perfume around us as we went.

At the top of the garden, Elizabeth grows her vegetables in high, ridged beds. These are also used in Glenveagh, and designed to making heavy retentive soil easier to work. I admired an abutilon on the wall behind the rows of leeks and spinach, to be told that it came from a seed taken from New York's Central Park. Beside it we looked at a shrubby *Clematis heracleifolia* with purple bells, and a creamy greeny white *Clematis rehderiana*. The herbaceous borders run perpendicularly away from these massed shrubs. Grass paths allow the visitor to get right in between big drifts of daylilies, phlox and white sanguisorba. Flowers drift in all directions, including upwards and into the trees in the shape of a climbing aconitum twining through the branches of variegated azara. Close by, the fascinating striped snake bark on an *Acer forrestii* acts as a reminder that no garden should be without one of these exquisite acers.

This is a garden that is maturing – and has matured so much that a digger was recently brought in to move a path from out of the way of a maturing *Viburnum tinus*. It was as I thought – the plants rule.

❖ COUNTY DOWN

BALLYWALTER PARK |
BALLYWALTER, NEWTOWNARDS, COUNTY DOWN, BT22 2PP

Contact: Mrs Sharon Graham
Tel: (+44) 048 4275 8264
e-mail: enq@dunleath-estates.co.uk
www: www.ballywalterpark.com
Open: All year by appointment. Groups welcome.

Supervised children welcome.
Special features: Teas by arrangement.
Directions: Turn off the A20 at Greyabbey. Take the B5 and turn right at the T-junction. Continue to the gate lodge on the right.

Out on the windy Ards Peninsula, Ballywalter Park was built in the 1850s by the English architect Charles Lanyon for the Mulholland family, later the Lords Dunleath. I arrived for my most recent visit to see the blue European flag flying cheerfully over the house. This seemed only proper, as the house was designed along the lines of an Italianate Renaissance palazzo for Andrew Mulholland when he moved here from Belfast.

There was, however, something puzzling about the approach to the house. It was not quite as I remembered. The drive toward the house appeared to be much more open, well-tended and much more of a feature than the dark, wood-encroached drive I thought led to the house. Thinking memory failure, it was a relief to be told that Lord Dunleath – with

the help of one other man and some great machinery – has spent the past few years 'clearing' the woods. He could have used the phrase 'completely rejuvenating'. The results of this ongoing work are stunning: the drive now runs past stretches of wild flower and meadow grass and stands of impressive trees, through which there are excellent views. These light-splashed openings are all recent and owe their existence to the clearances. As they worked, all sorts of surprises were thrown up, including a pond and several groves of magnolias that had been completely lost and forgotten under decades of rampant *Rhododendron ponticum* growth.

The greater gardens are chiefly comprised of a landscape park. In addition to the house, Lanyon also laid out a plan for the grounds and a great gardening programme was undertaken with 93,500 trees and shrubs planted in the winter of 1846. There are walks and rides past a lake through impressive rhododendron, such as *Rhododendron falconeri* and *Rhododendron sinogrande*, with huge leaves and creamy yellow flowers. A series of streams cuts through the park. These gently meandering, bridged waterways were also designed as part of a naturalistic, picturesque landscape. Informal plantings of ferns, rodgersia and primula edge the water. The views over the well positioned bridge towards the house or down to the woods are like pictures of nature perfected. Among the small groves of trees there are two fine Monterey pines, both in the Irish Tree Register.

The house stands unhampered and handsome on a terrace overlooking the park. Attached to it is the restored conservatory. This award-winning glass construction was also designed by Lanyon. Along with the house, it had degenerated over the years until a major restoration of both began in the 1960s. The work had been first recommended by the poet Sir John Betjeman when he visited for tea in 1961. In any case, after decades of work, the whole place sparkles today. Lord Dunleath is particularly proud of the restoration overseen by him on the conservatory, and describes with pleasure the painstaking operation involved in getting the details right, such as re-creating staging for plants using small sections of the original iron work.

I arrived on a bright sunny day to see a gleaming edifice, full of citrus fruits and bananas in pots, showy displays of alpine pelargoniums on staging along the walls and an inviting table in the middle, set up with cake and tea. Unusually, instead of lilies in the little pond there are shoals of skittish tropical fish.

Behind the house, there are long wall-backed mixed borders full of scented fennel, hebe, euphorbia, tree paeonies and crocosmia. Leaning up against the wall, a dramatic red flowering embothrium stands out, as it is not a tree often seen outside the shelter of a wood garden. Long draping lengths of wisteria cover the rest of the wall. The walk from here takes you to the walled garden, where four statues guard the entrance. These are goddesses depicting the four seasons – minus the wheat sheaf Miss Summer should be carrying.

Inside the walled garden the chief feature is a long rose walk and pergola made of red brick uprights and oak beams. The roses twine around the pillars, which are all under-planted with rich, black Sweet William and cornflowers. Walking between the black and blue flowers on the ground and the scented roses around and over ones head is a real pleasure.

The fruit garden can be found behind a wall of yew. The fruit trees themselves are divided into twelve sections, or rooms, recalling the Bible passage 'in my father's garden there are many mansions'. This new development is still being worked on.

The rose walk leads up to a huge range of glasshouses, the first of which is fronted by a line of tall cardoons. There are actually seven greenhouses in the walled garden; they are all still standing, but in need of work. It is unusual to see such a number still intact. Usually it is only the footprints that remain of old greenhouses. It is hoped that they will be able to restore some of them.

The work on Ballywalter continues.

GUINCHO | 69 CRAIGDARRAGH ROAD, HELEN'S BAY, COUNTY DOWN

....

Contact: Nick Burrowes, Head Gardener
Tel: (+44) 048 9048 6324
Open: April to September, by appointment to groups of fifteen or more only and for charity days. See local press or National Trust Garden Scheme for details. Supervised children welcome. Dogs on leads. **Directions:** From the main Belfast to Bangor road (A2), take the Craigdarragh Road to Helen's Bay. The garden is 0.5km along on the left-hand side.

The gardens at Guincho are known as one of the best private gardens on the island. They were created by Mrs Vera Mackie in 1948 on a sloped, twelve-acre wooded site near the County Down coast.

Guincho seems like it has been here for a lot longer than just over sixty years, particularly in the case of the four acres of woodland. The garden is substantial, full of variety and beautifully maintained. In 1982 it was added to the Northern Ireland register of gardens of outstanding historical importance.

The greater garden is made up of huge sweeping lawns wrapped by a wide collar of woods, filled with unusual and rare plants, some of which came from the Kingdom Ward plant gathering expeditions as well as collectors like Lord Talbot of Malahide. (See The Talbot Botanic Garden, County Dublin.) Guincho is a garden on the grand-scale. The woods contain and shelter long walks past hellebores, ferns and hydrangea, all under sheltering oak, pine, eucryphia, cordyline and rhododendron. These winding, mossy paths open every so often onto expanses of lawn, letting in daylight and lending the walker views across the garden to well designed combinations of plants, like the massive silver fir beside a large plantation of gunnera or a sea of blue hydrangea.

The path leads alongside a huge *Cryptomeria japonica* that looks like a monster climbing-frame or a one-tree adventure playground. Continuing along, there is a stream garden in another clearing that feels tropical, full of wet tree ferns and trachycarpus. The mood changes again as it reaches a mixed wood of oak, ash, horse chestnut, beech and sweet chestnut. The paths rise and fall at the side of the stream, eventually leading down to a grove of large-leaved rhododendron.

Emerge from the wood to a cultivated area of lawns edged with myrtle and willow, with splashes of geranium, osteospermum, *Fascicularia pitcairnifolia* and cotoneaster draping over a stone wall. Among the special plants found at Guincho is a handsome *Rehderodendron macrocarpum*. This is a rare plant to find in Ireland. It carries white, creamy flowers and shiny, tapered leaves.

In the area close to the house there are smaller, more domestic-sized garden rooms with select and unusual small trees and flowering shrubs knotted through with climbers. A series of tiny gardens come as a surprise. Some are sunken, some are circled by tall architectural walls of phormium, some by hedges. Within these little rooms there are small lily ponds marked by mop-head bays and topiary in pots. The champion *Banksia marginata* here is worth the visit alone.

Sambucus nigra 'Guincho Purple' is a famous as well as handsome shrub, with blackish-purple leaves and pale-pink flowers. It was found growing in a hedge by Mrs Mackie while walking in the Scottish highlands in the 1960s; she took cuttings and grew them on. She gave some of these to Sir Harold Hillier, whose nursery brought it into cultivation. Mrs Mackie's original still grows here.

The terraces and balconies around the house are cleverly decorated with old varieties of apples and pears trained as balcony fences and boundaries. This is a most unusual, space-saving and clever – if technically difficult – way to work with fruit trees. Standing on the terrace and looking down from a height, over these and to flowering magnolias and cherries in the garden below, is an experience.

One last touch is the slim arch of cotoneaster wound tightly around and over the front door – a little touch of genius.

11 LONGLANDS ROAD | ISLAND HILL, COMBER, COUNTY DOWN

. . . .

Contact: David McMurren
Tel: (+44) 048 9187 2441
e-mail: davidmcmurren@btinternet.com
www: www.ulstergardensscheme.org.uk
Open: For one weekend each year. Contact in spring for annual details. **Directions:** Take the A21 To Newtownards from Comber and travel for aproximately 1 Km. Turn right and the house is 300m along on the right, clearly visible.

I arrived to visit David McMurren's garden on a day when the rain was pouring down, Monsoon-style, to find him not well pleased with his hedges. The plans to cut them were going awry.

Hedges are a vital part of this garden. The straight, smart, green lines frame and enclose, divide and wrap around swathes of herbaceous plants throughout the place. This is a virtuoso small garden in which David manages to pack a huge number of plants and features into a site of only about a half acre.

The trick is that he divides the space into small, self-contained garden rooms. Yet from each little space there are a number of views across hedges or through arches into other rooms and areas. Add real skill in choosing plant combinations and a perfectionist's attention to detail and the result is a polished gem of a garden.

There are sharp ideas at play everywhere – such as the 'secret' gravel walk down the centre of a wide herbaceous border. From head-on, this appears to be one solid border. But a little path through it divides it in two, and the splashes of Jacob's ladder, daylilies and other self-supporting perennials can be enjoyed from different angles as one walks between them. In a smaller site, this is a clever way to incorporate a double border and single border on one piece of land. Close by, what looks like the outside of a large maze is in effect an unusually shaped and placed privet hedge that splits the space.

David has been developing this garden since 1989 and in that time he has learned much about maximising space. As an example of this, we studied one corner where he pulled a philadelphus in to play host to *Rosa* 'Zephirine Drouhin'. Planting them together like this allowed him to double the floral possibilities of both plants without taking up any extra space. Working the soil to this extent means that the garden needs to be kept very fertile; liberal doses of organic matter are needed regularly if everything is to be maintained at full tilt.

Rather unusually, the plants wash right up to the edges of the building and the garden seems as though it might invade the house: a bulging hosta pond placed right beside one of the windows gives the indoor onlooker more to look at than any television could. The *Acer palmatum* 'Osakazuki' beside this is under-lit, so it can be seen at night as well during the day. Lights are used fairly widely through the garden so that much of it can be seen and enjoyed at night.

At the front of the house there are two long serpentine herbaceous borders, cheerfully advertising this as a must-see garden. Perfect striped lawns and well maintained box walls between these borders all display impeccable old-school upkeep.

Peeping around the outer boundary, I saw too that the urge to expand has been too strong to resist. Along the outside of the hedge, he is busy beautifying what would otherwise be a plain place, planting shade-loving, ground-covering hellebores, spring bulbs and woodland plants.

I left with the recipe for a good container from this sunny, talented gardener: use one-third drainage and a fibre liner on the inside of the pot to save it from frost damage.

MOUNT STEWART |

NEWTOWNARDS, PORTAFERRY ROAD, NEWTOWNARDS, COUNTY DOWN, BT22 2AD

Contact: Paul Rowlinson, Head Gardener
Tel: (+44) 048 4278 8387 / 4278 8487
e-mail: mountstewart@nationaltrust.org.uk
www: www.ulstergardensscheme.org.uk
Open: March, daily 10am-4pm / April, 10am-6pm / May to September, 10am-8pm / October, 10am-6pm.

Supervised children welcome. Dogs on leads.
Special features: Partially wheelchair accessible. Sensory garden trail. Tearoom. Sales of plants raised in the garden. House and garden tours. Garden fairs. Jazz concerts. Events.
Directions: Situated on the A20 between Newtownards and Portaferry.

Everything about Mount Stewart is aimed to impress: its size at ninety acres, the enormous variety within its many gardens, the care employed in its upkeep, the wit of the design and even the standard of the guided tours. My most recent visit was preceded by tea in the gardener's canteen, surrounded by both the professionals, and a number of the fifty garden volunteers. One was reading *The Professional Gardener*, while a group of others were arguing about the placement of a particular and special shrub. It was every bit the hub of horticulture one would expect of such a famous garden.

Mount Stewart House is an impressive pile in honey-coloured stone, and somewhat unusual in that it does not stand in splendid isolation on a lawn or on a wide spread of gravel or a restrained terrace. Standing just a hundred metres from the wide steps that lead to the door, one could equally be in a jungle of the finest plants. The house has to do battle with vegetation for attention. Even the paving around it is colonised by lavender. Tall, peeling eucalyptus, elegant conifers and seas of variegated phlox, waving anemones, great Florence Court yews, cordylines, wonderful clipped bays, irises and a thousand other plants all distract from the house in every way possible.

The garden was designed by Edith, Lady Londonderry, in the 1920s, when she arrived to live in Mount Stewart, a place she declared 'damp and depressing', situated as it was between the Irish Sea and Strangford Lough on the Ards Peninsula. Employing first twenty, then another twenty and then yet another twenty gardeners and ex-servicemen, she set to turning her ideas for a garden into reality. By the time she had finished, Mount Stewart was home to an extraordinary series of formal gardens. The warm, damp climate, once thought to be Mount Stewart's drawback, allowed her to grow a great number of tender plants. As a result, the place has more than a touch of the tropics about it. Tree ferns, fruiting kiwis (*Actinidia chinensis*), acacias and olive trees all grow happily in the temperate climate.

This was designed as a pioneering garden, and not one designed to be frozen in aspic. Today, the whole garden is undergoing a major bout of restoration with a view to improvements that will bring it firing on all cylinders into the next century.

The parterre beds, always lovely, have undergone a rethink and subsequent restoration. They look better than ever as a result. Experiments with low hedges of berberis, heather and hebe around the beds are also being carried out. And the surrounding stone monkey heads have had their head-dresses replanted with *Agave americana* as they once would have been.

The formal gardens are broken into large rooms. Between the Spanish and Italian gardens, the huge, iconic leyandii cypress or *Cupressocyparis leylandii* hedge is cut with nail-scissors perfection into a series of arches that resemble a huge green viaduct. Saline incursion into the Lough is causing concern and could cause long-term problems for the plants that grow here, including this famous hedge, and it is being monitored carefully.

Another of the gardens is surrounded by the most remarkable yew hedge, on top of which used to romp devils, hunters, the whole Londonderry family in a boat, riders on horseback and stags – all in topiary. Only a few of these characters are left of the original thirty. There are plans to reintroduce some of the lost characters, however. The hedge surrounds Mount Stewart's most famous feature: the Shamrock garden with its huge Red Hand of Ulster picked out in red bedding, begonias and double daisies set into gravel. The hand is set off against a green topiary harp, which towers four and a half metres over it.

The most romantic of all the gardens is the Mairi garden, created for Edith's daughter, Lady Mairi. This was where she would be brought for her daily turn in the pram. A little bronze fountain incorporates a statue of the baby girl spraying water in a haphazard way that will please children more than parents, as they get squirted by the little imp. The original layout of this garden was drawn up by the English gardener Graham Stuart Thomas, who planned it as a rose garden. The roses never quite took however, and the planting was replaced by a blue-and-white garden

There are wonderful statues of gryphons, turtles, crocodiles and dodos scattered throughout the Ark Garden. These are references to a long-lost political and family in-joke, but fortunately also appeal to the uninitiated. Meanwhile, the great bay umbrellas and drums flanking the house were bought for £99 8s 9d as a job lot in the 1920s.

Mount Stewart is a full day's visit, and it might even be two if you really want to study the individual gardens, and then take in the lake and woodland walks, as well as the famed Temple of the Winds overlooking the lough, reckoned by some to be the finest garden building in Ireland. It was built in 1782 to designs of James 'Athenian' Stuart, and based on the first-century BC building of the same name in Athens.

The lake walk is becoming more and more beautiful, as acers, magnolias and other fine shrubs grow ever bigger. The once evenly mown lawns are today left to become wild flower meadows in many areas. The number of natives that have appeared as a result is wonderful. Populations of orchids that had been mown down for decades are now thriving. While it is a fine idea to take a guided walk, the specimens are clearly marked and identified, so an unescorted browse can be just as enjoyable and instructive.

Rowallane Garden |
Saintfield, Ballynahinch, County Down, BT24 7LH

Contact: The Manager **Tel:** (+44) 048 9751 0131
e-mail: rowallane@nationaltrust.org.uk
Open: 17 March to October, Monday to Friday
10.30am-6pm, Weekends 12.00-6pm /
November to 17 March, Monday to Friday
10.30am-5pm. Children welcome.

Dogs on leads. **Special features:** Walks for the
visually impaired can be arranged. Home of the
National Collection of penstemon. Tearoom. Gift
shop. Second-hand garden book shop.
Directions: 1.5km south of Saintfield, off the A7.

In 1903, Hugh Armytage Moore, a man deeply interested in plants, inherited this 1861 house and garden just outside Saintfield from his uncle, the Rev. John Moore. He started growing some of his special plants in the yards and fields around the farm and went on to create the garden we know as Rowallane today, a fifty-acre spree of landscaped gardens, wild flower meadows, rhododendron plantations, woods, rock and walled gardens.

Arriving at the gate, a strange set of features immediately attract attention. These are like huge stone cairns or pyramids made of boulders, lining the drive. They advertise Rowallane as a garden out of the ordinary.

The larger garden is a natural, wild, Robinsonian-style garden that ranges over the hilly, rocky drumlins of south County Down. It is renowned for its spring displays, when vast numbers of daffodils and rhododendrons burst into flower. But it is a garden that looks wonderful twelve months of the year. Mr Moore subscribed to all the great plant-hunting expeditions and he planted rhododendron seeds from these, creating a large collection of special specimens in well arranged combinations through the gardens. They reach their flowering peak in May. The rhododendrons, usually grown under a canopy of trees, are grown here in the open.

The famous Rowallane rock garden was created by relieving a huge outcrop of the local stone, called whinstone, of its soil and scrub. Pockets were then filled with acid soil and planted up with meconopsis, including the locally bred *Meconopsis* x *sheldonii* 'Slieve Donard', gentians, primulas, bulbs, erythroniums, celmisias, heathers and leptospermum.

To the side of the house, I stopped to admire the huge yew cones. The man cutting them told me that it takes two weeks each summer to clip them.

It is in the walled gardens that many of the treasures are to be found. In the outer walled garden *Chaenomeles* x *superba* 'Rowallane' and a variety of lace-cap hydrangeas are stationed. Large wisteria and a *Hoheria sexstylosa* stand by the entrance to the outer walled garden and the greenhouse.

The walled garden covers two acres and varies between strictly clipped, box-enclosed ten-metre runs of agapanthus, even longer runs of glorious yellow *Cephalaria gigantea*, penstemon and looser beds of tumbling peony and bergenia, inula and camellia. The dates 1828-1883 are carved on one of the gateways. In fact, throughout the garden there are dates scattered around, pointing intriguingly to landmarks in the garden's history but I could find no-one able to throw further light on these carved dates.

There are a series of lovely stone buildings scattered about the greater grounds. These house second-hand gardening bookshops, tea rooms and shelters from the rain. The wider pleasure grounds are also marked at various points by old stone walls and boundaries. They are pretty and serve to render the directionally challenged visitor even more lost than they might otherwise be. One is never quite sure whether a wall or a little stone building up ahead means that the centre of the garden is ahead or if one has become hopelessly lost. I love it.

At one point, a hilly grass path leads between groves of spectacular trees towards the most beautiful *Cornus kousa* var. Chinensis I have ever seen. When in flower, it is like a magnet in the centre of the garden attracting mesmerised visitors from all corners, a beacon in the midst of a maze-like garden.

If it is raining, retreat to the little shed where the stock of old garden magazines is kept, and dry off while poring over the thoughtfully provided publications. Having met some of the garden staff, an incredibly welcoming and enthusiastic crew, I was not surprised at the inclusion of such a generous facility at this fine garden.

Seaforde Gardens |
Seaforde, Downpatrick, County Down, BT30 8PG

. . . .

Contact: Charles Forde

Tel: (+44) 048 4481 1225

e-mail: plants@seafordegardens.com

www: www.seafordegardens.com

Open: April to September, Monday to Saturday
10am-5pm, Sunday 1pm-6pm. Groups welcome.

Guided tours can be booked.

Supervised children welcome.

Special features: Butterfly house. Tearoom.
Home to the National Collection of eucryphia.

Directions: On the Belfast–Newcastle road. Look
out for the signposts in the village of Seaforde.

The drive up to Seaforde is like driving through a mossy valley under tunnels of mature trees, between walls of ferns. It is magical, as are the almost infestation numbers of preening peacocks loping around the car park.

The garden dates back to the 1750s and was probably the work of great landscape gardener, John Sutherland. It originally involved extensive woodlands, shelter belts and screens. There was also a network of winding drives, including the charming present entrance drive.

But it was in the nineteenth century that many of the trees seen here today were planted, including the Wellingtonias and Monterey pines. Seaforde is made up of the woods and a walled garden encompassing five acres, full of rare and interesting shrubs. Many of these specimens are the fruits of Patrick Forde's numerous seed-collecting expeditions abroad, particularly to Vietnam.

The main body of the walled garden was at one time formal, laid out in the type of smart beds still seen in many walled gardens today. This format had descended into a wilderness of bramble and laurel until the mid-1970s, when Mr Forde took it in hand and began to bring the garden back to a presentable state.

He planted a maze of hornbeam in 1975, which is now a large puzzle complete with an arbour and statue of Diana. It could keep visitors away from the rest of the garden for too long. The area around the maze has been formalised through the addition of new wide gravel paths.

Next to the maze, the garden proper begins with well laid-out groves of rhododendron (including over one hundred different *R. falconeri*) and large shrubs, such as an incredibly tall mahonia, used to accommodate climbing roses. Huge echiums and mimosas are grand by

themselves but even more diverting with melianthus and hostas planted in numbers underneath. The peafowl population makes itself useful by eating slugs and saving the hostas from attack.

It is not hard to get lost, coming across a eucryphia walk in the process, with its laden-down branches of white and pink flowers, in the case of *Eucryphia lucida* 'Pink Cloud' and *E. milliganii* 'Whisper', both of which have shell-pink blooms. These are part of the National Collection of twenty-three species and hybrids.

Scattered through the woodland garden are surprise clumps of large, sweet-scented white *Lilium* 'Casa Blanca' and tree ferns. The path eventually leads into a clearing where a damp, wet area and pond garden could probably be described as infested with primula. The place is full of rarities. I loved the unnamed rose originally collected in Bhutan, on the border between China and India. It has strange, hairy orange hips.

One of the great pleasures of this garden is standing back and enjoying the sight of maturing groves of trees, shrubs and climbers, many of them rare and unknown in any other garden on the island.

The responsibility for caring for and developing Seaforde has now fallen to the late Patrick's son, Charles. He too displays a great enthusiasm both for the garden and its special plants, continuing to collect seed in the wild. We should give thanks for that.

There is a butterfly house to occupy non-gardeners. This tropical butterfly house is set in a huge greenhouse planted like a jungle and home to hundreds of colourful butterflies, flying freely about, settling on branches and leaves, camouflaging themselves only to surprise visitors by suddenly taking flight in front of them.

Acknowledgements

First and foremost I want to thank my husband Michael, always enthusiastic and willing to back me up on every endeavour. The encouragement he, Mary Kate and Michael junior give makes what I do possible.

Meanwhile Mum and Dad, Mary and Billy have always been at the front of the queue with help and back-up.

Dor and Michael Lanigan senior are the sort of cheerleaders that most people can only dream of.

On several occasions, Ray McNally, Niall Lanigan and Dor Keane have kindly and patiently answered my uninformed questions about technological things and I am grateful to them for that. I will separately thank Dor in advance for rashly promising to 'deliver' the book club for me.

I could only wish a best friend like Paddy Friel on all of us – under what she calls 'the full beam', I have been showered with praise, spot-on advice and a nicely swelled head.

A big thank you must go to a real human person, John Keane and the staff at the *Kilkenny People*.

I want to thank Jonathan Williams. As an agent, going above and beyond the call of duty seems to be his standard practice.

As an editor, Daniel Bolger has the unquantifiable talent of making the hassled business of bringing out a book a pleasant and smooth experience.

I want also to thank Sean O'Keefe, Caroline Lambe, Alice Dawson and everyone at Liberties Press. They are a professional and civilised lot.

Gerry Daly and Mary Davies of the *Irish Garden* have been kind and generous for years, issuing me with interesting work projects and welcome advice.

Lastly, I want to thank the gardeners and owners of all the gardens I have visited. Without their hard work there would be no point in mine. In particular I need to thank Dorothy Jervis of Mountcharles in Donegal, a wonderful gardener and a woman of great kindness. Along with another admirable ambassador for the village of Mountcharles, Sean Gillespie and two Polish ambassadors, Pawel and Pieter, Dorothy organised the rescue of a complete stranger from the ditch outside her garden gate. To top it off she fed me scones. Thank you Dorothy.

BORD BIA

Bord Bia's mission is to grow the success of a world-class food and horticulture (food and ornamental) industry by providing strategic market development, promotion and information services. The role of Bord Bia is to act as a link between Irish food, drink and horticulture suppliers and existing and potential customers in Ireland and around the world.

Visit www.bordbia.ie.

FÁILTE IRELAND

Fáilte Ireland provides strategic and practical support to develop and sustain Ireland as a high-quality and competitive tourist destination. We work with the tourism industry in areas including business support, enterprise development, training and education, research, marketing and regional development. With a dedicated team working across five regions, Fáilte Ireland offers tourism professionals and service providers a wide range of support services to help them grow their business.

For further information, visit www.failteireland.ie.

Opposite: Ballymore, County Wexford.

Photograph Credits

Airfield	Airfield
Altamont Gardens	Con Brogan
Annes Grove	Jane Annesley
Ardcarraig	Lorna McMahon
Ardgillan Demesne	Istockphoto
Ballymaloe Cookery School Gardens	Ballymaloe Cookery School
Ballymore Garden	Paul Sherwood
Ballynacourty	Sebastian Stacpoole
The Cottage Garden Plant Center	Maurice Parkinson
Ballywalter Park	The Lady Dunleath
Bantry House and Gardens	Fáilte Ireland
Beaulieu House and Gardens	Beaulieu
Beechwood	Ned and Liz Kirby
Bellefield House	Paul Barber
Belvedere House	David Knight and Belvedere and Garden
Benvarden Garden	Val Montgomery
Birr Castle Demesne Foundation, Istockphoto	Birr Scientific and Heritage
The National Botanic Gardens	Con Brogan
Buchanan Garden	Brian Webb
Bunratty	Istockphoto
Burtown House	James Fennell
Caher Bridge Garden	Carl Wright
Cedar Lodge	Neil Williams

Coolcarrigan House	Robert Wilson-Wright
Coolaught Gardens	Harry Deacon
Coosheen	Hester Forde
Derreen	David Bingham
Dromboy	Charlie Wilkins
17 Drumnamallaght Road	Shirley Lanigan and Frank Brown
The Duignan Garden	Carmel Duignan
Fairbrook House Gardens	Clary Mastenbroek
Farmleigh	PHP Photography
Fota Arboretum and Garden	David O'Regan
Gash Gardens	Ross Doyle
Glanleam House and Garden	Meta Kreissig
Glebe Gardens and Gallery	Rohan Reilly
Glenarm Castle	Conor Tinslon
Glenveagh Castle Garden	Con Brogan
Glenveagh Castle Garden	Sean O'Gaoithin
Guincho	Gail Cairns
Hampstead Hall	Hall Brian Webb
Heywood Garden	Con Brogan
Hotel Dunloe Castle Gardens Beaufort	Hotel Dunloe Castle
Hunting Brook Gardens	Jimi Blakes
Illnacullin	Cormac Foley
Inish Beg Gardens	Paul Keane

The Japanese Gardens and St. Fiachra's Garden	Irish National Stud Co.	Mount Stewart House and Gardens	National Trust
June Blake's Garden	June Blake	Muckross Gardens	Cormac Foley
Kilfane Glen and Waterfall	Richard Mosse	Patthana Garden	TJ Maher
Kilgraney House Herb Garden	Martin Marley	Phoenix Park Walled Victorian Garden	Richard Johnston
Kilgraney (Main House)	Rai Uhlemann	Portumna Castle Gardens	Con Brogan
Killineer House and Garden	Charles Carroll	Poulnacurra	Harpur Garden Images
Killurney	Shirley Lanigan	Powerscourt Gardens	Suzanne Clarke
Kilmacurragh Botanic Gardens	Seamus O'Brien	Primrose Hill Gardens Lucan	Gay O'Neill
Kilmokea Manor House and Gardens	Emma Hewlett	Rowallane Garden	Averil Milligan
Kilravock Garden	Phemie Rose	Royal Hospital Kilmainham	Gráinne Larkin
Kilruddery House and Gardens	James Fennell	Salthill	Elizabeth Temple
Knockpatrick Gardens	Tim O'Brien	Seaforde Gardens	Charles Forde
Kylemore Abbey	Gareth McCormack, Istockphoto	Boyce Gardens	Dick Boyce
Lakemount	Harpur Garden Images	The Dillon Garden	Helen Dillon
Lismore Castle Garden	Lismore Castle	Talbot Botanic Gardens	Istockphoto
Lissadell	Pamela Cassidy	Tourin House and gardens	Kristen Jameson
Lodge Park Walled Garden and Steam Museum	Patrick Ardiff	Tullynally Castle	Thomas Pakenham
Marlay Demesne and Regency Walled Garden	Dun Laoghaire Rathdown County Council	Turlough Park Museum of Country Life	Noreen Hennigan
Terra Nova Garden	Martin and Deborah Begley	Woodstock Gardens and Arboretum Department	Kilkenny County Council Parks
Mount Congreve	Richard Cutbill		

Every effort has been made to contact copyright holders. In the event of any omissions please contact the publisher in writing.

Overleaf: Ashtown Walled Garden, Phoenix Park, County Dublin © Richard Johnston.